a practical guide to

USING
PANEL
DATA

SAGE was founded in 1965 by Sara Miller McCune to support the dissemination of usable knowledge by publishing innovative and high-quality research and teaching content. Today, we publish more than 750 journals, including those of more than 300 learned societies, more than 800 new books per year, and a growing range of library products including archives, data, case studies, reports, conference highlights, and video. SAGE remains majority-owned by our founder, and after Sara's lifetime will become owned by a charitable trust that secures our continued independence.

Los Angeles | London | Washington DC | New Delhi | Singapore

a practical guide to

USING PANEL DATA

*Simonetta Longhi &
Alita Nandi*

Los Angeles | London | New Delhi
Singapore | Washington DC

Los Angeles | London | New Delhi
Singapore | Washington DC

SAGE Publications Ltd
1 Oliver's Yard
55 City Road
London EC1Y 1SP

SAGE Publications Inc.
2455 Teller Road
Thousand Oaks, California 91320

SAGE Publications India Pvt Ltd
B 1/I 1 Mohan Cooperative Industrial Area
Mathura Road
New Delhi 110 044

SAGE Publications Asia-Pacific Pte Ltd
3 Church Street
#10-04 Samsung Hub
Singapore 049483

Editor: Jai Seaman
Assistant editor: Lily Mehrbod
Production editor: Ian Antcliff
Copyeditor: Neville Hankins
Proofreader: Kate Campbell
Marketing manager: Sally Ransom
Cover design: Francis Kenney
Typeset by: C&M Digitals (P) Ltd, Chennai, India
Printed and bound by CPI Group (UK) Ltd,
Croydon, CR0 4YY

Library of Congress Control Number: 2014940794

British Library Cataloguing in Publication data

A catalogue record for this book is available from
the British Library

MIX
Paper from
responsible sources
FSC
www.fsc.org   FSC® C013604

ISBN 978-1-4462-1086-4
ISBN 978-1-4462-1087-1 (pbk)

At SAGE we take sustainability seriously. Most of our products are printed in the UK using FSC papers and boards.
When we print overseas we ensure sustainable papers are used as measured by the Egmont grading system.
We undertake an annual audit to monitor our sustainability.

Contents

List of Figures

List of Tables

List of Acronyms

ASCII	American Standard Code for Information Interchange
BHPS	British Household Panel Survey
CDF	Cumulative Density Function
CI	Confidence Interval
CNEF	Cross-National Equivalent File
CPI	Consumer Prices Index
ECHP	European Community Household Panel
EU	European Union
EU-SILC	European Union Statistics of Income and Living Conditions
FAQ	Frequently Asked Questions
GLS	Generalised Least Squares
GOR	Government Office Region
IID	Independent and Identically Distributed
IMR	Inverse Mills Ratio
ISER	Institute for Social and Economic Research
LFS	Labour Force Survey
LPM	Linear Probability Model
LSDV	Least Squares Dummy Variables
ML	Maximum Likelihood
MLE	Maximum Likelihood Estimator
MSE	Mean Square Error
OECD	Organization for Economic Co-operation and Development
OLS	Ordinary Least Squares
ONS	Office for National Statistics
OSM	Original Sample Member
PDF	Probability Density Function
PH	Proportional Hazard
PMF	Probability Mass Function
PPS	Probability Proportional to Size
PSID	Panel Study of Income Dynamics
PSM	Permanent Sample Member
PSU	Primary Sampling Unit
SEO	Survey of Economic Opportunity
SMSA	Standard Metropolitan Statistical Area
SOEP	German Socio-Economic Panel

SRC	Survey Research Center
SRS	Simple Random Sample
SRSWOR	Simple Random Sample Without Replacement
SRSWR	Simple Random Sample With Replacement
TSM	Temporary Sample Member
UKHLS	UK Household Longitudinal Study
VIF	Variance Inflation Factor

About the Authors

Simonetta Longhi is Research Fellow at the Institute for Social and Economic Research at the University of Essex. She is also Research Fellow at the Institute for the Study of Labour (IZA) and Research Affiliate at the Centre for Research and Analysis of Migration (CReAM). Her research interests are on migration and labour economics and she has published various journal articles using individual and household datasets. For many years she has taught courses on how to analyse the British Household Panel Survey and the Understanding Society datasets, and she is currently teaching a course on applications of data analysis.

Alita Nandi is Research Fellow at the Institute for Social and Economic Research. Her research interests include issues of ethnicity, identity, personality, family formation and dissolution. She has conducted empirical research in these areas using cohort and household panel datasets and published in various journals. She has been part of the Ethnicity Strand of Understanding Society since 2007. For the last few years she has taught courses on applications of data analysis and on how to use and analyse the British Household Panel Survey and Understanding Society datasets.

Acknowledgements

For many years the Institute for Social and Economic Research (ISER) at the University of Essex has taught a course called 'Introduction to the British Household Panel Survey Using Stata'. This book is a spin-off of that course and a course on 'Applications of Data Analysis' which we teach at the Department of Economics.

We are in debt to all those who – over the years – have contributed to the development of the course 'Introduction to the British Household Panel Survey Using Stata'. Among these: Nick Buck and Stephen Jenkins who developed the very first version of the course and Annette Jackle with whom we developed the most recent version of the course. We also had valuable feedback from Gundi Knies, Alexandra Skew and course participants. We are grateful to Szilvia Altorjai, Feifei Bu, Francisco Perales and Dorothee Schneider for detailed comments on some of the chapters, and to Olena Kaminska and Peter Lynn for helpful discussions on weighting techniques.

We have developed and written this book while working at ISER; we are grateful for the support of the Institute, where we have benefitted from discussions with various colleagues.

Finally, we would like to thank Jai Seaman and Lily Mehrbod for their support during the production of this book and two anonymous reviewers for their extremely useful comments on a previous version.

Introduction

This book is an introduction to data management and data analysis for cross-section and panel data. This book will guide you step by step through the whole process from data management to model estimation and interpretation of the results. We explain how to prepare panel datasets for analysis, what the differences between the most commonly used panel datasets are, and how the data preparation techniques should change depending on the dataset used and on the type of analysis we want to perform. We discuss which techniques are commonly used in the literature, how to choose among different estimators, how to interpret the results and how to prepare output tables and graphs.

The main focus is on the practical use and issues of the data, such as data cleaning, data preparation, computation of descriptive statistics, use of sample weights, choice of the right estimator and interpretation of the results. Because of the introductory focus of the book, we only discuss estimation techniques that are of relatively straightforward implementation, but refer to Stata books, online tutorials and user-written commands for more advanced techniques.

This book can be used as a modular textbook and self-study book for undergraduate, Master and PhD students undertaking their first empirical (longitudinal) analysis, and for academics unfamiliar with data analysis or unfamiliar with panel datasets and with the complexity of their file structure. The book is aimed at readers who already have some knowledge of statistical methods for quantitative analysis but do not have practical knowledge of using data (particularly panel data) to implement these techniques.

To better illustrate the techniques, most of the chapters are structured as hands-on exercises. Chapters 1 to 5 discuss data management techniques with references to the British Household Panel Survey (BHPS), the Panel Study of Income Dynamics (PSID), the German Socio-Economic Panel (SOEP) and Understanding Society (UKHLS). These are all household panel surveys. They are some of the panel datasets most commonly used by social scientists and we have chosen them because household panel surveys generally entail more complex data manipulation than other types of longitudinal datasets such as cohort studies. Users will learn about data manipulation required not only for simple panel data, but also for data at multiple levels (for example, individual and household level) and event history data.

Although different datasets may pose different problems in terms of data manipulation, the estimation techniques do not vary according to the dataset used. The hands-on exercises discussed in Chapters 6 to 14 all use the BHPS. Details of where to download these datasets can be found at the end of this introduction.

These are 'large-scale' panel surveys, with a relatively complex data structure. Readers using small-scale panels and other datasets may encounter slightly different data manipulation needs. However, the techniques discussed in this book should cover most of the issues that may be encountered. Caution may be needed in applying the estimation techniques to datasets with very small sample sizes (less than 50–100 individuals).

This book is complemented by an online appendix (https://study.sagepub.com/longhiandnandi), which is divided into three parts. Appendix A gives practical details of the datasets used in the book. Appendix B gives the full syntax for the data manipulation and estimation exercises discussed in the book, and Appendix C contains the whole set of results that the estimations produce. The reader can go through each chapter, type the suggested commands on the computer, and double-check the syntax and results against the online appendix. As an alternative, the reader can use the online appendix as a solution manual to the exercises proposed in the book without needing to download the data or even use a computer.

Nowadays any type of analysis involving large datasets has to be done using software for statistical analysis. For this book we have chosen Stata. The book does not require any prior knowledge of this software. Besides guiding the reader through the data management and estimation process, this book can also be seen as an introduction to how best to use Stata for data manipulation and statistical modelling. We include tips on how to improve readability of the syntax files and how to make the analysis and results easy to reproduce and update.

Why Stata?

All exercises in this book are based on Stata 12 (www.stata.com/). Stata is statistical software widely used for econometric and statistical analyses. It is relatively easy to use compared with software such as SAS, R or Limdep, and much more flexible than SPSS or Eviews.

The way Stata is structured and the large user community mean that a large number of user-written routines (for meta-analysis, for spatial econometrics, or to estimate novel estimators proposed in recently published journal articles) are freely available for download. This makes it straightforward to implement many complex estimation techniques. The Stata website also hosts discussion groups (www.statalist.org) focusing on different aspects of the software and its commands, and discussing how to perform different types of tests and estimations. Furthermore, the possibility of writing programs (ado files) makes Stata flexible enough to implement novel estimators. Stata tutorials can also be found on YouTube (www.youtube.com/user/statacorp and http://blog.stata.com/tag/tutorials/); some of this material can be accessed via the Stata Help Manual.

There are different versions of Stata currently available. We focus on Stata for Windows, although Stata also provides versions for different operating systems such as Unix or Mac. The syntax we use is that for Stata version 12, although in the book we also discuss older and more recent versions if there are relevant differences. The SE (Special Edition), MP (multiprocessor), 'Small Stata' packages are also different versions of Stata, which differ mostly in terms of the size of data they can handle (more details are available at www.stata.com/products/which-stata-is-right-for-me/). For example, SE and MP are able to deal with datasets with a larger number of variables than the Small Stata version, but the syntax of the commands is exactly the same. Where such capabilities may be relevant, we discuss ways to deal with them. What we discuss in this book is applicable to all these versions of Stata.

Structure of This Book

The book is divided into four main parts. Part I is about data management and how to prepare the data for cross-section and panel analysis, while Part II focuses on estimation methods and techniques for cross-section and panel data. Part III is about event history analysis, which requires different types of data manipulation and analysis than the ones discussed in Part II. Finally, Part IV discusses the best way to present the results and produce output tables.

Chapter 1 describes what panel or longitudinal surveys are and how they differ from cross-section data, and discusses the advantages of using longitudinal data. Chapter 2 discusses the different types of (large) panel datasets (household versus individual panels, rotating versus perpetual panels, and so on) that are commonly used for analysis, and briefly describes various commonly used household panel surveys that have been collected around the world. Many of these surveys have a similar file and data structure; the four datasets discussed in this book cover the main possible structures that one may encounter. The lessons to be learnt using these datasets in the hands-on exercises should be easily translated to other datasets.

Chapter 3 starts with a short primer on Stata: how to use it interactively and how to use the basic programming tools. The chapter also discusses best practice tips to ensure reproducibility of the analysis and of the results. It shows how to open and inspect the data, compute some basic descriptive statistics and deal with missing values.

Chapters 4 to 6 focus on data preparation. Chapter 4 discusses how to combine data on individual respondents from any number of interview years into one dataset ready for panel analysis, and how to create lagged variables and compute first differences. Household and panel datasets include multilevel data stored in separate data files (some at the individual, some at the household level) that often need to be combined before they can be used for analysis. Chapter 5 discusses how to combine household- and individual-level data, how to aggregate individual-level data to obtain household-level variables, and how to merge these new household-level variables to the individual-level file. Chapter 6 discusses how to identify different relatives in the household (such as father, mother or daughter) and how to match information on these relatives to that of the respondent. Often survey datasets on individuals can be matched with other datasets such as administrative records or geographical data. Chapter 6 concludes with a brief discussion of the advantages and difficulties of this type of matching.

At this point the final dataset is ready for cross-section and panel data analyses, which are discussed in the second part of the book.

The first chapter of this second part of the book (Chapter 7) discusses an issue often neglected in most books: whether and how to use survey weights. Most estimation techniques assume that the data are a simple random sample, although empirically this is rarely the case. For cost reasons the sample may be clustered, a part of the intended sample may be lost due to non-response, a minority group may be oversampled to allow separate analyses of this group, and so on. To reinstate the representativeness of the sample most datasets include sample weights. This chapter discusses the usefulness of sample weights, the different types of sample weights available in the different datasets, their meaning, and when and how to use each of them correctly.

Chapter 8 discusses estimation techniques for cross-section data and the main differences among the most commonly used techniques. This is in preparation for the discussion of panel data estimations in the following chapters. In Chapter 8 we discuss how to estimate different types of models (coefficients, marginal effects and standard errors), how to compute linear and non-linear tests on the coefficients, how to obtain predictions and residuals, and their meaning. The discussion includes estimation methods for continuous dependent variables and for discrete dependent variables, and the main differences between them. Chapters 9 and 10 focus on estimation techniques commonly used for panel data. Chapter 9 focuses on the analysis of continuous dependent variables and discusses how to estimate fixed versus random effects models (coefficients, marginal effects and standard errors), how to compute linear and non-linear tests (including the Hausman test), how to obtain predictions, and residuals. Chapter 10 discusses estimation methods for panel data for discrete dependent variables, how to obtain different types of estimates (coefficients, marginal effects, odd ratios) and how to interpret them.

While collecting current information at regular intervals, most panel datasets also collect retrospective information on events referring to the period before the beginning of the survey, or to the period between two successive interviews. Examples are employment, fertility and marital histories; these data give a more complete picture of a person's history and are typically used for event history analysis. Event history data and analysis are the focus of Part III of this book. Chapter 11 gives a brief overview of what duration analysis is, what the data requirements are, and how to set up the dataset for this type of analysis. Chapter 12 discusses the general structure of retrospective data files and problems that are often encountered when combining retrospective data with prospective data (prospective data concern current – rather than past – status) such as date inconsistencies. Chapter 13 discusses the most common estimation techniques for event history analysis, and how to choose among the different types of estimators.

Throughout the book we discuss and compare estimation techniques and highlight the correct way of interpreting the results of the analysis. Chapter 14 concludes the book by describing how to present such results in professional-looking tables and graphs.

The Data Discussed in This Book

The datasets discussed in this book are available from the following websites:

- The British Household Panel Survey (BHPS) and Understanding Society (UKHLS) are available free of charge for non-commercial purposes from the UK Data Archive to registered users: www.data-archive.ac.uk/home.
- The Panel Study of Income Dynamics (PSID) is available free of charge to registered users: http://simba.isr.umich.edu/data/data.aspx.
- The German Socio-Economic Panel (SOEP) is available from the German Institute for Economic Research (DIW Berlin): www.diw.de/en/diw_02.c.221178.en/about_soep.html.

PART I

DATA PREPARATION IN MICRO PANEL SURVEYS

1

WHY PANEL SURVEYS?

Aim

Different types of data are available for analysis. This chapter is a very brief introduction to longitudinal data and discusses their advantages over cross-section data.

1.1 What Are Longitudinal Data?

Cross-section data consist of one set of observations for each unit of observation. It gives us a snapshot of the population of interest at a particular point in time. In contrast, longitudinal data represent multiple snapshots of the same units of observation. Units of observation may be individuals, households, firms, schools, countries, and so on. While cross-section data may show who is poor, unemployed or in poor health at any point in time, longitudinal data also show whether people move into and out of poverty, how often people are unemployed, whether poor health follows periods of unemployment or vice versa.

Longitudinal data may be collected from one single interview by asking people about both their current and their previous situation. For example, people may be asked about the characteristics of their current job but also about their previous jobs and spells of unemployment and inactivity, or they may be asked about their current marriage but also their previous marriages and spells of cohabitation. These are often referred to as retrospective data. Alternatively the data may be collected via multiple interviews asking about the current situation (for example, marriage or employment) at the time of the interview. In this case we have repeated observations for each unit of observation and these successive interviews are often called 'waves', 'sweeps' or 'rounds' (of interviews). Longitudinal data collected using these prospective methods are referred to as panel data. The datasets discussed in this book fall into this category although they may include some retrospective data as well. In most of the surveys discussed in this book, households are randomly selected at a point in time and all household members are interviewed at that time and at regular intervals after that. We discuss different aspects of panel surveys in detail in Chapter 2.

Some surveys do not interview the same set of people or households at each point in time, but sample new ones at each wave. In this case we do not have a longitudinal dataset – of the same people – but pooled cross-sections. These are also known as repeated cross-sections; one example is the Family Resources Survey, where a sample of approximately 25,000 UK households is selected and interviewed each year. While these datasets do not qualify as longitudinal data, if we are interested in group averages, say regional average pay, we can use these surveys to compute average pay of all people living (or working) in the same region and construct longitudinal data of regions, thus creating a macro or pseudo panel.

Another common type of longitudinal data consists of macro or pseudo panels. Macro panels consist of aggregates such as unemployment rate, inflation, and so on, observed over time for a certain number of areas. In this case the cross-sectional part of the panel is not made of people, but may be made of, for example, countries or regions. Typically, in these types of panel datasets the number of units of observation is much lower than in the case of individual or household panels, where we often have thousands of people or households.

Although there are commonalities, econometric techniques used for macro panels can be rather different than those used for individual and household panels. For example, individual and random effects, discussed in Part II of this book, have a different interpretation when they refer to regions rather than individuals. Techniques such as spatial econometrics are applied to macro panels, but not to individual and household panels. It is also worth noting that while individual and household surveys generally include only a sample of the population of interest, macro panels tend to include the whole universe of areas the researcher is interested in. In this book we focus on individual and household data and their related econometric techniques.

1.2 Advantages of Longitudinal Versus Cross-Section Data

Compared with longitudinal data, cross-section data are quite common and perhaps easier to deal with. However, since they represent a snapshot of a population at a specific point in time, the type of econometric analysis that they allow is relatively limited. These types of data rarely allow analyses of transitions or changes over time.

The first advantage of longitudinal data is that repeated observations for the same individual also allow us to use econometric techniques such as fixed and random effects methods. These methods allow us to control for certain types of individual-specific time-invariant factors that are not observed in the dataset (often referred to as individual unobserved heterogeneity). For example, we may observe that those people who change their residence are more likely to earn higher wages than those who do not move. One reason why some people earn higher wages may be that they have higher levels of motivation. Those who have higher levels of motivation may also be the ones who are more likely to change place of residence. So, if we observe that those who move earn more than those who do not, does that mean that by changing the place of residence of individuals we can increase their earnings? No: since motivation levels are not observed in the data and we cannot directly include them in the models, the correlation between wages and the probability of changing residence may simply reflect differences in wages between the high and less motivated. If these unobserved characteristics do not change over time, panel data methods such as the fixed or random effects method can be used to better identify such causal effects. These and other panel data methods are described in Part II of this book.

The second advantage of having repeated observations is that they allow a better study of dynamics. For example, if we want to analyse the correlation between bad health and unemployment, observing people over time allows us to see whether bad health tends to appear before unemployment or after it. The causation (unemployment leads to bad health instead of bad health leading to unemployment) is likely to be clearer when longitudinal data are available.

The key advantage here is the possibility to measure change. For example, we may know that the unemployment rate in a certain country has been 6% for the last four years. However, this figure does not tell us if it is the same few people who are unemployed over a long period of time, or if there are many people who transition into and out of unemployment and experience short spells of unemployment. While it is possible to study the macro-level phenomenon with repeated cross-sections (6% unemployment rate for four years), longitudinal data are necessary to analyse transitions into and out of unemployment. More generally, duration or survival analysis methods which investigate what drives staying in a particular state such as unemployment or poverty and what determines transitions out of these states can only be used with longitudinal data. These methods are described in Part III of this book.

1.3 Missing Data, Balanced and Unbalanced Panels

In panel surveys, sometimes it is not possible to obtain further interviews with all individuals, households or firms who were interviewed in the first wave.

The different reasons for non-interviews are discussed in Chapter 7. We have 'wave non-response' if some non-interviews are followed by interviews in successive waves, and 'panel attrition' if the units of observation drop out of the survey permanently. Together these are referred to as unit non-response.

Even those interviewed in every wave may not answer all questions in every interview, resulting in 'item non-response'. There are serious implications of non-response and attrition on analysis and extensive efforts are made to minimise non-response and attrition in surveys. But despite these efforts non-response and attrition are present in almost all surveys and analysts often use statistical methods to minimise these problems.

Unit and item non-response also result in the data being unbalanced: that is, each individual unit is not observed at every interview wave. For example, if we have a panel of 100 people interviewed for three years, we should have three interviews for each of the 100 persons. However, this may not happen because of attrition and non-response. We can convert an unbalanced into a balanced panel by dropping all people who have missed at least one interview; this, however, would reduce the sample size, sometimes considerably. Luckily, most estimation techniques and estimation commands work effectively for both balanced and unbalanced data and researchers often use panels that are unbalanced (see, for example, Baltagi 2009).

1.4 Summary and Suggestions for Further Reading

For those who are unfamiliar with longitudinal data, in this chapter we have very briefly discussed the main differences between longitudinal and cross-section data, and the advantages of being able to use longitudinal data. Although this book focuses on longitudinal and panel data, data management techniques such as those discussed in Chapters 3, 5 and 6, and econometric estimations such as those discussed in Chapter 7 and 8, are relevant also for the analysis of cross-section data.

Key points

- Cross-section data provide only one observation at a particular point in time per individual/household/firm, while longitudinal data provide multiple observations at different points in time per individual/household/firm (either collected once or in repeated interviews).
- Longitudinal data allow us to analyse changes, transitions, temporal order of events, and persistence in particular states. More importantly, longitudinal data allow us to

control for the effects of individual-specific time-invariant unobserved factors. None of this is possible with cross-section data.

- Data may not be available for all units of observation at all points in time when the data were collected, either because of unit non-response (wave non-response and attrition) or because of item non-response (specific questions not answered). This results in unbalanced panels. Estimation techniques for unbalanced panels are the same as those for balanced panels. However, non-response also has serious consequences for population estimates based on these data. Estimation methods are available to address these issues.

Suggestions for further reading

- For a more detailed discussion on the advantages and disadvantages of panel data see:

  ○ Chapter 1 of Baltagi, B.H. (2009) *Econometric Analysis of Panel Data*. London, Wiley.
  ○ Chapter 1 of Hsiao, C. (2003) *Analysis of Panel Data*. Cambridge, Cambridge University Press.

- For a discussion of different types of longitudinal data see Chapter 1 of Taris, T.W. (2000) *A Primer in Longitudinal Data Analysis*. London, Sage.
- For a discussion of survey non-response see Groves, R.M., Dillman, D.A., Eltinge, J.L. and Little, R.J.A. (2001) *Survey Nonresponse*. New York, Wiley.

DIFFERENT TYPES OF PANEL SURVEYS

Aim

Panel surveys can be collected for different purposes and, like other surveys, they have different features. In this chapter we discuss the main aspects of panel surveys: who is interviewed, how many times, how the data can be collected. We then give a short overview of some frequently used panel datasets.

2.1 Introduction

In this book we discuss four major panel surveys in the world and how to use them to implement different longitudinal estimation methods. These four surveys are: the Panel Study of Income Dynamics (PSID) in the USA, the German Socio-Economic Panel (SOEP), the British Household Panel Survey (BHPS) and Understanding Society: the UK Household Longitudinal Study (UKHLS).

The SOEP, BHPS and UKHLS started by interviewing a set of private households selected from all private households in a specific country at a particular point in time, and then continued to interview these same household members (and their descendants) at regular intervals. The PSID is slightly different since it focuses on individuals rather than households (see Section 2.4). In all four surveys most of the information collected during the interviews is related to the household members' current situation. Some of these surveys also collect information about respondents' labour market, partnership and fertility activities before the start of the survey. In Section 2.7 we discuss the specific features of each of these surveys. To understand why these particular features were chosen it is important to understand the advantages and disadvantages of various survey features. We provide an overview of these in Sections 2.2 to 2.6.

2.2 Censuses Versus Sample Surveys

All surveys, including panel surveys, can be categorised into two main types: censuses and sample surveys. The panel surveys discussed in this book belong to the latter category; sample surveys are more popular than censuses.

The purpose of empirical analyses is often to estimate population parameters such as means, proportions and correlation between certain characteristics. Depending on the purpose of the research, a population could be all individuals, or households or firms in a country. It could also be all residents of a city, or all pupils in a school, and so on. For example, we may want to know whether in the UK the average pay of men differs from that of women, what proportion of single mothers participate in the labour market, or what is the effect of living in an economically deprived neighbourhood on the chances of getting a job.

To answer such kinds of questions, ideally we would want to gather information from every member of the population of interest. This type of survey is referred to as a census or a complete enumeration survey. Unfortunately, a census of a relatively large population geographically spread over the whole country is often too costly in terms of money and time. However, we can use information gathered from sample surveys to infer parameters and correlations of interest in the population. Sample surveys collect information from a subset of the population of interest, referred to as a sample. The four surveys discussed in this book are all sample surveys, not censuses.

A sample can be drawn from a population using different methods; in this book we discuss different types of sampling techniques. The quality of an estimator based on a sample depends on the sampling technique; we discuss these issues in Chapter 7.

The estimation techniques we discuss in the second and third parts of this book are some of the most popular methods used to estimate population parameters (quantities in the population) from sample statistics (the same quantity in the sample). For example, the average pay of adults living in the UK in 2010 is a population parameter, while the average pay of a sample drawn from this population is a sample statistic. A sample statistic used to estimate the population parameter is referred to as an estimator. Statistical techniques are then used to determine the quality of the estimate.

2.3 Surveys Versus Administrative Data

There are a variety of sources of longitudinal data; an important distinction is between surveys and administrative data. Administrative data are collected by government agencies or regulating bodies for their own administrative purposes. For example, government departments may collect certain information on people's characteristics to verify whether they are entitled to certain types of benefits, and record the actual amount of each type of benefit paid to claimants, for the whole duration of the claim. Administrative databases therefore usually include a large number of individuals; in some cases, they include information on the whole population. For example, if our population of interest is that of people on unemployment benefit, then administrative data on unemployment claimants are essentially censuses. If our population of interest is that of people who are searching for a job, including those who do not qualify or apply for unemployment benefit, then these data are a (possibly selected) sample of the population of interest. To the extent that they refer to the whole population of interest, administrative data can be considered better than survey data. Since they refer to a sample of the population, survey data are subject to sampling error.

Because administrative data are collected for administrative purposes only, they often include only basic information on the relevant individuals and quite often lack detailed socio-demographic information that may be useful for research purposes. Furthermore, because of confidentiality reasons, these types of data may be difficult to access for research purposes.

Also note that, depending on the purpose of data collection, some administrative data may be cross-section rather than longitudinal. The longitudinal data are often collected only over the period of time that the person satisfies certain criteria for inclusion. For example, data on unemployment benefits include information about individuals currently receiving unemployment benefits. Anyone who stops claiming such benefit falls out of scope and is from that moment on excluded from the data.

In contrast to administrative data, surveys are specifically collected for research purposes. We may distinguish between multipurpose and specific-purpose surveys. While in multipurpose surveys a large number of questions are asked on different aspects of people's lives, specific-purpose surveys may be commissioned to collect detailed information on specific aspects of people's lives (for example, environmental behaviour, consumption patterns, and so on).

The information reported by individuals in sample surveys may not always be accurate, for example when respondents do not remember certain events or facts, when they have difficulties understanding the question, when they do not feel comfortable answering sensitive questions such as questions about their income (see Groves et al. 2004). On the other hand it could be argued that administrative data may also be subject to error.

With the explicit consent of survey respondents, survey data can be linked to administrative data such as hospital episodes, benefits or educational records. This is becoming more common since such data linkage allows a set of substantial and precise information to be imported into the survey data. The linkage is more valuable the higher the proportion of survey respondents who give consent to the linkage, and the higher the success of the linkage itself (the linkage between survey and administrative records often relies on individual information such as name, year of birth, and so on, being recorded unambiguously across surveys).

2.4 Who is Included in the Survey and for How Long?

Surveys differ in terms of population of interest, which in turn determines who is included in the survey and for how long. One important distinction is between individual and household surveys.

Individual surveys ask questions to individual respondents about different aspects of their lives. Information on other members of the household may also be collected, but the interview is with only one person in the household. Household surveys instead ask questions to all people living in the household, thus producing multiple individual interviews for households with more than one adult. Household surveys add another layer of complexity for data management. Among the datasets discussed in this book, the PSID started as an individual panel survey, while the SOEP, BHPS and UKHLS started as household panel surveys.

Another important distinction is between individual panels and cohort surveys. While panel data include people of all ages living in a certain country at a certain point in time, cohort surveys focus on individuals with a common experience at a specific time period, such as being born in a particular year, or entering a country in a particular period, or graduating from high school in a particular year or decade. The most common types of cohort surveys are birth cohort surveys. These are individual surveys which collect information on individuals born in a particular short time span and follow them over their life cycle with interviews at specific points in time, often determined by age. As the sample members are of similar age, this increases comparability across respondents, but may reduce the range of research questions that can be answered with these types of data; for example, even if we combine data from different cohort surveys we may not be able to analyse the impact of the most recent recession on different age groups.

Various birth cohort surveys have been commonly used for research. The National Child Development Study follows a sample of people born in the UK in a single week in 1958, with interviews at ages 7, 11, 16, 23, 33, 42, 46, 50 and currently 55. The 1970 British Cohort Study follows a sample of people born in the UK in a single week in 1970, with interviews at ages 5, 10, 16, 26, 30, 34 and 38 and most recently 42. The Millennium Cohort Study follows a sample of people born in the UK in 2000–01, with data collected at the ages of 9 months, 3, 5, 7 and currently 11 years. The National Longitudinal Survey of Youth 1979 follows a sample of people born in the USA between January 1957 and December 1964 with annual interviews from 1979 (when the respondents were aged between 16 and 22) to 1992 and biennial interviews after that. The National Longitudinal Survey of Youth 1997 follows a sample of people born in the US between January 1980 and December 1984 with annual interviews from 1997, when the respondents were aged between 13 and 17.

In contrast to cohort surveys, panel surveys include a sample of people who are resident in a certain area at a certain time period and follows them, and sometimes their descendants as well. For example, the PSID started with a sample of people resident in the USA in 1967–8; the SOEP started with a sample of households living in West Germany in 1983–4; while the BHPS started with a sample of households living in Great Britain in 1990–91; and the UKHLS started as a sample of households living in the UK in 2008–09. The inclusion in the survey of people of all ages increases the heterogeneity of the respondents in terms of their life experiences; for example, the sample may include respondents both born and grown up during periods of boom and periods of recession.

Finally, surveys differ in terms of their length. The length of a survey is often determined a priori depending on the needs of the commissioning body and of the survey itself. In fixed life surveys respondents are followed up to a certain number of periods, after which they are typically substituted by a new set of respondents. Fixed life surveys are often used in rotating panel surveys, such as the UK Labour Force Survey (LFS). Respondents in the LFS are interviewed quarterly for up to five successive quarters, after which they are substituted by a new set of respondents sampled from the population currently living in the UK. Hence, the sample is divided into five parts: each quarter, one-fifth of the LFS respondents have their first interview, one-fifth each have their second, their third and their fourth interviews, while one-fifth have their fifth and final interview.

In contrast to fixed life surveys, perpetual surveys have indefinite life, with no scheduled end: individuals are interviewed as long as they remain within the scope of the survey (for example, as long as they live in the country). The household panel surveys discussed in this book are all perpetual life surveys (the BHPS officially ended after 18 waves but the surviving sample became part of Understanding Society after that).

2.5 Methods of Data Collection

The main methods of data collection are face-to-face personal interviews, telephone interviews and self-completion interviews (where the respondents complete a questionnaire by themselves). Self-completion questionnaires are often mailed to respondents, although are now increasingly implemented via the Web. Each of these methods has different implications on cost, non-response and quality in general; see Roberts (2007) for a review of advantages and disadvantages of the different modes of data collection. Nowadays surveys are increasingly being administered in multiple modes (De Leeuw 2005). Some parts of the interviews may be conducted in a different mode, or some of the sample members may be interviewed in a different mode. For example, most BHPS sample households are interviewed face-to-face but around 500 are interviewed by telephone, and those interviewed face-to-face also receive self-completion paper questionnaires to fill in.

As discussed in Chapter 1, retrospective and prospective surveys are the common types of longitudinal surveys, deriving their names from the different data collection methods employed.

In retrospective surveys, sample members are interviewed (often only once) and asked about their past history, so that the longitudinal element of the survey (the repeated information) is built very quickly and relatively cheaply, as generally only one interview is necessary.

In prospective surveys, sample members are interviewed every year (or every few years) and are asked about their current situation each time they are interviewed. In this case the longitudinal element of the survey is constructed (slowly) year by year via successive yearly interviews, although note that not all prospective surveys are annual, or even take place at regular intervals. Hence, prospective surveys are more expensive than retrospective ones. However, compared with retrospective surveys, prospective surveys are more likely to produce better quality data (see Chapter 1 of Taris 2000). The first reason is that people may forget details or the exact dates of events, especially when these happened a long time in the past; retrospective surveys are more likely to suffer from recollection bias than prospective surveys. The second reason is that retrospective surveys also suffer from survivor bias. By design, retrospective surveys are collected from those who have survived (in the literal sense or more generally those who are still present in the population of interest) until the time of the interview. If those who survived are systematically different from those who did not in terms of the variable of interest then estimates based on these data will be biased, hence survivor bias. Take for example a retrospective survey on a sample of migrants to study outcomes such as labour market success. If, by the time the survey is conducted, those migrants who had poor labour market success have returned to their home country (hence they left the population of interest or did not survive) then estimates of labour market success of migrants based on these data will be biased upwards.

It is worth noting that most prospective surveys also collect some data retrospectively (see the online appendix for details on the data collection of some commonly used panel datasets).

2.6 Attrition and Refreshment Samples

As already mentioned in Chapter 1, not all sample members are interviewed in every interview wave (unit non-response). For example, some people may change their residence without communicating the change to the survey organisers, who may therefore be unable to locate them for further interviews. Even when people can be located, the survey organiser may not be able to get in touch with them to fix an interview date (for example, some people may be away or too ill to answer the door or the phone). Some of them may have decided they no longer want to be part of the survey and refuse to give further interviews. In Chapter 1 we also discussed the difference between wave non-response and attrition: the former refers to intermittent non-response and the latter to dropping out of the survey permanently.

Non-response or attrition is a serious problem for sample-based estimations. First, it reduces sample size, thus reducing the precision of estimates based on these data. Secondly, attriters and non-respondents may be systematically different from respondents so that the estimates based on respondent reports may also be biased. In Chapter 7 we discuss the relevance of non-response and attrition in more details. If the sample size reduces to such a level that it greatly reduces the precision of estimates based on these data, then sometimes refresher samples are drawn from the original population to replenish the reduced sample.

Since panel and cohort surveys collect information from a sample of residents which is drawn at one particular point in time, these surveys may miss out on population changes. New births are usually incorporated in the sample design by determining who, from the original sample, should be followed: for example, respondents and their current and future offspring. Nevertheless, new waves of immigration are likely to be missed by many sample designs (exceptions are rotating panels, which incorporate regular refresher samples into the sample design). Hence, sometimes refresher samples drawn from the new population (for example, new immigrants) may be added to the original sample at a later stage in the life of the panel to account for the population changes.

2.7 Household Panel Surveys Around the World

There are various panel surveys collected around the world. Below we discuss the main characteristics of some of the most commonly used ones: namely, the PSID, SOEP, BHPS and UKHLS.

Although most of the examples in this book are based on the BHPS, in Chapters 3 to 6 and in Chapter 12 we discuss all four datasets. Below we focus on the most important characteristics of these surveys and refer to the online appendix for more details.

Further details about each of the four surveys can be accessed through their user guide as well as through technical papers focusing on specific aspects of the survey. There is also excellent online interactive documentation which is a good place to start. The questionnaires and other materials used during surveys, user guides and technical papers are also available online. Some people find it helpful to join the respective user groups and attend training workshops offered by the data managers.

These surveys are multipurpose surveys and collect information on socio-demographic characteristics (such as gender, age, ethnicity or race, region and country of birth), family background (such as living arrangement and parents' employment when respondent was a child), education and training, labour market activities, partnership and fertility, income, wealth and assets, self-reported physical and mental health, and values and opinions. In addition, the UKHLS includes information on bio-markers for a subsample.

2.7.1 The Panel Study of Income Dynamics (PSID)

The PSID is one of the oldest ongoing household panel surveys. The survey started in 1968 with a sample of about 18,000 individuals in 4,802 families living in the USA, with data collected annually from the head of the household. This is the male for married couples, and either the male or the female for other families (for a recent overview see McGonagle et al. 2012).

The respondent provides information about him- or herself and other members of the family, although in specific supplements (like the ones about retrospective histories) both members of the couple are interviewed. From the 1970s, however, the PSID collects the same details also from the spouse of the head of the household. The survey intends to follow members of the original family unit and their offspring (note that the PSID focuses on families while the other three datasets discussed below focus on households).

The 1968 PSID sample comprised two independent subsamples: the 'SRC' (Survey Research Center) and the 'SEO' (Survey of Economic Opportunity), referred to as the 'core samples'. The SRC sample was collected by the Survey Research Center, at the Institute for Social Research, University of Michigan, and the SEO sample was collected by the Bureau of the Census for the Office of Economic Opportunity.

The SRC sample was a sample representative of the US population, with equal selection probabilities in the 48 coterminous states. This sample produced 2,930 interviews. In the SEO sample, low-income families had comparatively higher selection probabilities. The SEO sample included only people living in Standard Metropolitan Statistical Areas (SMSAs), and people living in non-SMSAs in the southern region. This sample produced 1,872 interviews. The 18,000 individuals living in these interviewed households became permanent sample members or were said to have the 'PSID gene'. These individuals and all their biological or adopted descendants would be followed over time. In 1990, an additional sample of 2,043 Latino individuals (Mexican, Cuban and Puerto Rican) was added but dropped after 1995 due to lack of funding and under-representation of immigrants of Asian descent (this short-lived subsample is rarely used by researchers for analysis). Two additional immigrant samples were added in 1997 and 1999, respectively, and are referred to as the 'immigrant samples'. To reduce costs, 57% of the SEO sample was also dropped in 1997; this was also the year when the interview frequency changed from annual to biennial. Interviews in the PSID were conducted face-to-face from 1968 to 1972 and by phone from 1973. This change led to much shorter interviews.

2.7.2 The German Socio-Economic Panel (SOEP)

The SOEP is a household panel survey of the non-institutionalised resident population in Germany. It started in 1984 with a sample of private households in West Germany which included a sample of households with non-ethnic minority household heads (called subsample A) and an oversample of households with household heads of Turkish, Greek, Yugoslavian, Spanish or Italian origin (called subsample B).

In 1990 an oversample of private households with a German Democratic Republic citizen as head of household was added (subsample C), followed by an immigrant boost sample in 1994 and 1995 (subsample D), a refreshment sample with similar design as subsample A (subsample E) in 1998 and a boost sample of high-income earners in 2002 (subsample G). In 2000 an innovation sample with a similar design as subsamples A and E was added.

All household members aged 16 and over are eligible for personal interviews, which are conducted primarily face-to-face with a small self-completion component. Information is collected prospectively, with some retrospective elements such as employment, partnership and fertility histories. In addition to the information collected in personal interviews, the head of the household is also asked questions about the household, parents about their children, and interviewers about the interview process.

All members of households who participated in the first wave and their descendants are followed as long as they live in Germany; people who join these households are also interviewed and since 1998 are also followed as long as they live in Germany.

2.7.3 The British Household Panel Survey (BHPS)

Similar to the SOEP, the BHPS is a household panel survey, of people living in the UK. The data collection began in 1991 on a sample of approximately 5,500 households and 10,000 adult respondents in England, Wales and (most of) Scotland.

To allow analyses separately for the three British countries, since 1999 the survey includes additional samples of about 1,500 households living in Scotland, and a further 1,500 households living in Wales. In 2001 a sample of about 2,000 households living in Northern Ireland was added to the BHPS sample.

Interviews are carried out annually with each adult member (aged 16 and over) of the selected households, with youth self-completion questionnaires for children aged 11–15 added from 1994. All members of households who participated in the first wave and their descendants, referred to as Original Sample Members (OSMs), are followed as long as they live in the UK. Respondents who join these households after the first wave, referred to as Temporary Sample Members (TSMs), are also interviewed, but only as long as they are living with the original household members. When TSMs have children with OSMs, they become Permanent Sample Members (PSMs) and are followed even when they stop living with an OSM.

Among the panel surveys discussed in this book, the BHPS is the only one which is not currently ongoing. As a stand-alone survey, the BHPS finished in 2008. From 2010 the sample of surviving households from the BHPS has been incorporated into a new and larger UK household longitudinal survey Understanding Society.

2.7.4 Understanding Society: The UK Household Longitudinal Study (UKHLS)

The UKHLS is a household panel survey drawn from the non-institutionalised resident population of the UK. The UKHLS includes a sample of approximately 26,000 households living in the UK, and a sample boost of about 4,000 households belonging to selected ethnic minorities. The BHPS sample of 6,500 households that survived after the eighteenth wave became part of the UKHLS sample from the second wave onwards.

The large sample size is a peculiar characteristic of the UKHLS compared with other panel surveys. This allows analysis of specific subpopulations such as pre-retirement workers, single mothers, and so on; the ethnic minority boost sample makes it possible to analyse the selected ethnic minority groups separately.

All household members who are aged 16 and over are eligible for personal face-to-face and self-completion interviews; young people aged 10 to 15 are asked to complete a self-completion questionnaire. Most information is collected prospectively, with some retrospective elements such as partnership and fertility histories. Similar to the BHPS and SOEP, the household reference persons answer questions regarding the household, and parents answer questions about their children. In addition, interviewers provide information about the interview process.

The following rules for the UKHLS are similar to those of the BHPS with some exceptions: only children of OSMs who are women become OSMs; only TSMs who are men and who have children with an OSM become PSMs and are followed as long as they are in the UK. While the BHPS sample members maintain their sample status when they join the UKHLS, once they become part of the UKHLS, the following rules of UKHLS apply.

An additional sample, called the Innovation Panel, with a sample of approximately 1,500 households is interviewed one year prior to the UKHLS main survey. The Innovation Panel is used for research on survey methodology issues and survey 'experiments'. It is essentially a different survey from the main UKHLS dataset, and should not be used in conjunction with the main UKHLS sample.

Compared with the other three surveys discussed above, the UKHLS puts a much greater emphasis on health measures, particularly direct health measures such as grip strength, blood pressure, lung function test, and so on. Cognitive ability tests have also been administered. These measures have been collected at one point in time from subsamples of respondents.

2.7.5 Other Panel Surveys

Quite a few countries have now started their own household panel surveys, which often have a structure very similar to the SOEP and BHPS. However, these surveys are also rather heterogeneous across countries since questions are often asked differently in each national survey. In an attempt to produce datasets that allow cross-country comparisons, the Development of Policy Analysis and Management at Cornell University in collaboration with a number of institutes around the world has developed the so-called Cross-National Equivalent File (CNEF). The 1970–2009 CNEF contains harmonised variables for the PSID, the SOEP, the BHPS, the Household Income and Labour Dynamics in Australia, the Canadian Survey of Labour and Income Dynamics, and the Swiss Household Panel. Recent additions to the CNEF are the Korean Labor and Income Panel Study and the Russian Longitudinal Monitoring Survey.

The CNEF provides a simplified version of the national panels and guidelines for formulating equivalent variables across countries. The CNEF files also include a set of constructed variables that are not directly available in the original surveys and that can be merged into the national surveys and included in the analyses.

In Europe, some panel datasets have been collected in harmonised ways across countries. One of these is the European Community Household Panel (ECHP). Data are available annually from 1994 to 2001, when the survey officially ended. ECHP data have been collected using a standardised questionnaire. The first wave of data was collected from about 60,500 households (130,000 adults aged 16 years and over) in the 12 European Community Member States (Belgium, France, Italy, Luxembourg, the Netherlands, Germany, Denmark,

Ireland, the United Kingdom, Greece, Portugal and Spain). Data collection for Austria started in 1995; data for Finland have been added since 1996, and for Sweden since 1997.

Cross-country comparability in the ECHP is achieved by means of common survey structure and procedures, common questionnaires and common standards for data processing.

A more recent source of household panel data harmonised across EU countries is the European Union Statistics on Income and Living Conditions (EU-SILC). EU-SILC data cover the 25 EU Member States, Norway and Iceland. The EU-SILC is intended to be a finite-life sample, in which households are interviewed for up to a maximum of four (consecutive) years. In contrast to the ECHP, EU-SILC data are not based on a common questionnaire, but on a list of harmonised target variables, collected following common guidelines, procedures and concepts.

2.8 Summary and Suggestions for Further Reading

In this chapter we have discussed the different types of longitudinal data that can be used for analysis. In the rest of the book we focus on panel surveys rather than census or administrative data, although most of the data management and econometric techniques discussed are relevant for most types of longitudinal datasets. The book mostly uses the BHPS in its examples, but data management techniques (and the online appendix) also include detailed explanations of PSID, SOEP and UKHLS data.

Key points

- Surveys differ in many aspects: who is interviewed (households or individuals), how the data are collected (prospectively or retrospectively), and so on.
- There are numerous panel surveys around the world, with different degrees of cross-country comparability.
- Attempts have been made – and are ongoing – to produce data that are comparable across countries.

Suggestions for further reading

- For a good primer on survey methodology including inference, sampling, non-response, interview modes and questionnaire design, and see Groves, R.M., Fowler, J.F.J., Couper, M.P., Lepkowski, J.M., Singer, E. and Tourangeau, R. (2004) *Survey Methodology*. Hoboken, NJ, Wiley-Interscience.

- There is extensive research on different methods of data collection and some that recommend using mixed modes and designing surveys so as to minimise any differences in response due to differences in interview mode (unimode design). See:

  o De Leeuw, E. (2005) To Mix or Not to Mix Data Collection Modes in Surveys. *Journal of Official Statistics* 21(2): 235–55.
  o Dillman, D.A. (2007) *Mail and Internet Surveys: The Tailored Design Method.* Hoboken, NJ, Wiley.
  o Roberts, C. (2007) Mixing Modes of Data Collection in Surveys: A Methodological Review. NCRM Methods Review Papers (NCRM/008).

- A concise overview of different data collection methods, specifically administrative and sample surveys, their advantages and disadvantages, can be found on the Statistics Canada website: www.statcan.gc.ca/edu/power-pouvoir/ch2/5214911-eng.htm.
- The Administrative Data Liaison Service provides support and help to researchers using UK administrative data for their research. See www.adls.ac.uk/.
- Nowadays the most detailed user guides for the panel datasets we have briefly discussed here are all online. See the US PSID: http://psidonline.isr.umich.edu/. On this website, you will find that the PSID also offers short video podcasts which clearly explain some key aspects of the study: http://psidonline.isr.umich.edu/videos.aspx. Although created to train interviewers, it is quite useful for new users as well. A short overview outlining the main features is available from www.uncg.edu/bae/people/ribar/teaching/ECO725/notes/intro_PSID.pdf. See also the SOEP: www.diw.de/en/soep; the UK BHPS: https://www.iser.essex.ac.uk/bhps and UKHLS: www.understandingsociety.org.uk/; the CNEF: www.human.cornell.edu/pam/research/centers-programs/german-panel/cnef.cfm; the ECHP: epp.eurostat.ec.europa.eu/portal/page/portal/microdata/echp; and the EU-SILC: epp.eurostat.ec.europa.eu/portal/page/portal/microdata/eu_silc.

A FIRST LOOK AT THE DATA USING STATA

Aim

In this chapter we give a short introduction to Stata and to its basic commands, including best practice tips. These are followed by a description of how to open different types of datasets and how to deal with datasets provided in different formats. We then describe the commands commonly used to inspect the data, compute descriptive statistics, recode values, create new variables, label variables and values, and produce graphs.

3.1 Introduction

Any analysis starts with a first look at the data. It is good practice to familiarise ourselves with the dataset before starting any new analysis: what variables are available, how are they coded, how many missing values do they have? For large datasets, looking at the data generally means looking at summaries of the data by producing frequency distributions, cross-tabulations and descriptive statistics such as means and standard deviations. In this chapter we use the individual respondent file for the first wave of the BHPS (the file is called aindresp) to illustrate these issues. In this chapter we analyse in a descriptive way if there are differences between the marital status of men and women and in what they think about their neighbourhood. For those who are employed, we also want to look at the distribution of wages. First, we need to open Stata.

3.1.1 Stata Windows and Help

As Stata opens, at least four windows are shown by default (see Figure 3.1); all these windows can be moved, resized or closed. The 'Command' window at the bottom of the screen is used to type the Stata commands and run them interactively. The results of the commands that we have run are shown in the 'Results' window immediately above. The 'Command Review' window on the left of the screen shows the list of commands that we have typed, while the 'Variables' window lists the names, labels and other characteristics of the variables in the dataset currently open in memory.

Stata offers different forms of help. For help with a specific command, use the drop-down menu: Help → Stata command → then type the name of the command. Alternatively, in the 'Command' window type help followed by the name of the command (for example, help regress). A new window will open describing the syntax for the command. All the documentation is available in pdf (portable document format): clicking on the name of the command will open the relevant part of the Stata pdf manual.

Command Review: shows the list of the commands that have been typed (interactively) in the 'Command' window

Results: shows the results of the commands that have been run

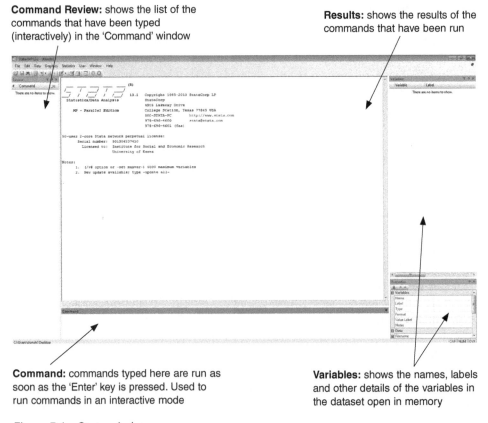

Command: commands typed here are run as soon as the 'Enter' key is pressed. Used to run commands in an interactive mode

Variables: shows the names, labels and other details of the variables in the dataset open in memory

Figure 3.1   Stata windows

For more general help, use the drop-down menu: Help → Search → then type a keyword. Alternatively, in the 'Command' window type search followed by a keyword (for example, search dummy variable). When using the menu, the help is provided in a new window, but when using the 'Command' window the help is provided in the 'Results' window. The command search with the option all performs the search across both the local keyword database and the material available on the Internet. This is particularly useful when we do not know the name of a specific command. The best way to search for information across all sources, including the online help, the frequently asked questions (FAQs) on the Stata website, the *Stata Journal* and all other Stata-related Internet sources, is the command findit. If the search produces results such as user-written programs, a link is provided to the source page, which in most cases includes further links to the program files which can be used to install the command, if it is not installed in the current version of Stata (for an example see Section 3.3, where we discuss how to install the command fre).

Some commands can be used in all versions of Stata; one example discussed below in Section 3.3 is the command use which is used to open datasets that are in Stata format.

Sometimes certain commands are replaced by newer versions. If a command is no longer available in a version of Stata but was available in earlier versions, the Stata help for this command specifies that the old command has been replaced with a new one and points to the command that has replaced it.

3.1.2 Stata Commands

In Stata many commands can be called by using drop-down menus. Although the menus are a good way to start for those commands with many options, such as graphs, it is good practice to learn the structure of each command. First, not all Stata commands can be called using the drop-down menus. Second, learning the syntax of the command is important to allow reproducibility of the analysis (see Section 3.1.7).

Stata is case sensitive: most of the commands are all in lower case and have the following structure:

```
command [optional qualifiers], [options]
```

The name of the command (in the example above, command) is followed by parts which are optional. In the Stata help the optional parts of the command are specified between square brackets (these square brackets are not to be included when writing the command). Everything which is not between square brackets is needed to make the command work; the options of the command are typed after a comma.

Most command names and options can be abbreviated, sometimes to one letter only! The Stata help underlines the shortest abbreviation possible for the command. In the example above, it would be equivalent to typing command, options or co, opt. For example, if we look at the Stata help for the command used to compute summary statistics we find the following description:

```
summarize [varlist] [if] [in] [weight] [, options]
```

where varlist is the list of variables for which we want summary statistics. However, the only part which is necessary is su. We notice that varlist is within the square brackets. The command summarize alone produces summary statistics for all the variables in the dataset. The command summarize followed by a list of variables produces summary statistics for the specified variables. For example, the command summarize age produces summary statistics for the variable age.

It is generally good practice to write the full command (for example, summarize instead of the minimal abbreviation su) to make it easier to read the do file at a later stage. This also facilitates collaboration with colleagues who will find it easier to interpret a do file where all the commands are written in full.

3.1.3 Variable Types and Names

Variable names can be between 1 and 32 characters in length and may contain letters, numbers and underscores. The letters can be either in upper or lower case, or a combination of both. Hence, Stata will recognise Apaygu and apaygu as two distinct variables.

Besides the name of the commands, also the name of the variables can be abbreviated, as long as there is no confusion. For example, if a dataset includes two variables paygu and pay, and we type the command tab1 payg, we obtain a tabulation of the variable paygu even though the last letter of the name (u) is missing and the variable payg does not exist. The command tab1 pay would tabulate the variable pay, while the command tab1 pa would generate an error message since the name of more than one variable starts with the letters pa. However, the command tab1 pay* or tab1 pa* tabulates both pay and paygu. The symbol * is used as a placeholder for an unspecified list of characters (of any length): for example, the command sum pa* would summarise all variables whose name starts with the letters pa.[1]

----

[1]Note that this characteristic of Stata can create problems when combining files from datasets in which variable names might change slightly over time (more details in Chapter 4): when combining files into long format, variables will be appended only if they have exactly the same name. In some datasets – such as the quarterly Labour Force Survey for the UK – variable names might change slightly over time as a reflection of a change in their collection or definition; for example, a variable that was named occupation up to 2007 might suddenly become occupation08 from 2008. If we were to append two files, one for 2007 with the variable occupation and the other for 2008 with the variable

```
                                                Closest to
Storage                                         0 without
type                 Minimum          Maximum   being 0      bytes
-------------------------------------------------------------------
byte                      -127            100   +/-1            1
int                    -32,767         32,740   +/-1            2
long            -2,147,483,647  2,147,483,620   +/-1            4
float   -1.70141173319*10^38  1.70141173319*10^38  +/-10^-38   4
double  -8.9884656743*10^307  8.9884656743*10^307  +/-10^-323  8
-------------------------------------------------------------------

Precision for float  is 3.795x10^-8.
Precision for double is 1.414x10^-16.


String
storage        Maximum
type           length           Bytes
-------------------------------------------
str1             1                 1
str2             2                 2
...             .                 .
...             .                 .
...             .                 .
str244          244               244
-------------------------------------------
```

Figure 3.2   Types of variables in Stata

In addition, suppose that in the dataset we have two other variables called paymen and paywomen and we want to summarise only these variables, and not pay and paygu. In this case we can abbreviate the names of the variables by using an asterisk as a placeholder in the following way: summarize pa*n. This command summarises all variables that start with the letter pa and end with the letter n.

As in most software, variables can be of two types: numeric or string. Strings can be of different lengths (ranging from 1 to 244 characters in Stata), while numeric variables range from bytes (the smallest) to double, which are used to store exceptionally large numbers, such as identification numbers (for example, the variables pid and hid in the BHPS, see Chapter 4). Figure 3.2 lists the possible options.

When generating a numeric variable, by default this is stored as a float variable. Float variables have seven digits of accuracy, although the magnitude of the number itself does not matter. If the content of the variable is an integer or a dummy, storing it as a float variable would waste space. If the value of the variable is between –127 and 100 it can be stored as a byte; if its value is between 32,767 and 32,740 it can be stored as an integer (see also Figure 3.2). Similarly, storing a 6-character string in a string which is 20 characters long

occupation08, the resulting file would include both variables (that is, these two variables would not be appended to each other). For 2008, the variable occupation would include only missing values, and for 2007 the variable occupation08 would include only missing values.

would be a waste. Although it is good practice to specify the type of variable when generating it, this can be cumbersome. A useful alternative is to type the command `compress`, alone or followed by a list of variables, before saving the final version of the file. The aim of the command `compress` is to reduce the amount of memory used by the dataset by using the appropriate data type to store variables. The command `compress` converts variables that are stored as `double` to `long,` `int` or `byte` formats; it converts variables that are stored as `float` into `int` or `byte`, and so on; this is done for all variables as long as the new format does not involve loss of information. Although the data are logically unchanged, the size of the final dataset might be substantially smaller.

Note that a `float` variable has (only) seven digits of accuracy. If we want to create a variable containing numbers more than seven digits long (as would be the case for variables which represent unique identification numbers in large datasets) we need to store the variable in `double` or `long` format. If we use a `float` type of variable and the original person identification number is formed of 10–12 digits, Stata would round this number to the nearest seven-digit number. The original number would be lost and all individuals whose person identification numbers start with the same seven digits would be given the same identification number. In this specific case we need to specify the size of the numeric variable while we define it (see Section 3.4 for how to create new variables).

3.1.4 do Files

In the previous sections we talked about accessing Stata commands using the drop-down menu and typing the commands interactively. There is a third option: writing the commands and storing them in a 'do file'. A do file is a text file where we store a sequence of Stata commands. When we execute the do file, Stata runs all these commands in the order in which they appear in the do file. Although a variety of text editors can be used for this purpose (like Notepad), Stata provides its own text editor (see Figure 3.3).

Typing the commands interactively might be a good idea when deciding which new variables to compute or which model to use; however, to allow reproducibility of the analysis it is always better to keep track of the commands that we have chosen for the analysis by storing them in the do file. When using do files we can also add comments. Comments are pieces of text that we add to our do files but that are not commands. We use special symbols to distinguish the comments from the Stata commands (see below). Comments may be included in the do file to better explain the choices of variables and estimators, for example why we have used estimator A instead of estimator B, or why we have not included variable C in the final model specification. Such comments are particularly useful when working with others on the same project and for the future when we may not remember every detail of the choices we made earlier.

We can open the do file using the drop-down menu: select Windows → Do file editor → New Do file editor. To run (or execute) the do file, from the do file drop-down menu we select Tools → Execute (do) or Tools → Execute quietly (run). While the first option (do) shows all the results of the commands in the 'Results' window, the second option (run) runs all the commands 'quietly', without showing any of the results in the 'Results' window (Figure 3.3). We can also use the do and run icons in the toolbar at the top of the Stata's do file editor (sometimes the run icon may not be there by default and we may have to add it in). We can also use the shortcut keys Ctrl + D to execute the do file or Ctrl + R to run it quietly.

Click here to open a do file

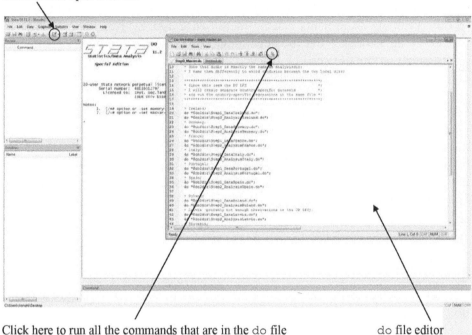

Click here to run all the commands that are in the do file   do file editor

Figure 3.3   do files

When typing the commands interactively, each command has to appear in one line: the 'Enter' key indicates the end of the command. In do files it is possible to split commands into different lines by using three forward slashes (continuation lines: ///) at the end of the line to indicate that the command continues on the next line. This is the approach we use throughout this book, and in the do files provided in the online appendix. Note that we need to leave at least one space between the command and the three forward slashes or we will get an error message.

An alternative way to split commands into different lines in do files consists of defining the semicolon (;) as a delimiter. This can be done by adding the following command at the beginning of the do file.

```
#delimit ;
```

From this point onwards in the do file we can use more than one line to write the command since it is now the semicolon – rather than the 'Enter' key – which identifies where the command ends.

Note that the three forward slashes (///) and the #delimit command only work in do files, and do not work when typing the commands interactively. When working interactively, it is necessary to type the whole command in one line.

As already mentioned, another advantage of do files is the possibility of including comments. To avoid Stata interpreting comments as if they were commands, and therefore producing an error message, comments are identified by specific symbols. Comments can be identified either by two forward slashes (//), or by an asterisk (*) at the beginning of the line containing the comment. Alternatively, comments can be placed between the /* and */ delimiters. Also note that the three forward slashes (///) placed at the end of a line mean that the command continues on the following line, but when they are placed at the beginning of the line they denote a comment. Furthermore, the different comment indicators may be used in different ways. For example, when we are typing our commands interactively we can use the asterisk (but not the other symbols) to identify the comment. In a do file we can use the /* and */ delimiters (but not the other symbols) to include comments in the middle of a command line. Look at the Stata help for more details.

3.1.5 Best Practice

It is good practice to start each do file with some housekeeping. Here are some useful commands:

```
version 12

clear all

set more off

capture log close
```

With every new version of Stata new commands are added, which might not work in older versions of the software. The command version specifies the version of Stata in which the commands have to be run. This command can be very useful when working on two different computers which have two different versions of Stata installed, for example version 12 on one computer and version

13 on the other. This command ensures that all commands, even when typed in version 13, are compatible with version 12. Hence, in the command `version` we should specify the older version of Stata we may use. This book uses commands compatible with version 12.

The command `clear all` clears the working directory of any data that might already be open and of older results that might be stored in the temporary memory (see also Section 3.3).[2]

By default, Stata displays the results in the 'Results' windows page by page; we will then be prompted to press any key or click on the `-more-` link at the bottom of the page to display the next page. We use the command `set more off` to show the entire set of results, even if longer than one page, without pausing after each page. This command is useful when we are executing do files and when we are using Stata interactively and want to store all the results appearing in the 'Results' window in a file which can be consulted later. Such files, where all the results that appear on the screen are stored, are called `log` files. We discuss them in more detail in Section 3.1.7.

Generally we include the commands to create a new `log` file at the beginning of our do file, and include the commands to close the `log` file at the end of our do file. The command to create a new `log` file is `log using`, while the command to close a `log` file (if one `log` file is already open in memory) is `log close`. Note that the command `log close` generates an error message if there is no `log` file currently open in memory.

Sometimes the execution of the do file stops because of an error. We correct the error and run the do file again. In this case, however, we have a `log` file already open in memory because Stata has executed the command `log using` but the execution of the do file terminated before the command `log close` (the do file never completed running and never got to the point where the command `log close` is written). If we run our do file again, now the command `log using` will generate an error message because there is already a `log` file open

---

[2]In versions of Stata older than version 12 it may be necessary to set the size of the memory. When working with individual-level data, the size of the memory provided by default in Stata 11 and older versions might not be enough to open the data file. It might therefore be necessary to increase the size of the working memory to be able to open large files. This can be done using the command `set memory 20m` (note the m after the 20, and that 20 is much smaller than 20m). This command increases the size of the working memory to 20 megabytes. As a rule of thumb, we need at least as much memory as the size of the dataset we want to open.

Remember that the size of the working memory can only be changed when there is no data file open in memory. Technically there is no maximum in the amount of memory that can be allocated, and each computer and operating system will impose different limits. In Stata 12 and more recent versions, there is no need to set the memory size as memory adjustments are performed on the fly automatically. Also in Stata 12 and more recent versions, the command `set memory 20m` is ignored and does not generate an error.

in memory. As with datasets, it is not possible to open a `log` file if one is already open in memory. This is the reason why we type the command `log close` at the beginning of our do file.

However, here we run into another problem. The command `log close` closes the `log` file if one is already open, but gives an error message if no `log` file is currently open, thus terminating execution of the do file. To prevent this happening, it is enough to type `capture` before the command that might generate the error message. The command `capture` prevents Stata from terminating the do file even if the command cannot be successfully completed (for example, because the command is not typed correctly or because the action cannot be undertaken). If the command generates an error message, its return code (which is a short description of why the command failed) is stored in the built-in scalar `_rc` (this is a number identifying the type of error that occurred). If there was no error and the command completed successfully, the return code stored in `_rc` is zero.

3.1.6 Global and Local Macros

Before discussing the Stata commands we need to discuss how Stata stores information. We can think of the Stata memory as being divided into separate 'boxes', each dedicated to different types of information (see Figure 3.4). In one of these 'boxes' Stata stores the dataset (the variables, value labels, variable labels attached to the data) that have been uploaded to its memory. For example, one of these variables may be called `age`. To upload these variables in the correct 'box' we use the command `use` (see Section 3.2). When we want to use this variable we type its name (`age`). For example, if we want to produce means and standard deviations of this variable, we use the command `summarize age`.

In other such 'boxes' Stata stores objects called macros. Macros are sequences of characters or bits of text, to which we give a name. When we call a macro within a command, Stata replaces it with the sequence of characters we have specified earlier and then executes the command. This is very useful as we can use short names in place of long sequences of characters, particularly when we are using the same piece of text repeatedly. This reduces the possibility of errors and is very efficient when we need to make changes, since it means we only need to make the change once, when we define the macro.

Macros can be local or global. While a local macro is only available within the do file (or within a loop when working interactively), a global macro is available throughout the Stata session (that is, until we close Stata or overwrite the macro). Global macros and local macros are stored in separate 'boxes' in the Stata memory. To define a local macro and upload it in the appropriate 'box' we use the command `local name`, which may be followed by an equals (=) sign; see the Stata help for more details (we use local macros in Chapter 4, Section 4.3.1). The name of the local macro can be exactly the same as the name of a variable, but because they are stored in different 'boxes' there is no confusion between them. When we want to use the local macro within a command we type its name enclosed between a grave accent ' and an apostrophe ' (`name'). For example, if we want to use a set of variables at different points in the do file, once to compute descriptive statistics, once as explanatory variables in one or more estimation models, and so on, we can use a local macro. We first define the local macro using, for example, the command:

```
local name age sex region education
```

This command creates a local macro called name, and the content of this local macro is the name of four variables that are in our dataset (age sex region education). If we now want to produce descriptive statistics for all these variables, instead of typing

```
summarize age sex region education
```

we can type: summarize `name' and obtain exactly the same result.

To define a global macro and upload it in the appropriate 'box' we use the command global name, which, again, may be followed by an equals (=) sign. Also in this case there is no confusion if we have a local macro and a variable with exactly the same name. To use the global macro we type its name after the symbol $: $name. Note that there should be no spaces between the dollar sign and the name of the global macro. The dollar sign tells Stata to look for an object (in this case called name) in that 'box' in memory where global macros are stored. Section 3.1.7 gives an example of how to use a global macro.

Figure 3.4 summarises these different types of 'variables' that we can use in Stata. There are other types of 'boxes' in the Stata memory where other types of variables are stored. We discuss some of these in Chapter 5.

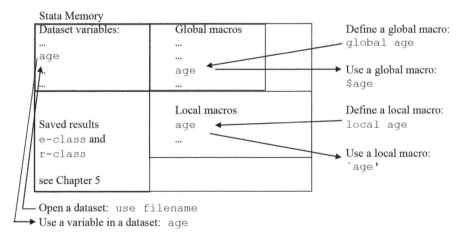

Figure 3.4   Local and global macros

3.1.7 Portability and Reproducibility

When working with collaborators or using different computers, issues of portability may arise. For example, often the directory where the data are stored has different names and paths in different computers. To make the do file more portable it is good practice to store the file paths to the relevant directories in global macros. The advantage of defining the path using a global macro at the beginning of the do file is that, when moving across different computers, it is only necessary to change the content of this global macro, rather than the file path throughout the do file. As already mentioned in Section 3.1.6, we define global macros using the command global. For example, to store the file path "C:\My Documents" in a global macro called datadir we type

```
global datadir "C:\My Documents"
```

Are quotation marks always necessary? No. However, Stata would not accept paths including spaces unless written within double quotes: only paths that do not include spaces do not need quotation marks.

It is possible to define more than one global macro, for example one for the path to where the data are stored, and one for the path to the folder where we want to save the output. If we do not use paths to specify where the results should be stored, by default Stata saves all the output in the current working directory (displayed on the bottom left of the Stata screen, below the 'Variables' window). This is often different in different computers. To avoid losing or misplacing our output, we can either specify the path every time we want to save any type of output, or change the working directory to the folder specific to the project. Once we have specified the new working directory, we do not need to specify the path. We can directly change the working directory using the command cd (for example, cd "C:\My Documents\Project1").

All the results that appear on the screen eventually disappear. Hence, we may want to save everything that appears on the screen in a text file, called log file, which can be consulted at later stages. We can create or open a log file, which we can call "Example_Chapter3", using the command log using:

```
log using Example_Chapter3.log, replace
```

The log file is automatically saved every time a new result appears in the 'Result' window. If a log file with the same name already exists, we can use the option replace to overwrite the old file, or use the option append to append the new results to the old ones (note that in this case the file might quickly become very large).

By default, Stata creates a log file with the extension .smcl. This type of file can only be opened within Stata, but if we use the extension .log instead, the file is written in ASCII, and can be read in almost all text editors. We can also save a `log` file in text format by adding the option `text`:

```
log using Example_Chapter3, replace text
```

Alternatively, we can specify the file format of the `log` file at the beginning of the do file using the command `set logtype text`. All the `log` files will then be saved as text files without the need to specify the file format (`.log` or `text`).

3.2 How to Open Datasets

3.2.1 Opening Datasets in Stata Format

Now that we are familiar with Stata, we can open the dataset we want to analyse. Most datasets, such as the BHPS, UKHLS and SOEP, are provided in Stata format (`.dta`), and data for different waves of interviews are provided in separate files (we discuss how to combine these files in Chapter 4). To open the data we can use the drop-down menu (File → Open) or click on the 'open' icon. However, it is always best to write down the appropriate command in a do file. The command to open datasets in Stata format is `use`, which can be used in different versions:

```
use filename [, clear nolabel]
```

or

```
use variable1 variableN using filename, clear
```

The first version of the command opens the whole dataset and is most useful when the exact content (for example, the names of the variables) of the dataset is not known. However, it might not be feasible if the dataset is very large. If the content of the dataset is known in advance and we know which variables are needed for the analysis, we can open only part of the dataset after specifying the name of the variables that have to be uploaded in memory, as in the second version of the command. Note that the maximum number of variables we can upload in memory depends on the version of Stata we use, and may vary from 99 for Small Stata to 32,767 for the MP and SE versions.

How can we use the second version of the `use` command if we do not know the names of the variables in the dataset? We can use the Stata command `describe using` followed by the path and the name of the file, to get a description of the data without opening the data itself. The command shows the names of all variables included in the dataset, their type (string, numeric float, byte, and so on) and labels (labels are short descriptions of the variables, see Section 3.4 for more details).

In datasets such as the BHPS the variable names have the same root across waves but a different letter prefix representing each wave (`` `a' `` for the first wave, `` `b' `` for the second, and so on). For example, if wage data collected in the first wave are called `awage`, wage data collected in the second wave are called `bwage`, `cwage` for the third wave, and so on. The UKHLS follows the same rule, but the prefix includes an underscore: `a_wage`, `b_wage`, etc. Hence, if we want to use only the variables `aage` and `asex` from the BHPS file `aindresp`, stored in the folder `S:\final` (remember that we have already stored this path in the global macro `datadir`), we can use the following command:

```
use aage asex using $datadir/aindresp, clear
```

where the dollar sign ($) indicates that `datadir` is the name of a global macro that we have defined earlier in the `do` file. The option `clear` is used to clear the memory in case another dataset is already open. Besides uploading in memory only some of the variables, we can decide to upload only some of the records, for example only data for men, by adding an `if` statement:

```
use aage asex using $datadir/aindresp if ///

    asex == 1, clear
```

(remember that `if` always goes before the comma). Note that Stata identifies equalities by a double – rather than a single – equals sign. A single equals sign is used to assign values to a variable. A list of the most common Stata operators that we can use to compute arithmetic operations and to perform logical comparisons is given in Table 3.1.

In some datasets, such as the SOEP, variable names do not follow rules. In the SOEP there are three types of variable names: some variables have one common root and a wave prefix as in the BHPS, while other variables have the same root but a year suffix instead of a wave prefix (for example, `wage84`; `wage85`). Most variables, however, have names which refer to the question number in the

Table 3.1   Stata operators

Arithmetic		Logical		Relational (numeric and string)	
+	addition	&	and	>	greater than
-	subtraction	|	or	<	less than
*	multiplication	!	not	>=	greater than or equal to
/	division	~	not	<=	less than or equal to
^	power			==	equal
-	negation			!=	not equal
+	string concatenation			~=	not equal

questionnaire and bear no resemblance to the content of the variable itself. These variables have a wave prefix (a, b, etc.), which is followed by a unit of analysis prefix (p for individual and h for household questionnaires). Because new questions are added, old questions removed and/or shuffled around, variable names might change significantly across waves (for example, the variable for marital status in wave a is called ap58 but in wave b is called bp87). In these types of datasets we may prefer to use the first version of the use command and open the whole dataset.

A quick way of locating variables with the same content is to use the command lookfor, which searches for a specified keyword or sequence of characters across all variable names and variable labels (but not value labels; see Section 3.4 for how to use labels). For example, the command lookfor marital used in the wave-specific individual datasets, in this case ap.dta and bp.dta, gives the results shown in Figure 3.5.

We can then tabulate these variables to see their exact content and decide whether they are suitable for our analysis.

```
. use "$datadir/ap.dta", clear
(AP: 09/10/10 10:14:13-634 DB09)

. lookfor marital

                  storage  display      value
variable name     type     format       label      variable label
-------------------------------------------------------------------------
ap58                       byte     %22.0g       ap58       Marital Status



. use "$datadir/bp.dta", clear
(BP: 09/10/10 10:14:13-634 DB09)

. lookfor marital

                  storage  display      value
variable name     type     format       label      variable label
-------------------------------------------------------------------------
bp87              byte     %22.0g       bp87       Marital Status
bfamstd1          byte     %8.0g                   Marital Status One
bfamstd2          byte     %8.0g                   Marital Status Two
bfamstd3          byte     %8.0g                   Marital Status Three
```

Figure 3.5 The lookfor command

3.2.2 Opening Datasets That Are Not in Stata Format

In some cases the data are not provided in Stata format. Long (2009) includes a detailed discussion of different data formats and how to use them in Stata. Here we focus on the most common options.

To open data files that are in ASCII format we can use the drop-down menu: File → Import → ASCII data created by a spreadsheet. The corresponding Stata command is called insheet. Regardless of the creator of the file, insheet reads text (ASCII) files in which there is one observation per line and the values are separated by tabs or commas. The syntax for the command is the following:

```
insheet [varlist] using filename [, options]
```

where filename can include the extension of the file; if no extension is specified, .raw is assumed. Among the options:

tab: if the data are tab-delimited
comma: if the data are comma-delimited
delimiter("char"): if the data use a certain sequence of characters as delimiter
case: to preserve a variable name's case
[no]names: if variable names are included (or not) in the first line of the file

Other commands can be used to open data which are not in Stata format, such as infile. Check the Stata help and Long (2009) for more details. To save data in spreadsheet-style format, we use the commands outsheet or outfile. Files stored in this format usually require less disk space than a Stata-format dataset. We can also read data in MS Excel format using the command import excel (more on this in Chapter 5).

There are programs, such as StatTransfer, that convert files across different formats (Excel, Stata, SPSS, and so on). These are easy to use but we need always to double-check that the conversion has been done properly, for example all records have been converted. However, almost all software allows us to save the file in ASCII or in comma- or tab-delimited format, which can also be read by almost all software packages. Hence, it is worth considering using this type of file format when moving between software packages rather than relying on a third package for the conversion.

3.2.3 Opening PSID Data

Some datasets, such as the PSID (see Hill 1992), are not provided in Stata format. For the PSID, a Stata do file is provided with the dataset, which opens the data and assigns names and labels to all variables. The name of this file varies depending on the release of the data; in the 2009 release the do file is called IND2009ER.do. Hence, the first step in opening the individual data for the PSID consists of opening the do file, which looks like the one shown in Figure 3.6.

Here the three dots (. . .) stand for the lines of the file we have omitted for illustrative purposes. We use this style repeatedly throughout the book.

```
#delimit ;

**********************************************************************
    Label           : Panel Study of Income Dynamics:  1968-2009 Individual Data File
    Rows            : 71285
    Columns         : 1446
    ASCII File Date : July 7, 2011
**********************************************************************;

infix
        ER30000          1 -  1       ER30001        2 -  5       ER30002       6 -  8
        ER30003          9 -  9       ER30004       10 - 12       ER30005      13 - 13
    ...
        ER34041       3212 - 3212     ER34042     3213 - 3214     ER34043    3215 - 3216
        ER34044       3217 - 3218     ER34045     3219 - 3225     ER34046    3226 - 3230
using [path]\IND2009ER.txt, clear
;
label variable  ER30000     "RELEASE NUMBER" ;
label variable  ER30001     "1968 INTERVIEW NUMBER" ;
    ...
label variable  ER34045     "CORE/IMM INDIVIDUAL LONGITUDINAL WT   09" ;
label variable  ER34046     "CORE/IMM INDIVIDUAL CROSS-SECTION WT  09" ;
```

Figure 3.6   Stata do file for opening PSID data

Since the file is for general use, the do file does not specify any path for the dataset. Instead, the letters '[path]' are a placeholder for the pathname of the folder where the data are stored on the user's computer; before running the do file we need to substitute [path] with the path to the folder where our data are stored. We can either type the path or use global macros.

After the do file has run successfully, we can save the data in Stata format. In summary:

1. Open the do file provided with the data.[3]
2. Add the path where the PSID data are stored.[3]
3. Save the do file for later use.
4. Run the do file.
5. Save the data in Stata format for later use.

For more details on the file structure of the PSID see the PSID online user guide at http://psidonline.isr.umich.edu/Guide/FileStructure.pdf.

In contrast to the BHPS and UKHLS, and similar to SOEP, the variable names in the PSID are not related to their content. Variables are identified by the letters ER followed by a sequence of five numbers. The variable ER30000 is the release number; variables from ER30001 to ER30866 refer to waves from 1968 to 1993 and are arranged by wave; ER31990-ER31999 and ER32001-ER32050 are

---

[3]One characteristic of the PSID data files is that for the individual-level data all waves are provided in the same data file, which, therefore, is very large. Hence, if we are working with Stata 11 or older versions, before running the do file we need to increase the size of the memory significantly: for the 2009 release the minimum amount of memory needed to open the whole dataset is around 300m. This command can go between steps 2 and 3.

summary variables such as sex, order of birth or year of birth of parents; variables from ER33101 to ER33150 refer to the 1994 Public Release Individual data; variables from ER33201 to ER33299B refer to the 1995 Public Release Individual data; and so on. The variables from ER34001 to ER34046 refer to the 2009 Public Release Individual data. It is relatively simple to identify the year to which the data refer from the label of each variable: for example, the label of the variable ER30004 is 'Age of individual 68', while the label of the variable ER30023 is 'Age of individual 69', which are the ages of the individual in 1968 and in 1969. Similarly, the label of the variable ER34004 is 'Age of individual 09', which is the age of the individual in 2009.

Because of the way the PSID data are structured, the file contains almost 1,450 variables. Not all versions of Stata might be able to open such a large number of variables. In this case the best thing to do is to modify the do file provided with the dataset. To upload in memory only the relevant variables we delete from the command infix the name (and corresponding position numbers) of the variables that we do not need for our analysis. We also need to delete the corresponding label variable commands (see Figure 3.6). We can then run this modified version of the do file, which will only upload in memory the specified subset of variables.

3.3 Inspecting and Recoding Variables

Once the dataset is open in memory we can inspect the data, and rename and recode the variables to make them suitable for our analysis. Stata provides different commands to perform essentially the same operations. Here we suggest alternative commands from which to choose. First of all we upload in memory the variables of interest:

```
use ahid pid asex amastat aage aqfachi ///
    alknbrd apaygu using $datadir/aindresp, clear
```

The command describe describes the variables that are contained in the dataset open in memory; the command list in 1/20 lists the first 20 observations in the dataset. The observations listed are the ones in rows 1 to 20 and may vary according to the way the dataset is sorted. It is possible to list any number of observations between the two rows specified (1/20; 15/29 etc.). The command summarize gives information on means, standard deviations, minimum, maximum and sample sizes. The results of these commands are in the log files provided in the online appendix.

Write the commands and compare with the do file in the online appendix

In most datasets all data are stored in numeric variables – rather than strings – even when they refer to non-numeric characteristics. For example, in the BHPS the variable asex can be either 1 or 2, where 1 indicates that the respondent is a man and 2 indicates that the respondent is a woman. When tabulating the variable asex (tabulate asex), however, the possible options appear to be 'male' and 'female' rather than 1 and 2. This does not mean that this variable is a string; rather, value labels have been attached to the numeric values to make their meaning (1 = man, 2 = woman) clearer. Hence, 'man' is the label of the value 1, while 'woman' is the label of the value 2. Note that some datasets such as the PSID do not include value labels: it is necessary to consult the codebook to check what the numbers 1 and 2 mean; that is, to check whether also in this case 1 refers to men and 2 refers to women. Section 3.4 explains how to attach labels to the values of a variable.

The correspondence between the values and the value labels of a variable can be clearly seen by comparing the output of the commands list or tab, which shows labels, and sum, which shows the corresponding numeric values. The command label list lists the names and contents of the value labels in the dataset.

Another way in which we can look first at the data is the stem-and-leaf plot, using the command stem followed by the name of the variable. The command shows the different values of the variable and the number of observations that have each specific value. Try the commands stem amastat or stem apaygu.

Write the commands and compare with the do file in the online appendix

A useful user-written command, fre (see Jann 2007a), creates one-way frequency tables showing both numeric values and value labels of the variable categories. Note that the command fre is not automatically installed in Stata; to install it, first type findit fre in the 'Command' window. A new window will open, listing the results of the search. Once we have found the fre command within the list, we click on the link and follow the instructions ('click here to install') to install the command. We can now use the command (for example, fre asex).[4]

Write the commands and compare with the do file in the online appendix

Alternatively, we can tabulate the variable (in this case asex, and alknbrd – whether the respondent likes the neighbourhood where she lives) with and without labels:

---

[4]Often, different versions of the same program are available. We can type which fre to check which version of the fre command is installed, and check if this is the most recent version. We can also type ssc install fre to make sure that the latest version is installed.

```
tabulate asex

tabulate asex, nolabel

tabulate alknbrd

tabulate alknbrd, nolabel
```

The option `nolabel` shows the numeric values rather than their labels. We can also use the command `numlabel _all, add` to add the value number to the label. For example, for the variable `asex` the command changes the label `male` into `1. male` and `female` into `2. female`. The option `_all` specifies that this change has to be done for all variables in the dataset. If we want to remove the numeric values from the labels we use the option `remove` rather than the option `add`. Try tabulating the variables `asex` and `alknbrd` again after these commands.

Write the commands and compare with the do file in the online appendix

Looking at the variable `alknbrd`, we can see that, in the BHPS, as in most datasets, negative values identify (different types of) missing values. For example, in the BHPS and the UKHLS–1 means 'don't know', –2 means refusal, –8 means inapplicable; while in the SOEP –1 means no answer or 'don't know' and –2 means inapplicable. A coding error or some other error that could not be corrected is coded as –9 in the BHPS and UKHLS, and –3 in the SOEP; variables related to questions not asked in the proxy or telephone questionnaire in the BHPS and UKHLS are coded –7 (see the online appendix for more details on these datasets).

In the PSID missing values follow a different schema: generally, code 8 (or 98 or 998 etc.) represents 'don't know', while code 9 (or 99 or 999 etc.) represents other missing data or refusal. Inappropriate/inapplicable questions (such as age of the individual in a variable referring to waves before the individual was born or entered the sample) are coded as zero. Since in the PSID the missing values differ across variables, it is good practice always to double-check the codebook.

The reasons for missing answers are often relevant for survey methodologists (we will not discuss these issues in this book). If we are not interested in the reason why the variable is missing we can recode all the negative values into Stata system-missing, which is represented by a dot (.). There are different ways to recode missing values; here are two options:

```
recode alknbrd -9/-1 = .

mvdecode apaygu, mv(-9/-1)
```

The command `recode` recodes the values specified before the equals sign (in this case all values from –9 to –1) into those specified after the equals sign (in this case Stata missing). The command `mvdecode` sets the values specified in parentheses (in this case all values between −9 and −1) to Stata missing. We can use the option gen if we want to recode into a new variable, but leave the original variable unchanged (see the Stata help for details).

Now we can look again at how the proportions of those who like/dislike their neighbourhood vary by gender using again the command tab, which accepts a list of two variables maximum.

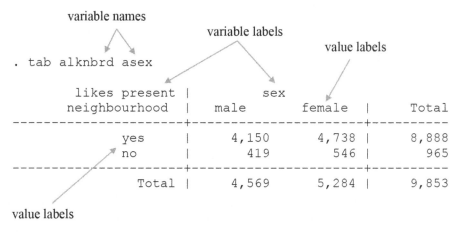

Figure 3.7   The tab command

Figure 3.7 shows the two-way tabulation of the two variables alknbrd and asex. The variable label for alknbrd is 'likes present neighbourhood' while the labels of its two values (1 and 2) are 'yes' and 'no'. Similarly, the variable label for asex is 'sex' while the labels of its two values (1 and 2) are 'male' and 'female'. The proportion of those who like the neighbourhood is around 90% and there do not seem to be relevant differences between men and women. We can also add proportions to the table. These proportions can be computed by row or by column; missing values can also be included in the table. Compare the different options:

```
tabulate alknbrd asex

tabulate alknbrd asex, col

tabulate alknbrd asex, row

tabulate alknbrd asex, col miss
```

Write the commands and compare with the do file in the online appendix

We can also test for the independence of the rows and columns by specifying the option chi2 in the following way: tabulate asex alknbrd, r chi2:

```
                        |     likes present
                        |     neighbourhood
            sex   |    yes           no      |      Total
      ------------------+--------------------------+-----------
           male   |    4,150         419 |      4,569
                        |    90.83         9.17 |     100.00
      ------------------+--------------------------+-----------
         female   |    4,738         546 |      5,284
                        |    89.67        10.33 |     100.00
      ------------------+--------------------------+-----------
          Total |    8,888         965 |      9,853
                        |    90.21         9.79 |     100.00

            Pearson chi2(1)  =    3.7486    Pr = 0.053
```

Figure 3.8   The chi2 option to the tab command

Figure 3.8 shows the results of the Pearson chi-squared test. The test shows that the chi-squared statistic has one degree of freedom and its observed value is 3.7486, which is statistically significant, but only at the 10% level of significance. In other words, the probability of observing this value of the statistic if the null hypothesis (that the two variables are independent) is true is 0.053.

3.4 Renaming, Creating and Labelling Variables and Values

We can change the name of any variable in the dataset using the command rename. For example, we can give the variable alknbrd a name which is easier to remember: LikesNeighbourhood. We can also change the name of the variable asex to sex:

```
rename alknbrd LikesNeighbourhood
rename asex sex
```

The variable apaygu, which is the usual gross monthly wage, is a continuous variable. In some cases we may want to summarise pay in a few categories. For example, we can create a new variable, called pay1, that has value 1 (which we will label 'low') if apaygu is less than 200; 2 ('medium') if it is between 201 and 400; and 3 ('high') if it is more than 400. We can do this using the commands generate and replace:

```
generate pay1 = 1 if apaygu <= 200

replace pay1 = 2 if apaygu > 200 & apaygu <= 400

replace pay1 = 3 if apaygu > 400 & apaygu < .
```

Note that Stata considers missing values as the highest values. Hence, if we only type `replace pay1 = 3 if apaygu > 400`, when `apaygu` is missing `pay1` has value 3. Adding `& apaygu < .` ensures that missing values in `apaygu` are also missing in `pay1`. An alternative way to generate the same variable (we can call it `pay2` in this case) consists of recoding `apaygu`:

```
recode apaygu (0/200 = 1) (200/400 = 2) ///

    (400/max = 3), gen(pay2) test
```

where the option `test` issues a warning message if there are overlaps with the new group formed. Compare with

```
recode apaygu (0/200 = 1) (200.01/400 = 2) ///

    (400.01/max = 3), gen(pay3) test

tabulate pay2 pay3
```

The command `recode` allows us to attach labels (low, medium and high) directly to the new values:

```
recode apaygu (0/200 = 1 low) ///

    (200.01/400 = 2 medium) ///

    (400.01/max = 3 high), gen(pay4) test

tabulate pay3 pay4
```

Note that in all the previous commands we have created new variables, each with a different name: `recode ..., gen(pay2)`; `recode ..., gen(pay3)`; and so on. Stata does not allow us to create new variables that have the same name as a variable that already exists in the dataset. Hence, to avoid getting an error message, if we want to create a new variable we must make sure that we choose a name that has not already been used for another variable.

We attached value labels to the variable `pay4` when we created it, but we have not attached any value labels to the variables `pay1`, `pay2` and `pay3`. We can attach labels to the values of the variables in a few steps. First we have to define the list of labels with the command `label define`; then we attach these labels to the values of the variable with the command `label value`:

```
tabulate pay1

label define pay1_labels 1 "low" 2 "medium" ///

  3 "high"

label value pay1 pay1_labels

tabulate pay1

label list pay1_labels
```

Although in most datasets the name of the label coincides with the name of the variable, this is not necessary: label names might differ from variable names, and any defined value label can be attached to more than one variable. However, similar to the case of creating variables, we cannot create a new label (`label define`) that has the same name as a label that already exists.

Finally, it is good practice to attach a short description to the variable itself using the command `label variable` (note the difference: `label define`; `label value`; `label variable`):

```
label var pay1 ///

  "Whether pay is low, medium, or high"
```

The command `label variable` can be shortened to `lab var` or `label var`.

We can also label datasets using the command `label data` followed by a sequence of characters enclosed between quotation marks. In Stata all types of labels can be up to 80 characters in length (244 in Stata SE for data and value labels).

If rather than a categorical variable we want to create a binary variable that has value 1 when specific conditions are satisfied and 0 otherwise (also known as a dummy variable), we can use the command `generate` in the following way:

```
generate highlypaid = (apaygu > 400 & apaygu < .)
```

This command creates a new variable called `highlypaid` that has value 1 when the condition within parentheses is satisfied (`apay` is higher than 400 and non-missing) and value 0 when it is not (`apay` is lower or equal to 400, including zero and negative values).

If we want to create a categorical variable identifying the position of the individual within the pay distribution, we can use the command `xtile`. For example,

```
xtile paidpctile = apaygu if apaygu < ., nq(5)
```

This command sorts the variable `apaygu`, identifies its quintiles by dividing the distribution into five groups of equal size (`nq(5)`) and assigns a value of 1 to all people in the first group (first quintile, the bottom 20% of the pay distribution), a value of 2 to all people in the second group, and so on. The new variable `paidpctile` therefore has values between 1 and 5, corresponding to the quintile of the wage distribution the worker belongs to.

A useful extension to the command `generate` is the command `egen`, which allows more complex computations in the creation of variables. The command `egen` can be used to create variables containing means, medians, standard deviations, total sums, running sums, and much more. For example, to produce a variable containing the average pay we can type

```
egen MeanPay = mean(apaygu)
```

We can compute mean pay by gender, for example by computing mean pay for men and women separately, using the option `if`. In this case mean pay for men is missing for women, and vice versa. These two new variables, which we can call `MeanPayMen` and `MeanPayWomen`, can then be combined into one single variable which contains the mean pay for the gender of the respondent using the command `replace`.

Write the commands and compare with the do file in the online appendix

The same result can be obtained in one single step using the command `bysort`, which we will discuss in Chapter 5.

We can use the commands `generate` and `replace` also to create dummy variables from a categorical variable. However, the most efficient way to do this is to use the command `tab`:

```
tabulate sex, gen(Sex)
```

This command tabulates the variable `sex` and generates two new variables: `Sex1`, which is 1 when `sex` is equal to 1 and 0 when `sex` is different than 1 and not missing; hence, it is 1 for men and 0 for women. The second variable generated is `Sex2`, which is 1 when `sex` is equal to 2 and 0 when `sex` is different than 2 and not missing; hence, it is 0 for men and 1 for women.

Write the commands and compare with the do file in the online appendix

Finally, as already mentioned in Section 3.1.3, in some cases we want to create variables with higher precision than the default size (float). Typically a higher precision is needed for variables such as person identification numbers. Compare the two options

```
generate PersonId1 = pid
generate double PersonId2 = pid
list PersonId1 PersonId2 pid in 1/10
```

Figure 3.9 compares the three variables `PersonId1`, `PersonId2` and `pid`, and clearly shows that while `PersonId2`, which has double precision, is the same as `pid`, the variable `PersonId1`, which is only float, is approximated and therefore different from the other two.

```
list PersonId1 PersonId2 pid in 1/10

      +----------------------------------+
      |  Person~1    Person~2       pid  |
      |----------------------------------|
  1.  |  1.00e+07    10002251    10002251 |
  2.  |  1.00e+07    10004491    10004491 |
  3.  |  1.00e+07    10004521    10004521 |
  4.  |  1.00e+07    10007857    10007857 |
  5.  |  1.00e+07    10014578    10014578 |
      |----------------------------------|
  6.  |  1.00e+07    10014608    10014608 |
  7.  |  1.00e+07    10016813    10016813 |
  8.  |  1.00e+07    10016848    10016848 |
  9.  |  1.00e+07    10017933    10017933 |
 10.  |  1.00e+07    10017968    10017968 |
      +----------------------------------+
```

Figure 3.9   Double-precision variables

After running Stata commands that alter the data it is good practice to check that the commands do what we expect them to do. Do not underestimate the possibility of typos causing havoc. One way to check the data is to click on the Data Editor or on the Data Browse icons. Alternatively, we can type `list` to list out a few cases, or we can tabulate or summarise the new variables generated.

You may have noticed that the Stata codes in this chapter and in the accompanying do file in the online appendix have been written with indentations for codes referring to the same command. This was not done to make the code look prettier but rather to make it easier to spot errors. Most programmers develop their own way of writing code that allows them to spot errors quickly.

3.5 Graphs: Histograms and Density Plots

Besides summarising and tabulating our variables, we can also analyse them using graphs. One of the most useful graphs for discrete variables is the histogram. For example, we can plot the variable `amastat` (marital status) using the command

```
histogram amastat, discrete ///
    title(Histogram for Marital Status)
```

where the option `discrete` specifies that `amastat` is a discrete variable, and `title` specifies the title we want to give to the graph. This command generates a graph that uses the standard Stata format and colour scheme. There are various alternative preset schemes that can be used; in this chapter we use a black and white scheme called `s1manual`. We use it by adding the option `scheme(...)` to the `histogram` command (use the Stata help to learn about different schemes):

```
histogram amastat, discrete ///
    title(Histogram for Marital Status) ///
    scheme(s1manual)
```

The resulting graph looks like the one in Figure 3.10.

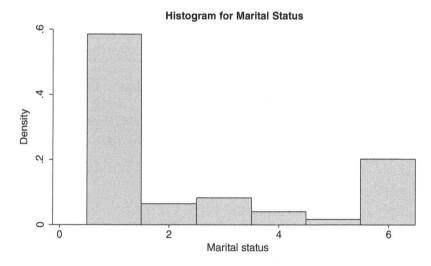

Figure 3.10   A simple histogram

We can also plot the variable of marital status by values of a second variable, for instance sex. For example we can require the histogram for marital status to be computed for men and women separately using the option `by()`:

```
histogram amastat, discrete ///

    title(Histogram for Marital Status) ///

    scheme(s1manual) by(sex)
```

The graph resulting from this command looks like the one in Figure 3.11.

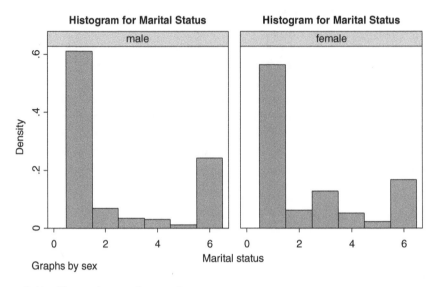

Figure 3.11   The option by for graphs

Note that in this case the title of the graph is repeated for males and females. Using the syntax below, the title of the graph will not be repeated. This is obtained by specifying the title of the graph as an option within by().

We can also show labels instead of the numeric values of the variables on the horizontal (x) axis using the option xlabel(,   valuelabel), where angle(45) specifies the appearance of the labels (at a 45 degree angle), and the numbers 1(1)6 specify the minimum and maximum values to be plotted, as well as the increment (the one in parentheses):

```
histogram amastat, discrete ///

    xlabel(1(1)6, valuelabel angle(45)) ///

    scheme(s1manual) ///

    by(sex, title(Histogram for Marital Status))
```

The graph should now look like the one in Figure 3.12.

Note that all these graphs show relative frequencies, but if we prefer to show counts rather than relative frequencies we can add the option freq. Compare for example the commands

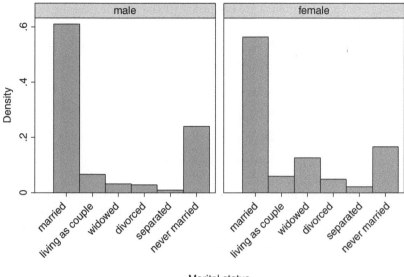

Figure 3.12   Using labels in graphs

```
histogram amastat, discrete ///
    title(Histogram for Marital Status) ///
    scheme(s1manual)
```

and

```
histogram amastat, discrete ///
    title(Histogram for Marital Status) ///
    scheme(s1manual) freq
```

In this specific case the dataset includes about 10,000 people. The frequencies vary between 0 and 0.6 and the count data range from 0 to 6,000.

Remember that at the beginning of the do file we had set more to be off. If we run the do file, all these graphs will be displayed in quick succession; this might not give us enough time to look at the graphs themselves. Also note that since the graphs appear in a separate window – instead of in the 'Results' window – they are not saved to the -log file.

We can use the command graph save Graph "path\graphname.gph" to save the graph in a file which we can open and analyse later on (note the capital letter in the command used to save a graph). We can also turn the more option on (set more on) and add the command more in the do file, where we want Stata to suspend temporarily execution of the do file (see the do file in the online appendix).

As an alternative, we can save the graph by specifying the option saving within the command which generates the graph:

```
histogram amastat, discrete ///

xlabel(1(1)6, valuelabel angle(45)) ///

by(sex, title(Histogram for Marital Status)) ///

saving("C:\MyGraphs\Graph1", replace)
```

The graph is then saved in C:\MyGraphs with the name Graph1. The replace option allows earlier versions of the graph to be overwritten. Graphs can also be saved in other formats such as pdf (see Chapter 14).

We can also use histograms to plot continuous variables, such as apaygu, and add a kernel density estimation of the variable, together with a normal distribution plot. Try the two commands

```
histogram apaygu, ///

    title(Histogram for Pay) scheme(s1manual)
```

and

```
histogram apaygu, normal kdensity ///

    title(Histogram for Pay) ///

    legend(on) scheme(s1manual)
```

In this graph the pattern of the lines of the normal and kernel density plots are almost indistinguishable. We can specify the colour, width and pattern of each line using appropriate options. Try the command

```
histogram apaygu, scheme(s1manual) ///

    normal normopts(lcolor(black) ///

    lpattern(solid)) ///

    kdensity ///

    kdenopts(lcolor(black) ///

    lwidth(thick) lpattern(dash)) ///

    title(Histogram for Pay) legend(on)
```

The option normopts(lcolor(black) lpattern(solid)) specifies the colour of the line or the normal density plot (black) and its pattern (solid).

The option for the kernel density plot `kdenopts(lcolor(black)`
`lwidth(thick)   lpattern(dash))` specifies that we want a black
(`lcolor(black)`), thick (`lwidth(thick)`) and dashed (`lpattern(dash)`)
line. Note that all the options are specified within the same parentheses. The

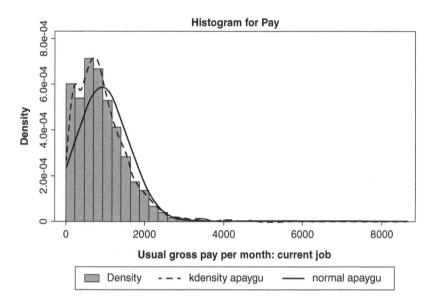

Figure 3.13   Adding densities to histograms

graph resulting from the last command looks like the one in Figure 3.13.

If we only want the kernel and normal density plots, we can use the command `kdensity`:

```
kdensity apaygu, scheme(s1manual)
```

and

```
kdensity apaygu, normal scheme(s1manual)
```

Once again, we want to specify the colour, width and pattern of the lines for the
density and normal plots. However, since we are using the `kdensity` graph command, the options for the kernel density line are specified directly after the
comma without the additional option `kdenopts(...)` that we used in the his-
`togram` command. The line for the normal plot, however, is considered as an
addition to the `kdensity` command and is therefore specified exactly as in the
`histogram` command:

```
kdensity apaygu, ///
    lcolor(black) lwidth(thick) lpattern(dash) ///
```

```
normal normopts(lcolor(black) ///
lpattern(solid)) ///
scheme(s1manual)
```

The last command generates a graph that looks like the one in Figure 3.14.

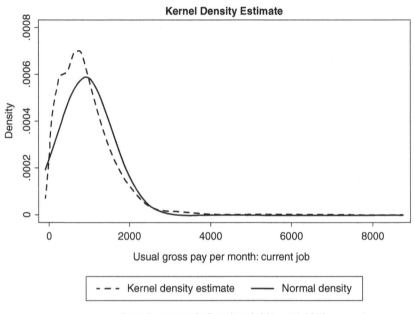

kernel = epanechnikov, bandwidth = 96.9276

Figure 3.14   Density graphs

These are only a few of the various types of graphs and adaptations that Stata supports. Besides the Stata Help Manual, various books discuss how to create professional-looking graphs; for example, see Mitchell (2012).

3.6 Clean Up and Save Datasets for Future Use

The dataset now contains some redundant variables: pay2, pay3, pay4. We can delete them from the dataset using the command drop:

```
drop pay2 pay3 pay4
```

The command drop deletes variables (drop variablename) or observations (drop if variable == specified_case). Note that if we type drop pay* we also lose the variable pay (not only pay2, pay3 and pay4). Similarly, instead of dropping, we can keep variables or observations, with the command keep. The two commands should give the same result:

```
drop if apaygu == .

* drops obs with missing apaygu

keep if apaygu < .

 * keeps obs where apaygu is not missing
```

We can also drop unwanted value labels with the command label drop labelname. To save files in Stata (.dta) format we use the command save:

```
save [filename] [, save_options]
```

where filename includes only the name of the file if we want to save it in the current directory, and the whole path if we want to save it in a specified directory. We can either type the path or save it in a global macro and recall it using the $ symbol. Useful options for the command save are replace, which we use if we want to overwrite an existing dataset, and emptyok, which we use if we want to save the dataset even if it includes no observations and no variables.

As mentioned in Section 3.1.3, before saving the file it is often useful to type the command compress. Finally, it is good practice to clean up after finishing the work. We can close the log file open at the beginning of the session using the command log close, and delete files no longer needed by typing erase name_of_file_to_be_erased.dta.

3.7 Summary and Suggestions for Further Reading

In this chapter we have discussed what Stata looks like and how it works, as well as the basic Stata commands, most of which we will use in the rest of the book. As will become clearer in the following chapters, sometimes Stata provides different commands that produce the same results. You can choose the type of syntax that comes easier to you.

Key points

- Remember that your analysis should be reproducible by others and on different computers: use do and log files, and also use macros.
- Open your dataset with the command use.
- Remember to inspect your data file and to recode missing values when needed. Clearly label your variables and values.

Suggestions for further reading

- In this chapter we have discussed the Stata do files editor; however, you can also use any other text editor. You can find a discussion of the advantages and disadvantages of alternative text editors at: http://fmwww.bc.edu/repec/bocode/t/textEditors.html.
- Stata has a large number of commands which no book can summarise. Here we discuss some of the most useful ones and focus on the most interesting options of each command. In some cases, which command to use is a matter of preference. Stata provides a very detailed manual that includes the description of all commands and their options: StataCorp (2013f) *User's Guide*. College Station, TX, Stata Press.
- The commands to construct graphics in Stata are very powerful but sometimes rather complicated. Check the publication StataCorp (2013e) *Graphics Reference Manual*. College Station, TX, Stata Press.
- Stata also has a manual dedicated to the data management commands: StataCorp (2013d) *Data-Management Reference Manual*. College Station, TX, Stata Press.
- To learn more about data management tips in Stata and how to automate processes look at Long (2009) *The Workflow of Data Analysis Using Stata*. College Station, TX, Stata Press.

④

PREPARING THE DATA FOR LONGITUDINAL ANALYSIS

Aim

In this chapter we discuss how to prepare the data for longitudinal analysis, starting from the simplest case of combining individual data for two waves. We then discuss how to use programming techniques to generalise the commands to combine multiple waves. Once the dataset is ready in its longitudinal form we discuss how to describe the panel data and compute lagged variables and wave-on-wave transitions.

4.1 Introduction

Panel data allow us to analyse changes over time. For example, we may want to analyse how people's wages change across two consecutive waves and whether this varies by sex or marital status. The first thing we need to do is to organise the data; in most cases this involves combining different data files into one dataset.

Most cross-section data files are structured to have one row for each unit of analysis (in our case individuals), with columns containing the variables. This is the same in most longitudinal datasets of individuals, because usually observations collected in different waves are often provided in separate files. It is the researcher's job to combine the data in a longitudinal way. The PSID is an exception in this regard, as the data at the individual level are combined before release, so that the individual-level file already includes all waves. However, data at the household level, as well as data for specific modules of the questionnaire, are still provided in separate files which need to be combined.

There are two main ways of combining the data: 'wide' and 'long' format (see Figure 4.1). The wide format contains one row per unit of analysis: variables referring to different time periods appear as different columns (as in the left part of Figure 4.1). The wide format is not ideal when the data contain a large number of waves, since the number of variables can quickly become unmanageable. In this case the long format should be preferred. The long format stacks the unit of analysis (individuals) observed over time one below the other. Observations for each individual appear in multiple rows and observations on a variable for different time periods are held in extra rows (as in the right part of Figure 4.1). It is possible to identify the matrix of observations on an individual over time by two identifiers: one for the individual (in the BHPS the variable is called pid, the person identification number); and one for time (wave or year). The long-file format is the most practical one when the data cover many waves. It is also the format needed by Stata to be able to use the set of panel data commands. In this chapter we focus on how to combine data into long format.

Wide File Format

- One row per case/individual
- Observations on a variable for different time periods are in different columns
- Variable name identifies time (via prefix)

pid	apay	bpay	cpay
	wave 1	wave 2	wave 3
10001	7.2	7.5	7.7
10002	6.3	missing	6.3
10003	5.4	5.4	missing
...			

Long File Format

- Multiple rows per case/individual
- Observations on a variable for different time periods held in extra rows for each individual
- Case-row identifier identifies time

pid	wave	pay
10001	1	7.2
10001	2	7.5
10001	3	7.7
10002	1	6.3
10002	3	6.3
10003	1	5.4
10003	2	5.4
...	...	...

Data are missing for wave 2

Figure 4.1   Wide and long format

The PSID provides a single cross-year file containing the data from the individual interviews. Hence, for this dataset there is no need to combine the individual-level files. However, the data are provided in wide format and need to be reshaped into long format before using the set of panel data commands; the reshape command is discussed in Section 4.4.

4.2 Merging Two Files into Long Format

We can combine two or more waves of data into long format using the command append:

```
append using filename [, nolabel]
```

This command appends a dataset which is stored on disk (called the 'using' file) to the end of the dataset which is currently open in memory (the 'master' file). When there are variables with value labels, the labels retained are those of the file currently open in memory, that is, the master file. In some cases labels vary across waves, for example when new options are added to possible answers to a certain question; hence, we should keep the most recent set of labels (see the Stata help for more details).

Variables are appended only if they are common in both datasets (and have exactly the same name). For those variables which appear in only one of the datasets the combined file will contain missing values in the rows corresponding to the other dataset. It is therefore crucial to ensure that the variables that we want to append have exactly the same name in both datasets. In most cases this means renaming the variables in one or both datasets before they can be appended.[1] In the case of the BHPS and UKHLS it is enough to remove the wave prefix. This can easily be done using the command rename * *.

The command rename a* *, for example, renames all the variables in the dataset starting with the prefix a (a*) with the same name without the prefix (*). This results in dropping the specified prefix from all variables in the dataset whose name starts with that prefix. Note that the command has no effect on the variable pid, since this does not start with a.[2]

For the UKHLS we would use the command rename a_* * since the wave prefix includes an underscore: a_, b_, c_, etc. Also note that in the UKHLS the

---

[1]There can be exceptions: in some cases we may want to keep the variables separate, for example because we need to harmonise them. In this case we can keep different names for these variables and then compute the final variable once the rest of the dataset is complete.

[2]In versions of Stata older than 12 the command rename * * does not work. For older versions of Stata use the command renpfix. For example, renpfix a renames all the variables in the dataset whose name starts with 'a' by dropping their a prefix.

unique cross-wave individual identifier is pidp and not pid as in the BHPS. In the UKHLS pid is also available, but this is the identifier of the BHPS respondents who have been included in the UKHLS. The variable pid corresponds to the BHPS identifier and can be used to match data for the BHPS respondents in the two surveys (UKHLS and BHPS). In the UKHLS the variable pid has a value of –8 (missing) for all respondents who were not part of the BHPS.

After the command rename * * the variables from the different waves all have the same name, for example age instead of aage, bage, cage, and so on. How do we know which observation refers to which wave? To be able to identify the wave each observation refers to, we create a new variable which we can call, for example, wave. This variable has value 1 for observations referring to the first wave of data and value 2 for those observations which refer to the second wave. To be able to use the Stata commands for panel data, the variable wave has to be numeric.

These steps (renaming variables and generating the new wave variable) have to be performed separately for each file before they can be appended. The whole sequence of commands needed to append two files is summarised in Figure 4.2.

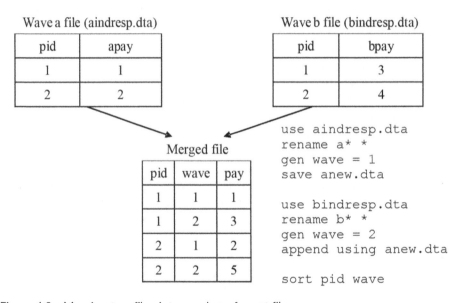

Figure 4.2   Merging two files into one long-format file

4.3 Generalisation to Multiple Waves

4.3.1 Appending Files in Datasets Where Variable Names Follow Rules

To append multiple waves we have to repeat the sequence of commands shown in Figure 4.2 separately for each wave; the most efficient way consists of using loops. In this case we use a `foreach` loop, which repeats the commands between curly brackets { } for each element in the `foreach` list (a b ... q r). The opening curly bracket must be on the same line as `foreach`, while the closing curly bracket must be in a line on its own:

```
foreach wave in a b c d e f g h i j k l m n o ///
   p q r {
  use `wave'hid pid `wave'sex `wave'mastat ///
    `wave'age `wave'qfachi `wave'paygu ///
    `wave'jbft `wave'region `wave'jbsoc ///
    `wave'jbbgy4 `wave'jbsemp `wave'jbstat ///
    `wave'cjsten ///
    using "$datadir/`wave'indresp", clear
  rename `wave'* *
  // deal with wave p
  capture rename id pid
  generate wave = ///
    index("abcdefghijklmnopqr","`wave'")
  save ind_junk`wave', replace
}
```

The command `foreach` creates a local macro, which can have any name. In our case we have called it `wave`. As we discussed in Section 3.1.6, to refer to the content of the local macro, we enclose its name between a grave accent and an apostrophe: `wave`. The content of the local macro has to be specified in the `foreach` list, which can have different forms. In our case the content list is a general one. Elements are separated from each other by one or more spaces: a b c d .... The content of the local macro changes each time Stata goes through the loop. For the first iteration, the content equals the first element in the `foreach` list (a → ahid pid asex...). For the second iteration, it contains the second element (b → bhid pid bsex ...), and so on.

Note the difference between the local macro `wave` used in the `foreach` loop and the variable `wave` created by the `generate` command. Macros, variables, etc., may have the same name but are distinct items within Stata.

Also note that the personal identification number `pid` never has a wave prefix. This produces a problem for wave p, where the command `rename p* *` would rename `pid` to `id`. Hence, in wave p we have to rename `id` back to `pid`. If we only typed `rename id pid` within the loop, we would get an error message which would terminate execution of the do file since for all waves other than wave p, there is no variable called id. If we add `capture` before the command, Stata will produce but not show the error message ('the variable id does not exist') for waves from a to o and would continue executing the do file. On wave p the variable id will be renamed pid, and, again, the error message would be suppressed for waves q and r.

An alternative to the command `capture rename id pid` is the command `if index("p","`wave'")` rename id pid. The command `index("p","`wave'")` identifies the position in the string "p" of the value in the local macro `wave'`. When `wave'` is equal to p, its position in the string is 1, and the command `index` returns a value of 1. In all other iterations the command `index` returns a value of 0, since the value of `wave'` (that is, a, b, c, ...) is not present in the string "p". When the result is 1, the `if` statement renames the variable id back to pid. Note that Stata provides another command that is equivalent to `index`; this is called `strpos` and has the same syntax as `index`. As a further alternative, we can use an `if` statement in the following way: `if "`wave'" == "p"` rename id pid. Note the quotation marks: these are needed because `wave'` and p are letters (strings) instead of numbers.

In the loop above we have also used the `index()` function to generate the numerical variable identifying the wave (`gen wave = index("abcdefghijk lmnopqr","`wave'")`. The new variable wave (not to be confused with the local macro `wave'`) is 1 when the local macro `wave'` is equal to a; 2 when it is equal to b; 3 when it is equal to c; and so on.

In many datasets some sets of questions are asked intermittently; hence, some variables might not be present in all waves. The easiest way to append waves in this case consists of uploading the whole dataset (that is, upload all variables), appending the different waves and then dropping the variables that are not relevant for the analysis. However, as this may require a lot of memory and computation time, a viable alternative consists of writing the extraction of the variables separately for each wave.

Once the data for each wave have been prepared and saved, we can use a similar loop to append all waves. Note that the wave r file at the end of the loop is still open. Hence, we have to append all other files to that one:

```
foreach wave in a b c d e f g h i j k l m n o p q {
    append using ind_junk`wave'
}
```

Rather than using two loops, we might more elegantly want to include the series of append commands in the first loop which opens the dataset and renames the variables. This will save running time and will avoid having to save a large number of unnecessary files. To do this we can use the command `indexnot()`.

In a similar way to the command `index()`, the command `indexnot()` returns the position in the first string of the first character which is not found in the second string, while it returns 0 if all characters in the second string are found in the first. Hence, we have to write the command so that the return code can be only 1 or 0: we want 0 for the first iteration, the only one when we do not want to append, and 1 for all other iterations, when we want to append the current dataset to the final one, which includes all previous waves.

Write the commands and compare with the do file in the online appendix

A close look at the individual respondent files should have revealed that the label of the variable `jbstat` (self-reported status in current job) in wave a differs from the label of the variable in the following waves. Specifically, 'family care' was coded as 5 in wave a and as 6 in all other waves; 'full-time student' was coded as 6 in wave a and as 7 in all other waves; 'long term sick/disabled' was coded as 7 in wave a and as 8 in all other waves. 'Maternity leave' was coded as 8 in wave a and as 5 in all other waves. This is also clear from the data documentation manual.

We should at this point recode the variable in the first wave (`if wave == 1`) to make it comparable with all other waves.

Write the commands and compare with the do file in the online appendix

4.3.2 Appending Files When Variable Names Do Not Follow One Rule

As already mentioned, in the SOEP many variables do not have the same root name. Hence, we cannot use a loop to generalise the `append` command to multiple waves; instead, we have to repeat the sequence of commands shown in Section 4.2, with the necessary wave-specific `rename` commands.

We can either prepare the files for each wave and append them to the final file, or prepare each file and save it with a different name. In the latter case we can then use a loop to append all the files. In the example below we keep only the unique person identifier (`persnr`), the survey year (`welle`), marital status and sex variables from the first three waves of the SOEP (ap, bp and cp). As the marital status and sex variables have a different name in each wave, we need to rename them to be able to append the datasets correctly:

```
use "$datadir\ap.dta", clear

keep persnr welle ap57 ap58

rename ap57 sex

rename ap58 marital_status

generate wave = 1

save DataFile.dta, replace
```

```
use "$datadir\bp.dta", clear

keep persnr welle bp85 bp87

rename bp85 sex

rename bp87 marital_status

generate wave = 2

append using DataFile.dta

save DataFile.dta, replace


use "$datadir\cp.dta", clear

keep persnr welle cp89 cp8801

rename cp8801 sex

rename cp89 marital_status

generate wave = 3

append using DataFile.dta

compress

save DataFile.dta, replace
```

4.4 Preparing PSID Data: Reshaping Files from Wide to Long and Vice Versa

As we have already mentioned, the PSID data are provided as a wide file and need to be reshaped into long format before we can use the set of Stata commands that are specific to panel data. We can convert the data from wide to long format (see Figure 4.1) by using the command reshape long followed by the list of variables that we want to include in the new dataset. After the comma we specify the variable that in the dataset identifies the individuals (var1) and the name of the new variable that will identify the wave of the data (var2). While we need to specify var1, the variable var2 is automatically created as a result of the reshape command:

```
reshape long list_of_variables, i(var1) j(var2)
```

Note that the names of the variables in the list_of_variables need to have the same root and have numbers as their suffix. Variables with the same root will be stacked below each other, and the suffix numbers will be used to create the new variable identifying the wave (var2); this variable needs to be numeric to be able to identify the data as panel data. Hence, once the PSID wide file is open we need to rename the variables of interest. In the example below we keep age and sex. While age data are in year-specific variables, sex is in one single cross-wave variable.

We first create the person identification number (what corresponds to `pid` in the BHPS and to `persnr` in the SOEP) by combining the variables ER30001 and ER30002 (see Chapter 3, Section 3.2.3). Since the variable ER30002 ranges from 1 to 262, we can generate the personal identifier by multiplying ER30001 by 1,000 before adding the variable ER30002. The new variable should be stored as long type (see Figure 3.2 in Chapter 3). We then rename all age-related variables using, for example, the root `Age` and adding the number of the year as a suffix:

```
* Generate the person id
generate long pid = ER30001 * 1000 + ER30002
label var pid "Person Identification Number"
* Rename variables we want to keep
rename ER30004 Age1968
rename ER30023 Age1969
* ... and so on ...
rename ER33904 Age2007
rename ER34004 Age2009
* Rename the variable identifying sex
rename ER32000 Sex
* Drop unwanted variables
keep Age* Sex pid
* Reshape
reshape long Age, i(pid) j(year)
```

Note that we have left the variable `Sex` out of the `reshape` command. This is because the dataset contains only one variable identifying the sex of the respondent. The `reshape` command keeps this variable in the dataset and repeats the value for all waves (this is also the reason why we need to drop unwanted variables). As for the age variables, we include in the `reshape` command only the root (`Age` instead of `Age1968`, `Age1969`, etc.). The variable `year` is created by the `reshape` command; its content is the remainder of the variable names, in this case `1968`, `1969`, etc.

Because of the structure of the PSID data file, the data have the form of a balanced panel, and include values for `pid`, `year` and `Sex` even for those waves when the person was not interviewed. We can see it from the PSID missing values on the variable Age. At this point we can drop from the data those obser-vations/rows with all missing values for Age or Sex:

```
drop if Sex == 9

drop if Age == 0 | Age == 999

* Age is 0 for those who have not yet

* entered the survey
```

Although this step is not necessary, it is a good way to reduce the size of the dataset. A smaller dataset needs less memory, opens more quickly, and estima-tion commands tend to run faster.

If we want to convert the data the other way round, from long to wide for-mat, we can use the command reshape wide followed by the list of variables that we want to include in the new dataset. After the comma we specify the variable identifying the individual (var1, which should be pid if we use the BHPS) and the one identifying the wave of the data (var2, which is the variable wave in the BHPS files we have constructed in Sections 4.2 and 4.3):

```
reshape wide list_of_variables, i(var1) j(var2)
```

4.5 Recoding Variables and Identifying the Data as a Panel

Going back to our example using the BHPS (Section 4.3.1), after all the waves have been appended into one long file we can start preparing the dataset for analysis. First, we recode all data missing into Stata missing. We can either recode each variable separately, or use another version of the foreach loop:

```
foreach var of varlist sex age region ///
   qfachi jbft ///
   jbstat paygu jbbgy4 jbsoc jbsemp mastat {
     recode `var' -9/-1 = .
   }
```

This loop repeats the command recode for each variable in the foreach list. In this case the list contains the name of the variables for which we want to repeat the command (sex paygu mastat ...). Note that in this case we have chosen to call the local macro var.

Alternatively, if we want to recode all variables in the dataset in the same way, we can use the command mvdecode _all, mv(-9/-1), which recodes all values between −9 and −1 into Stata missing for all variables in the dataset.

Note the difference between the previous (Section 4.3.1) and the current loop. In the first case we use `foreach wave in`; in the second case we use `foreach var of varlist`. The `foreach ... in` is a general list type, which can be used with a list of variables, numbers or other types of elements. The advantage of using a specified list type (`of varlist`), such as a list of variables, is that we can use shorthand conventions. For example, we can type `foreach var of var1-var10`, which would include all variables between `var1` and `var10`, in the order in which they appear in the dataset. Alternatively, we can use `foreach var of Var*`, which would include all variables starting with the three letters `Var`. If we want to repeat the series of commands for specified numerical values, we can use the command `forvalues` with shorthand conventions for numerical lists (consult the Stata manual for more details).

At this point we can declare the data to be a panel using the command `tsset panelvar timevar`, where `panelvar` is the cross-wave identifier, in our case `pid`, and `timevar` is the time-series identifier, in our case the variable `wave`. The `tsset` command specifies that the data have a panel structure, and allows us to use specific commands for time-series and panel data (all those starting with the letters `xt`); it also allows proper treatment of gaps in the panel:

```
tsset pid wave
```

As usual, we can use different commands to perform the same operation. The command `tsset panelvar timevar` declares the data to be a time series: while `timevar` is necessary, `panelvar` is optional and is used only when we want to declare the data to be a panel. For panel data we can also use the command `xtset panelvar timevar`, which declares the data to be a panel. In this case it is `panelvar` that is necessary, while `timevar` is optional. Hence, `tsset panelvar timevar` is equivalent to `xtset panelvar timevar`.

The commands `tsset` and `xtset` automatically sort the data by `panelvar` and `timevar`.

Now that we have declared the data to be a panel, we can summarise them using the command `xtsum` and describe them using the command `xtdes`. The results of these two commands are shown in Figure 4.3.

The command `xtsum` shows descriptive statistics for 'overall', 'between' and 'within'. The 'overall' statistics refer to the whole sample, while the 'within' statistics refer to each individual and to the variation from each individual average (T-bar). If a variable does not change over time, its 'within' standard deviation is zero. The 'between' statistics refer to individuals' means and their variation. N is the total number of observations in the dataset for that specific variable, while n is the number of individuals for whom we have data for that variable. T-bar is the average number of time periods – waves – for which the variable is observed. Since the panel is unbalanced, T-bar is not an integer; T-bar can be obtained by dividing N by n.

```
. tsset pid wave
        panel variable:  pid (unbalanced)
         time variable:  wave, 1 to 18, but with gaps
                 delta:  1 unit

. xtsum

Variable         |      Mean   Std. Dev.        Min        Max |    Observations
-----------------+--------------------------------------------+----------------
hid      overall |  1.08e+07     4940804    1000209   1.89e+07 |     N =  238996
         between |              4317334    1000209   1.89e+07 |     n =   32380
         within  |              3760499   -1328915   2.31e+07 | T-bar = 7.38098
                 |                                            |
sex      overall |  1.538223   .4985379          1          2 |     N =  236902
         between |             .4994418          1          2 |     n =   32336
         within  |                    0   1.538223   1.538223 | T-bar = 7.32626
                 |                                            |
pid      overall |  4.85e+07    4.39e+07   1.00e+07   1.89e+08 |     N =  238996
         between |             4.83e+07   1.00e+07   1.89e+08 |     n =   32380
         within  |                    0   4.85e+07   4.85e+07 | T-bar = 7.38098
                 |                                            |
mastat   overall |  2.539056    2.055286          0         98 |     N =  238942
         between |              2.06646          0   21.33333 |     n =   32379
         within  |             .9152662  -12.79428   85.20572 | T-bar = 7.37954
                 |                                            |
paygu    overall |  1335.755    1104.061   .0833333   72055.43 |     N =  120115
         between |             868.1677   4.333333      14064 |     n =   20167
         within  |             641.6543  -8009.365   65521.23 | T-bar = 5.95602
                 |                                            |
wave     overall |  10.43351    4.947756          1         18 |     N =  238996
         between |              4.27356          1         18 |     n =   32380
         within  |             3.838481  -1.995066   22.86208 | T-bar = 7.38098

. xtdes

    pid:  10002251, 10004491, ..., 1.893e+08               n =      32380
   wave:  1, 2, ..., 18                                    T =         18
          Delta(wave) = 1 unit
          Span(wave)  = 18 periods
          (pid*wave uniquely identifies each observation)

Distribution of T_i:   min      5%     25%      50%      75%     95%     max
                         1       1       2        6       10      18      18

    Freq.  Percent    Cum. |  Pattern
  -------------------------+---------------------
     4098    12.66   12.66 |  111111111111111111
     2559     7.90   20.56 |  ........1111111111
     1871     5.78   26.34 |  .........11111111
     1224     3.78   30.12 |  ......11111.......
      964     2.98   33.09 |  1.................
      840     2.59   35.69 |  ..........1.......
      632     1.95   37.64 |  ........1.........
      593     1.83   39.47 |  11................
      505     1.56   41.03 |  ................1
    19094    58.97  100.00 |  (other patterns)
  -------------------------+---------------------
    32380   100.00         |  XXXXXXXXXXXXXXXXXX
```

Figure 4.3 The xtsum and xtdes commands

The command xtdes describes the patterns of responses and highlights that the BHPS, as in most individual datasets, is an unbalanced panel (we could have

noticed this also from the results of the `tsset` command, which highlights that
`pid` has gaps). Figure 4.3 shows that 4,098 individuals (12.66% of the total)
responded to all 18 waves; 2,559 responded to all waves since the 9th; 1,871
responded to all waves since the 11th; and so on. By default only the nine most
common patterns are shown (to show a different number of patterns we can use
the option `patterns(#)`). The last row shows the number and percentage of all
remaining patterns.

This clearly shows that, if we were to choose to use a balanced panel, we
would be focusing on a small, and possibly highly selected, group of respondents. In most cases researchers choose to work with unbalanced panels since the
econometric tools for balanced and unbalanced panels are essentially the same
(see Part II of this book).

Also try typing the commands `iis` and `tis`: `iis` reminds us which variable
is used as the person identifier, and `tis` reminds us which variable is used as
the time identifier.

Write the commands and compare with the do file in the online appendix

4.6 How to Compute Changes over Time

We can compute changes over time in one variable using the operator `L.`,
which takes the lag of the variable following the dot (note that this command
can be used only after we have used either the `tsset` or the `xtset` command).
Hence, if we want to compute the lag of the variable identifying wages (`paygu`),
we can use `L.paygu`, which means $paygu_{t-1}$. Note that the first observation
will be missing since we have no data for the year prior to the first year of the
survey (see Figure 4.4). If we want a two-period lag we can use `L2.`. We can
obtain similar results using the operator for first differences (`D.`); there are also
operators for computing leads (`F.`) and seasonal differences (`S.`), which work
in a similar way. Consult the Stata help for more details on the time-series
operators:[3]

```
generate paych = paygu - L.paygu
label var paych "Change in pay"
```

---

[3]Although most of the commands described in this book apply to all longitudinal datasets,
we need to be careful when interviews are not conducted yearly or are not at constant
intervals (as in the case of cohort surveys). We may need to think how best to specify the
time variable in the `tsset` and `xtset` commands, and may need to be especially careful
when using the lag and lead operators.

pid	year	paygu	L.paygu
1001	2005	6.5	.
1001	2006	6.7	6.5
1001	2007	6.8	6.8
1002	2005	5.9	.
1002	2007	6.2	.
1002	2008	7	6.2
1003	2005	4.5	.
1003	2006	n.a.	4.5
1003	2007	4.1	n.a.

Figure 4.4   The lag operator

```
. tab sex, sum(paych)

                 |       Summary of Change in pay
         Sex     |         Mean      Std. Dev.           Freq.
-----------------+-----------------------------------------------
        male     |     103.65392      853.93596           44890
      female     |      67.852064     600.48718           48794
-----------------+-----------------------------------------------
       Total     |      85.007024     733.16378           93684
```

Figure 4.5   The `tab, sum` command

How does the change in wage vary by sex? As shown in Figure 4.5, the command `tabulate, summarize()` or `tab, sum()` produces one- and two-way tables of descriptive statistics for the variable in parentheses (in this case paych), broken down by the values of another variable (in this case sex). The results in Figure 4.5 show that both men and women experience an increase in their monthly wages from year to year, but the increase experienced by men (£104) is larger than the increase experienced by women (£68).

We can also compute changes in marital status. First of all, we should inspect the variable `mastat`. Here, a small number of observations refer to people aged younger than 16; these cases have code 0 and need to be excluded from the analysis by recoding 0 into Stata missing. We also recode the value 98, which is clearly a data error, to Stata missing. For simplicity, we also recode marital status into a smaller number of categories (married, living as a couple or civil partnership = 1; widowed, divorced or separated = 2; never married = 3), creating the new variable `ma`.

Write the commands and compare with the do file in the online appendix

Now we create a new variable which summarises different transitions across marital statuses by creating a two-digit summary of marital change. We call this variable `mach` (Figure 4.6).

```
. gen mach = (10*ma) + L.ma
(36870 missing values generated)

. tab mach

      mach |      Freq.      Percent       Cum.
-----------+-----------------------------------
        11 |    129,300        63.97       63.97
        12 |      1,302         0.64       64.61
        13 |      2,715         1.34       65.96
        21 |      2,442         1.21       67.17
        22 |     28,060        13.88       81.05
        23 |        158         0.08       81.13
        31 |      1,021         0.51       81.63
        32 |        138         0.07       81.70
        33 |     36,990        18.30      100.00
-----------+-----------------------------------
     Total |    202,126       100.00
```

Figure 4.6   Compute changes in marital status

The command gen mach = (10*L.ma) + ma is a useful trick that we often use when we want to 'concatenate' two numeric variables. We multiply the first variable by 10 and then add the value of the second variable. This works because the variable ma is an integer and its values have one digit only (it only has values between 0 and 9); if the second variable comprised two digits (it could assume values of 10 or higher, but lower than 100) then we would have to multiply the variable by 100 in order to be able to concatenate the values.

Using the command label var we can attach a short description to the variable ma, and using the command label value we can attach labels to the values of the variable:

```
label var ma "marital status"

label define malab ///

  1 "married, living as couple" ///

  2 "widowed, divorced or separated" ///

  3 "never married"

label value ma malab

tabulate ma

sort wave hid

list ma in 1/20, sepby(hid)
```

The option sepby(hid) in the command list draws a horizontal separator line every time the variable hid changes value; hence, it draws a line separating each household, thus making the table easier to read (sort by hid first).

Write the commands and compare with the do file in the online appendix

We can now analyse transitions using the command xttrans. We use xttrans to analyse whether marriage varies over time and by sex. To analyse whether the change in pay varies by type of marital status and sex we use the command table (note the difference between the command tab, short for tabulate, and the command table). The results of these two commands are shown in Figure 4.7.

```
. xttrans ma

  marital |            marital status
  status  |      1            2            3 |      Total
----------+---------------------------------+----------
        1 |    97.23         1.97         0.81 |     100.00
        2 |     4.51        94.99         0.50 |     100.00
        3 |     7.15         0.41        92.44 |     100.00
----------+---------------------------------+----------
    Total |    65.77        15.15        19.09 |     100.00


. table ma sex, contents (mean paych n paych) format (%9.2f)

------------------------------------------------------
                              |       sex
          marital status      | male       female
------------------------------+-----------------------
  married, living as couple   |     98.09       59.06
                              |     32,856      34,546
                              |
  widowed, divorced or separated |    75.52       50.22
                              |      2,314       5,296
                              |
            never married     |    129.21      112.26
                              |      9,717       8,948
------------------------------------------------------
```

Figure 4.7   The xttrans and table commands

The command xttrans shows the matrix of transitions between the different states, but without distinguishing the year in which the transition happened. Most people do not seem to change state: most of those who are married one year remain married. While 92.44% of those who are never married stay so, 7.15% do get married.

The command table ma sex shows a two-way tabulation of the two variables (ma and sex), but the option contents (mean paych n paych) specifies that the content of the table should instead refer to the variable paych. In this case the table shows the mean and number of observations (n) for the variable paych. The option `format(%9.2f)` specifies that the table should show up to nine integer digits, and up to two digits after the comma (see Figure 4.7).

4.7 Graphically Analysing Panel Data

We can descriptively analyse panel data using graphs. As in Chapter 3, we can use histograms to summarise the distribution of a variable. For example, we can plot the density of the variable `paygu` using the `kdensity` command. We can either plot the density for the whole dataset, thus ignoring that we have repeated observations per individual, or plot it for one specific year. We can also look at the distribution of the variable separately by year using the option `by`. Since this option is not accepted when using the `kdensity` command, we can use the `histogram` command instead. For example,

```
kdensity paygu, ///
   title(Distribution of Wages 1991-2008) ///
   scheme(s1manual)
```

or

```
kdensity paygu if wave == 15, ///
   title(Distribution of Wages 2005) scheme(s1manual)
```

or

```
histogram paygu, scheme(s1manual) ///
   by(wave, title(Distribution of Wages 1991-2008))
```

A useful alternative is the command `twoway`, which can be used to combine separate graphs:

```
twoway (kdensity paygu if wave == 1, ///
   lcolor(black)) ///
   (kdensity paygu if wave == 8, ///
   lcolor(gs4) lp(dash)) ///
   (kdensity paygu if wave == 17, lcolor(gs10)), ///
   scheme(s1manual) ytitle(Density) xtitle(Wage) ///
   title(Distribution of Wages)
```

With this syntax the graph shows three kernel density plots: one for the first, one for the eighth, and one for the seventeenth wave of data. The option `lcolor()` specifies the colour of the density line (in this case, either black or two different shades of grey), while the option `lp()` specifies the pattern of the line. Note that `lcolor()` and `lp()` are options of each sub-graph and, therefore, are within the parentheses of each graph. We can also add options to the `twoway` command after the comma at the end of the last sub-graph. The option `ytitle()` refers to the title of the vertical axis; `xtitle()` refers to the title of the horizontal axis; and `title()` is the title of the graph.

Note that the `twoway` type of graph may require a lot of memory for its computation. Hence, before running the command we might need to drop some variables, or drop some observations. For example, in this case we can drop all those individuals who are not in employment and/or have no data on wages. The graph would then look like the one in Figure 4.8.

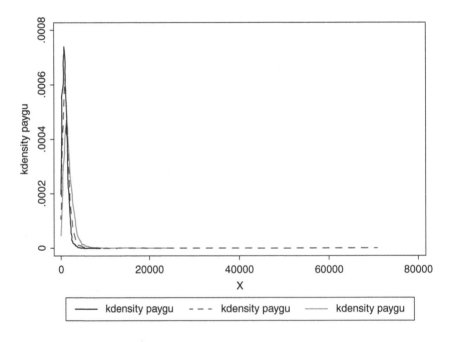

Figure 4.8   Graph of the wage distribution using the `twoway` command

Because there are few extremely high values of the variable `paygu`, this graph is difficult to read. Hence, we restrict it to values that are, for example, smaller than 5,000 by adding the `if` condition before the last comma. Furthermore, because of the way we have identified the variables to compare (using `if wave ==`), the legend does not clarify which line refers to each wave. We can overcome this problem by using the option `legend`. The new `twoway` command would then look like this:

```
twoway (kdensity paygu if wave == 1, ///

  lcolor(black)) ///

  (kdensity paygu if wave == 8, ///

  lcolor(gs4) lp(dash)) ///

  (kdensity paygu if wave == 17, ///

  lcolor(gs10) lwidth(thick)) ///

  if paygu <= 5000, ///

  legend(label(1 "Wage 1991") ///

    label(2 "Wage 1998") ///

    label(3 "Wage 2007")) ///

  scheme(s1manual) ytitle(Density) xtitle(Wage) ///

  title(Distribution of Wages)
```

The graph resulting from this command should look like the one in Figure 4.9.

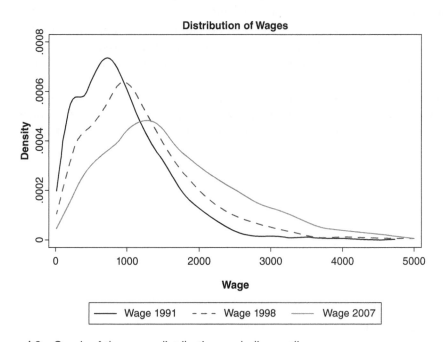

Figure 4.9   Graph of the wage distribution excluding outliers

Figure 4.9 shows that the wage distribution is clearly skewed to the left, with a majority of people earning up to £2,000 per month, and a small proportion of people earning more than that. The wage distribution clearly shifts to the right over time: in 1991 the majority of employed workers earned less than £1,000 per month, while in 1998 most workers earned about £1,000 per month. Part of this is likely to result from inflation. When computing descriptive statistics it might sometimes be preferable to deflate wages by using consumer prices indices (CPIs) which are normally published online by national statistics offices. For the case of the BHPS, since most interviews took place between October and December, we would use either the CPI for the last quarter of the year or the monthly ones for October, November and December (the dataset includes variables to identify the day, month and year of each interview). It is also interesting to note that the distribution not only shifts to the right between 1991 and 2007, but also becomes more spread.

We should be careful not to interpret this graph in terms of changes in the distribution of wages in the UK, since this is a sample of people which may or may not be representative of the population (Chapter 7 discusses why this is relevant and how to take it into account). First of all, since this is a panel, some people will contribute to the distribution in 1991 with the wages they earned when relatively young, and will appear in 1998 and 2007 with the wages of a 'mature' worker, with more seniority, experience and therefore higher wages. Second, from 1999, the BHPS oversamples people living in Scotland and Wales; this has an impact on the representativeness of the sample for the UK as a whole from 1999 onwards. This is relevant if the variable of interest, in this case average wages, differs across the three countries (for example, if wages in Scotland and Northern Ireland are comparatively lower than in England). We can overcome these caveats using the sample weights which are provided with the data. More details on sample weights, and when and how to use them, are given in Chapter 7.

Also, with this type of graph we can use the option by and, for example, show the distribution of wages plotted separately for men and women. The command looks like the one below, and the resulting graph looks like the one in Figure 4.10:

```
twoway (kdensity paygu if wave == 1, ///
   lcolor(black)) ///
   (kdensity paygu if wave == 8, ///
   lcolor(gs4) lp(dash)) ///
   (kdensity paygu if wave == 17, ///
   lcolor(gs10) lwidth(thick)) ///
   if paygu <= 5000, ///
   legend(label(1 "Wage 1991") ///
   label(2 "Wage 1998") ///
   label(3 "Wage 2007")) ///
   scheme(s1manual) ytitle(Density) xtitle(Wage) ///
   by(sex, title(Distribution of Wages))
```

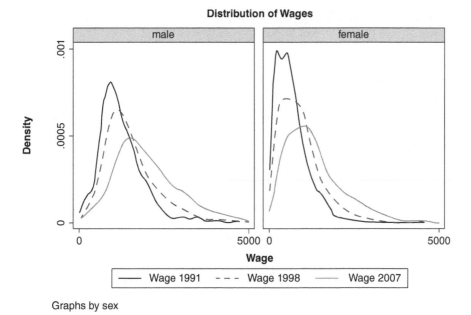

Figure 4.10   Graph of the wage distribution by gender

The graph in Figure 4.10 is consistent with the large literature on gender wage gaps, summarised by Weichselbaumer and Winter-Ebmer (2005), and suggests that on average women are paid less than men. This is especially clear for 1991, where we can see that for women the distribution of wages is more concentrated towards small amounts of monthly wages. The fact that in 2007 the wage distribution for women is more similar to that of men than in 1991 might suggest a reduction in wage gaps over time. We have to remember, however, that this graph includes workers with different levels of education, working in different types of occupations, and working different numbers of hours per month. A better comparison of gender wage gaps may use models such as those discussed in Part II of this book.

Stata also provides graph commands for panel data. One such command is xtline, which draws line plots for panel data by plotting a variable over time. The graph is presented separately by individuals; hence, it is not suitable when using a panel with a large number (more than five or six) of individuals. This command is more suitable in cases where we have only a few cross-sections and longer time series, such as unemployment or inflation rate across European countries over recent decades.

A different way of summarising individual longitudinal data has been suggested by Rabe-Hesketh and Skrondal (2012) who, when demonstrating growth curves, illustrate how to plot lines for random selections of individual cases.

4.8 Summary and Suggestions for Further Reading

In this chapter we have discussed how to prepare the data for longitudinal analysis, how to declare the data to be a panel, so that we can use the set of Stata commands for panel data. We have also discussed the most common commands to describe the data and compute lagged variables and wave-on-wave transitions.

Key points

- Preparing the data for longitudinal analysis usually requires merging together information from different data files.
- Check the naming conventions for the dataset: when variable and file names follow specified rules use loops to prepare the dataset.
- When the data are set up in long format, remember to declare the data as a panel using the commands `tsset` or `xtset` in order to use the Stata commands for panel data.

Suggestions for further reading

- For an overview of panel data see the introductory chapters in:

  - Baltagi, B.H. (2009) *Econometric Analysis of Panel Data*. London, Wiley.
  - Hsiao, C. (2003) *Analysis of Panel Data*. Cambridge, Cambridge University Press.

- Stata has a manual focusing on the `xt` set of commands, which are typically used for panel data: Stata (2013b) *Stata Longitudinal-Data/Panel-Data Reference Manual*. College Station, TX, Stata Press.

WORKING WITH
MULTIPLE DATASETS

Aim

In this chapter we discuss how to link household- and individual-level data and how to aggregate individual-level data to obtain household-level variables. We also discuss how to create a wide-format file; this complements the section on data set-up for longitudinal analysis in Chapter 4. We then discuss how these data matching techniques can be used to combine survey data with external data such as census data.

5.1 Introduction

The majority of the models we estimate in social science research deals with explaining individual behaviour: what level of education people acquire, what occupation they choose, which job offer (and wage offer) they accept, whether they remain single or enter into a partnership (and if so with whom), and so on. These models postulate that both characteristics of individuals and their surroundings affect behaviour. By surroundings we refer to characteristics of friends and families (such as family income and composition, age, race and gender of friends), regions of residence (such as local unemployment rate, sex ratio in the neighbourhood, local deprivation levels), workplaces (such as size of firm, type of firm), and so on. To allow analysis using information at these different levels (individual, household, family, region, workplace) all such data must be included in a single flat file as shown in Table 5.1.

Table 5.1   Flat file that includes individual-, family- and regional-level information

Personal ID	Age	Sex	Education	Family size	Local unemployment rate
1	23	Male	A levels	4	2.2
2	38	Female	PhD	4	2.2
3	55	Male	Masters	2	9.8

So, for example, people living in the same household will have the same household characteristics, and people living in the same neighbourhood will face the same level of local unemployment rate. However, data are often provided in separate files such as separate household- and individual-level files (see Table 5.2) as in the BHPS, SOEP, PSID and UKHLS. Additionally, some household-level variables may not be available and may need to be constructed from individual-level variables. We discuss how to handle both these issues in Sections 5.3, 5.4 and 5.5.

Table 5.2   Separate individual-, family- and regional-level files

Individual-level file

Personal ID	Age	Sex	Education	Household ID	Region ID
1	23	Male	A levels	32453534	1
2	38	Female	PhD	32453534	1
3	55	Male	Masters	24566567	2

Household-level file

Household ID	Household size
32453534	4
24566567	2
54682668	1

Regional-level file

Region ID	Local unemployment rate
1	2.2
2	9.8
3	7.0

In general, regional-level characteristics are not provided with the household or individual surveys but need to be retrieved from other data sources and then linked to these datasets. In Section 5.5 we discuss how to merge our survey datasets with external data sources using individual-level data from the BHPS and regional-level data from the 2011 UK Census. By this stage we would have learnt how to merge different datasets, but what is new in this section is a guide to the major issues one needs to contend with when merging datasets from completely different sources.

To illustrate these data management methods we will focus on a descriptive analysis of poverty using data from the last wave (wave r, year 2008) of the BHPS. Specifically, our aim is to identify individuals who are poor and then estimate the association between poverty status of an individual and some of their own characteristics such as gender, age, as well as characteristics of their household, such as the number of non-employed persons in the household, whether the household is a female-headed one, the number of young children in the household and household size. We discuss this analysis in Section 5.6. In Section 5.2 we discuss poverty measurement and the variables needed for this poverty analysis, some of which are directly available in the BHPS and some of which need to be created.

In the last section, Section 5.7, we deal with a different kind of data merge: we merge individual-level files from two interview years or waves into a wide format (see Section 4.4 for the definition of wide format) using the same techniques. Setting up the data in this fashion allows us to analyse transitions and changes over time. However, to analyse such transitions or for panel data analysis in general, it is more efficient and common practice to set up the data in long format (see Chapter 4). Having said that, there are some situations where it may be quicker to set up the data in wide format, especially if there are just two waves. In Section 5.7 we analyse poverty persistence by identifying the poverty status of BHPS sample members in both 2007 and 2008 (waves q and r).

5.2 Overview of Poverty Analysis

5.2.1 Defining Poverty

There are various ways of measuring poverty. In this chapter we will focus on one such measure, relative income poverty. This is the primary poverty measure used in the EU and many other developed countries. Another common poverty measure is absolute poverty, which is used mainly in developing countries. While absolute poverty measures the lack of basic items needed for survival, relative poverty measures the inability to achieve a standard of living that is typical of the society (see Citro and Michael 1995: Chapter 2; Frazer 2009).

There are different ways of defining the norm or typical standard of living, the most commonly used ones being the relative income poverty lines. These poverty lines are defined as 40%, 50%, 60% or 70% of the median income, 60% of median income being the most frequently used. Here, income is defined as the equivalised net household income, that is, the total income of all household members net of taxes, adjusted for household size and composition. This adjustment or equivalisation is needed to make the household income of different households comparable. First, the same amount of income needs to be divided between different numbers of people assuming income is shared equally between all household members. In most cases there is almost no information on intra-household sharing, so equal sharing is assumed. Second, the same amount of per capita income may be worth more for a two-person household than a single-person household because of economies of scale. For example, two persons living together need one television, one washing machine, one oven, but would have needed two of each had they lived separately. Also, children consume less than adults, so that a two-person household with one child and one adult will be able to afford a higher standard of living compared with a household with two adults on the same income. Analysts have defined different equivalence scales based on different assumptions about economies of scale, and adjustment for children (for further discussion see Citro and Michael 1995; Creedy and Sleeman 2005). Currently the most commonly used one in the EU is the modified OECD scale, although earlier it used to be the McClements scale. The BHPS only provides the McClements equivalence scale value for each household in the sample which we will use in this exercise. By using information on household size and composition it is possible to compute the modified OECD scale for each household.

5.2.2 Variables Needed for Poverty Analysis

Before we get started, let us make a list of variables that we need for poverty analysis (see Table 5.3). Among these, we need the equivalised household income to identify whether the household is poor. We may also want to identify whether the head of the household is a female to analyse whether these households are

Table 5.3   List of variables to be created, the corresponding input variable names and data sources

Variables to be created	Input variables (BHPS variable names)	
Poverty (0–1) indicator	(i) household monthly income (wfihhmn) (ii) McClements equivalence scale (wfieqfcb)	whhresp: household-level file of responding households
Number of non-employed persons in the household	(i) employment status of every adult in the household (whgemp)	windall: individual-level file of individuals in responding households
Female-headed household (0–1) indicator	(i) identify the person who is the head of household (whoh) (ii) gender of each person (whgsex)	
Number of young children in the household	(i) age of everyone in the household (wage)	

Note: The prefix w represents the wave prefix, which is a letter between a and r. As you know, the data files and variables in the BHPS follow a naming convention where the root name remains the same across all interview waves but the letter prefix signifies the interview. So, a represents wave 1, b wave 2, and so on.

more likely than male-headed households to be in poverty. We may also want to include in the dataset an index of deprivation to analyse whether there is a correlation between area characteristics and the probability of being poor.

A quick look at the online documentation for the BHPS will show that some of these variables are not directly available in the BHPS data files but need to be created from other variables which are available. The second column of Table 5.3 shows the BHPS variables we will use to create the variables specified in the first column. To the right of the table we specify the BHPS data files in which these variables are included. In the next section we will learn how to create these household-level variables (number of non-employed persons in the household, whether female-headed household, number of young children in the household) from the individual-level files.

5.3 Setting Up the BHPS Data for Poverty Analysis

5.3.1 Creating Household-Level Variables from Individual-Level Data

The file `rindall` contains some basic demographic information about everyone in a responding household, including children and non-responding adults from the last wave (year 2008) of the BHPS (see the online appendix). As this file has information on all household members, we will use it to create the household-level variables. First, let us open that dataset.

To create `numNotEmp`, the number of non-employed persons in the household, we will make use of `rhgemp`. The variable `rhgemp` records the employment status of each household member as reported by the household reference person in the household grid. However, to use it we need to know what the numerical codes of `rhgemp` mean. This information is stored in the value label of the variable. First we will find out what the value label is by making use of the command `describe` and then we can find out the details of the value label by using the command `label list` (see Figure 5.1).

The next step is to create a 0–1 indicator for being non-employed, `NotEmp`, using logical statements in Stata: if the condition within the parentheses holds, the new variable being generated takes a value of 1, and 0 otherwise:

```
generate NotEmp = (rhgemp ~= 1)
```

Note that all variables other than the individual and household identifiers, `rhid`, `pid` and `rpno`, have missing values for a few observations either because of coding errors or because the person refused to answer or did not know the answer. Whatever the reason, you need to decide what value the new variable

```
. describe rhgemp

                  storage   display    value
variable name     type      format     label       variable label
───────────────────────────────────────────────────────────────────────
rhgemp                byte    %8.0g      rhgemp      employment status - hh grid

. label list rhgemp
rhgemp:
           -9 missing or wild
           -8 inapplicable
           -2 refused
           -1 don't know
            0 under 16 years
            1 yes
            2 no
```

Figure 5.1   Value label for `rhgemp`

will take when the input variable is missing. We know that in the BHPS missing values are given negative values, so the above code will result in `NotEmp` being coded as 0 for cases where `rhgemp` is missing (that is, `rhgemp` < 0). So, to code `NotEmp` as missing for all cases where `rhgemp` is missing we can use

```
generate NotEmp = (rhgemp ~= 1) if rhgemp>=0
```

Check if the newly created `NotEmp` variable is what we expected it to be.

Write the commands and compare with the do file in the online appendix

Finally, we want to add up the number of individuals who are not employed (sum of `NotEmp`) within each household. Here we will make use of the `egen` command, which we came across in Chapter 3. We know it allows operations across a number of observations and the resulting value is assigned to all those observations. For example, the command `egen var2 = sum(var1)` will generate a variable called `var2` which is the sum of the variable `var1` across all the observations in a dataset. So, all observations in the dataset will have the same value of the variable `var1`. We will use this command to compute the number of non-employed persons in each household:

```
bysort rhid: egen numNotEmp = sum(NotEmp)
```

where `bysort rhid:` performs the operation specified after the colon (`:`) for each value of `rhid` separately; that is, for each household separately. But this means that `numNotEmp` will be incorrect for households where this information is missing for some of the household members. We will exclude these households from the analysis by assigning a missing value to `numNotEmp` for them:

```
bysort rhid: egen empmiss = sum(NotEmp==.)
replace numNotEmp=. if empmiss>0
```

Table 5.4 illustrates numNotEmp, NotEmp and rhgemp for a sample of seven individuals living in four households.

Table 5.4   Values of numNotEmp, NotEmp and rhgemp for three example households

rhid	pid	rhgemp	NotEmp	numNotEmp
1001	100001	1	0	0
1001	106702	1	0	0
1702	234505	1	0	2
1702	987578	1	0	2
1702	234598	2	1	2
1702	998499	0	1	2
3596	123123	2	1	.
3596	123124	-2	.	.
3560	730475	2	1	1

We can also create the variable numNotEmp by skipping the intermediate step of creating NotEmp:

```
bysort rhid: egen numNotEmp2 = ///
   sum(rhgemp ~= 1 & if rhgemp>=0)
bysort rhid: egen empmiss2 = sum(rhgemp <0)
replace numNotEmp2=. if empmiss2>0
```

The first command produces a variable, numNotEmp2, which is the sum of all non-employed persons in each household, and the second command does the same for the number of persons for whom employment status information is missing. The value of numNotEmp2 is incorrect for cases where employment status information is missing for at least one household member, so the third command sets the value to missing where this is the case. Check that both methods produce identical variables.

Write the commands and compare with the do file in the online appendix

Using the techniques discussed in this section we can create an indicator for female-headed households and a variable that counts the number of children in each household, where a child is defined as anyone less than 16 years of age.

Write the commands and compare with the do file in the online appendix

Let us save this dataset for later use, with the name tempIND. The next step is to create the poverty indicator, for which we need to merge this individual-level file with the household-level file, rhhresp, which contains information on household income.

5.3.2 Linking Household- and Individual-Level Data

The general principles for matching two files at two different data levels are shown in Figure 5.2 (also known as many-to-one or one-to-many matching). The steps to do this matching are as follows. First, we need to find out whether the unique identifier of the higher level file is present in the lower

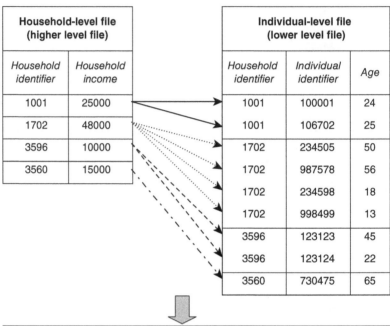

Figure 5.2   An illustration of the process of matching two datasets

level file. If it does not exist or cannot be computed from the existing variables, then the files cannot be matched. The unique identifier of the higher
level file may be present in the lower level file but have different names
across the two datasets. In this case one of the variables needs to be renamed
for the linking so that both datasets have the same variable name. This information should be available in any documentation about the data such as the
user guide. In the example shown in Figure 5.2, we see that the unique
identifier of the higher level file (household-level file) is the 'Household
identifier'.

Once we have identified the correct matching variable we can match the two
datasets using the unique identifier of the higher level file. Figure 5.2 shows how
these two datasets can be matched on the variable 'Household identifier' to
produce a third dataset with matched information.

If you do not need unmatched cases for your analysis, then drop them. Note
that matching two files at the same level, also known as one-to-one matching,
works on the same basic principle.

Here we will now match the individual-level file tempIND, which is a modified version of rindall, with the household-level file rhhresp. Notes on how to
do similar matching using the SOEP and PSID data files are in Section 5.3.5.

As outlined above, we need to determine the variable that uniquely identifies each row of observation. In the BHPS documentation we see that rhid is
the variable that uniquely identifies households in the rhhresp file. The same
variable is also available in the rindresp file. It is good practice always to
check whether the unique identifier does in fact uniquely define each row of
the dataset. We can check this by counting the number of observations for
each unique rhid. As this is a household-level file this number should be 1 for
all cases:

```
bysort rhid: generate uniqueHH = _N
```

As we saw earlier, the command bysort rhid instructs Stata to do the operation
following the colon separately for each group of cases with the same rhid, and
as _N counts the total number of observations in each group, this command asks
Stata to generate a variable, called uniqueHH, that counts the number of observations with the same rhid. We can check if uniqueHH is 1 for all cases by looking
at its frequency distribution (tab uniqueHH). Alternatively, we could use the
duplicates report or isid commands in Stata:

```
duplicates report rhid

isid rhid
```

While duplicates reports a frequency distribution of the number of times
each unique value of the variable rhid appears in the data, isid generates an
error message if there are multiple values of the identifier (and produces no

```
. tab uniqueHH
```

uniqueHH	Freq.	Percent	Cum.
1	8,144	100.00	100.00
Total	8,144	100.00	

```
.
. duplicates report rhid

Duplicates in terms of rhid
```

copies	observations	surplus
1	8144	0

```
. isid rhid
```

Figure 5.3   How to verify unique identifiers

results if each row of the data is uniquely defined by the identifier). So, if rhid is the unique identifier in this dataset then the duplicates report for the variable rhid should say that there is only one copy of data for each rhid (as is the case in Figure 5.3) and isid should produce no error message.

Now that we are convinced that rhid uniquely identifies each row, the next step will be to merge these data with the individual-level data.

At this point we may want to double-check that the file tempIND is an individual-level file and not a household-level file. Using the duplicates command we can check that rhid does not uniquely identify each row; rather there are multiple rows for each unique rhid. The result of the command is given in Figure 5.4 where we can see that 2,103 unique household identifiers, rhid, appear once, while 5,622 appear twice, and so on. In other words, Figure 5.4 shows that there are 2,103 single-person households, 2,811 two-person households, and so on. If we repeat the command on the unique individual identifier, pid, we find that each row is uniquely identified by pid. In other words, this is an individual-level file.

The final step is to instruct Stata to merge the two datasets using rhid as the matching variable. In Stata, when merging two files, one of the files needs to be open. As we mentioned in Chapter 4, the file open in memory is referred to as the 'master' file. The other file is then matched to it and this second file is referred to as the 'using' file. As tempIND is already open, to merge tempHH with this using rhid, type

```
merge m:1 rhid using tempHH
```

```
. duplicates report rhid
```

Duplicates in terms of rhid

copies	observations	surplus
1	2103	0
2	5622	2811
3	4107	2738
4	4888	3666
5	2315	1852
6	786	655
7	196	168
8	72	63
9	27	24
10	20	18
11	11	10
14	14	13
16	16	15

Duplicates in terms of pid

copies	observations	surplus
1	20177	0

Figure 5.4 Stata output for duplicates command in an individual-level file

The m:1 is to specify that this is a many-to-one matching. The command will work without this, but Stata encourages specification of the type of matching – one-to-one, many-to-one or many-to-many. Note that this is quite useful because it makes you think about the structure of both datasets and how you are matching them.[1] Also, although the datasets do not need to be sorted on the linking variable before merging, if they are sorted the merging process is much faster.

Other useful options are available with this command, such as update and replace. If some variables (other than those used for matching) appear in both

[1]In versions of Stata 11 or lower, both datasets need to be sorted on the matching variable(s) before they can be merged. Specifying the type of matching is not allowed in versions of Stata 11 or lower.

datasets, then by default Stata does not copy the values of the variables from the 'using' dataset over the values of the same variable in the 'master' dataset. By specifying `update` you are asking Stata to replace the missing values in the 'master' file with the values of the variables with the same name in the 'using' file; `update` together with `replace` ask Stata to replace the non-missing values as well.

After each `merge` command Stata outputs a frequency table of how many cases were matched (that is, were found in both datasets) and how many were unmatched. This information is stored in a Stata-created variable called `_merge`. An explanation of the different values of `_merge` can be found in the Stata help for `merge` (see Figure 5.5).

```
  numeric      equivalent
   code        word (results)    description
----------------------------------------------------------------
    1           master           observation appeared in master only
    2           using            observation appeared in using only
    3           match            observation appeared in both
    4           match_update     observation appeared in both,
                                 missing values updated
    5           match_conflict   observation appeared in both,
                                 conflicting nonmissing values
----------------------------------------------------------------
```

Figure 5.5   An excerpt from Stata (version 12) help for `merge`

After running the `merge` command Stata logs the output (see Figure 5.6) which shows that there are no unmatched cases in either dataset.

```
. merge m:1 rhid using tempHH

    Result                           # of obs.

    not matched                              0
    matched                             20,177    (_merge==3)
```

Figure 5.6   Stata output after `merge`

This is what you would expect given that `tempIND` is a modified version of `rindall`, which consists of all individuals in responding households, and `tempHH` is a modified version of `rhhresp`, which consists of all responding households.

Note that, whenever Stata is asked to merge datasets, it attempts to create the variable `_merge`. If a variable with the same name already exists in either of the datasets we want to merge together, Stata will produce an error message and stop the operation. If either of these datasets is the result of a previous merge operation, a _merge variable will already exist. So, it is always advisable either to drop _merge or rename it (if you think you will need it later) after a merge operation.

5.3.3 Relative Poverty Measure

To carry out the poverty analysis outlined at the beginning of the chapter we still need to create one more variable – the poverty status (see Section 5.2.1). The BHPS data files that we have been using do not include a net household income measure, only a gross one. A group of researchers have constructed net household income variables for the BHPS, which are available as a separate set of data files called 'British Household Panel Survey Derived Current and Annual Net Household Income Variables, Waves 1-18, 1991-2009'. These files can be downloaded from the UK Data Service website (UK Data Service Study Number 3909). For further details about this dataset see Levy and Jenkins (2012). For this exercise we will use gross household income instead of net.

To create the poverty status we first need to create the equivalised household income variable, equivHHinc, by dividing the household monthly income (rfihhmn) by the equivalence scale (rieqfcb), see also Table 5.1:

```
generate equivHHinc = rfihhmn/rfieqfcb ///
    if rfihhmn>=0 & rfihhmn<.
```

We can now compute the median equivalised household income by using the detail option of the summarize command. In addition to the usual mean, min, max this option produces some of the percentiles including the 50th percentile, which is the median. To get an unbiased estimate of a population statistic from sample data we will use the appropriate weight, which in this case is the enumerated cross-sectional weight for wave r (we discuss weights in more details in Chapter 7):

```
summarize equivHHinc [aweight = rxewght], detail
```

We can now compute the relative poverty line, PovertyLine, which is 60% of the median equivalised household income in the population. Instead of computing the poverty line manually, we will use commands to automate the process. A good data management tip is to automate as many operations as possible, to reduce human error and time spent on data management tasks. Stata has an excellent feature where it stores some of the outputs after descriptive statistics and estimation commands. The results from an estimation command are stored in the e() variables and those from a descriptive statistics command in `r()` variables. You can see what has been stored by typing `ereturn list` after an estimation command and `return list` after a descriptive statistics command. Note that these statistics are saved in these temporary variables only until the next estimation command. So if we need to use these variables, we must use them right after the estimation command. Figure 5.7 shows what content Stata has stored in the `r()` variables after the above `summarize` command.

```
. return list

scalars:
              r(N) =  10065
          r(sum_w) =  11023.22475796938
           r(mean) =  2703.679091031838
            r(Var) =  4154668.930140617
             r(sd) =  2038.300500451446
       r(skewness) =  4.980602030204397
       r(kurtosis) =  61.38689852694022
            r(sum) =  29803262.29386631
            r(min) =  0
            r(max) =  42690.1640625
             r(p1) =  323.3830871582031
             r(p5) =  820.5641479492188
            r(p10) =  1036.760131835938
            r(p25) =  1459.489990234375
            r(p50) =  2276.994873046875
            r(p75) =  3355.30126953125
            r(p90) =  4787.22509765625
            r(p95) =  5946.25048828125
            r(p99) =  9390.5146484375
```

Figure 5.7 Stata output for `return list` after `sum, ... detail`

The 50th percentile or the median is stored in `r(p50)` and, as shown in Figure 5.7, in our case it is equal to about 2277. Now we can create the poverty line and the poverty indicator, which is 1 if the household equivalised income is below the poverty line:

```
generate PovertyLine = 0.60*r(p50)

generate poor = (equivHHinc<PovertyLine) ///
    if equivHHinc<.
```

As already discussed in the previous chapters, Stata treats missings (.) as the highest values. If we do not specify the condition `equivHHinc<.`, then `poor` will have a value of 0 for cases where the equivalised household income is missing. The command creates a variable called `PovertyLine`, but as `r(p50)` is a scalar, any variable created using it will be the same for every observation.

Creating a new variable which is a constant is a waste of (data) memory. One way to save disk space is to store this number in Stata's memory and recall it later. This can be done by using a global `macro` (as discussed in Section 3.1.6):

```
global PovertyLine = 0.60*r(p50)

generate poor2 = (equivHHinc<$PovertyLine) ///
    if equivHHinc<.
```

You can compare `poor` and `poor2` to see that these are exactly the same.

Write the commands and compare with the `do` and `log` files in the online appendix

A quick look at the distribution of either of these variables shows that 22.6% of the sample in wave r is poor. Now save this dataset.

The next step is to link the BHPS data with regional information on the proportion of households which are in socially rented houses as a crude measure of regional deprivation from 2011 England and Wales Census data.

5.3.4 Linking External Datasets: Issues of Data Linkage

Quite often survey datasets can be linked with external datasets, such as population censuses or some administrative datasets. Protecting the confidentiality of respondents' information is of paramount importance. As linkage of survey data with external datasets may increase the risk of identification of the respondents, special measures are put in place to prevent this. There are two types of external data that may be linked with some surveys. The first type refers to administrative datasets such as tax records, or health records that are already linked in by the survey providers after receiving consent from the respondents. If you want to use these linked-in data then in almost all cases you will need to sign data confidentiality agreements and undertake special measures to protect the data. In some cases you will have to run the analysis using those data at the data provider's site rather than on your own computer. Also, note that these types of data require consent from respondents and not all respondents will provide it. If those who do not provide consent are systematically different from those who do, then you may need to examine how this might affect the interpretations of the results based on those data. More information on how to obtain and use such linked data is generally available in the user guides (for the SOEP see Section 2.8 of Haisken-DeNew and Frick 2005; for the UKHLS see Section 4 of Knies 2014).

The second type of data that can be linked to surveys are geographical data such as census data, or local environmental information, which are available directly from external sources but not linked to the survey data by the data providers. Most survey providers release geographical locator variables for each household in their data. These variables can be used to link the survey data with the geographical-level datasets. Access to some of these linkage variables may also be subject to special data access agreements and procedures. For high levels of geography with low risks of identification, such controls are minor. For example, in the BHPS and UKHLS, variables identifying the Government Office Regions (GORs) of all households are released with the rest of the survey data; no special licence is required.

5.3.5 Linking External Datasets: Matching Census Data with the BHPS Data

In this section we will discuss how to match external data, specifically England and Wales Census data, with the BHPS. The principles of matching these datasets are the same as those outlined in Section 5.3.2. The notable difference is the possibility that the common variable to link the two datasets may have different names as well as different coding frames. To illustrate these techniques we will match a crude measure of GOR deprivation, the proportion of households in social housing by GOR, obtained from the 2011 Census, with the individual-level poverty status file we produced using data from year 2008 (wave r) of the BHPS. Ideally, we should link information on deprivation measures such as the Townsend Scores, Carstairs Scores or Multiple Deprivation Indices (Payne and Abel 2012; Noble et al. 2006; Carstairs and Morris 1991; Morris and Carstairs 1991; Townsend et al. 1988; Townsend 1987) and at a much smaller regional level as these are more likely to be linked to individual poverty. However, to obtain geographical indicators at any lower level of geography than the GOR for BHPS households will require special permission, so for illustrative purposes we will continue with these measures at the GOR level. Furthermore, we should always try to match aggregated data to individual data which refer to the same year. However, since there was no census in 2008 (which is the year for which we use the BHPS data) we use data from the 2011 Census.

Data derived from the Census 2011 can be downloaded as an Excel file from the ONS website: https://www.nomisweb.co.uk/. Specifically, we downloaded a file consisting of the total number of households with different ownership types (also known as housing tenure) across all regions and saved it as "HHtenure2011UKcensus.xls". Table 5.5 is a replication of this file.

To read the Excel file into Stata we use the command import:

```
import excel using "HHtenure2011UKcensus.xls", ///

    clear cellrange(A11:E20)
```

As you will notice, we do not need information such as 'KS402EW - Tenure' in cell A1 or 'ONS Crown Copyright Reserved [from Nomis on 16 September 2013]' in cell A2. We do not need the variable names either, since the names in the file

Table 5.5   The 2011 England and Wales Census table of households that are social renters by GORs

KS402EW - Tenure

ONS Crown Copyright Reserved [from Nomis on 16 September 2013]

population	All households
units	Households
date	2011
rural urban	Total

	All households		Social rented	
region	number	%	number	%
North East	1,129,935	100.0	259,506	23.0
North West	3,009,549	100.0	550,481	18.3
Yorkshire and The Humber	2,224,059	100.0	402,653	18.1
East Midlands	1,895,604	100.0	300,423	15.8
West Midlands	2,294,909	100.0	435,170	19.0
East	2,423,035	100.0	380,331	15.7
London	3,266,173	100.0	785,993	24.1
South East	3,555,463	100.0	487,473	13.7
South West	2,264,641	100.0	301,520	13.3
Wales	1,302,676	100.0	214,911	16.5

In order to protect against disclosure of personal information, records have been swapped between different geographic areas. Some counts will be affected, particularly small counts at the lowest geographies.

are inconvenient; we will specify our own. As the information that we want to import is located in the block of cells specified by cell range, A11:E20, we need to specify this cell range in the import command. Since the file has only one worksheet, there is no need to specify from which worksheet we should read in the data.

Stata will read in the data, but as we have not asked it to read in variable names, it will assign letters as variable names to each column: A, B, C, D. We will change them to names we can understand:

```
rename B allhhs

rename D hhs_socialrented

rename E pr_socialrented
```

The variable 'A' represents the GORs. But before we plunge into the task of merging two datasets, we must find out whether there is a variable in the BHPS which identifies the GOR each household is located in. Looking through the documentation we find that `rregion2` in the BHPS wave r dataset, which we have already extracted, is that variable. But `rregion2`, like all variables in the survey datasets we discuss in this book, is numeric, while A is a string variable. The easiest thing to do is to create in the census data file a new variable called `rregion2` and code it using the coding frame for `rregion2` in the BHPS data:

```
generate region=1 if A=="North East"

replace region=2 if A=="North West"

replace region=3 if A=="Yorkshire and The Humber"

replace region=4 if A=="East Midlands"

replace region=5 if A=="West Midlands"

replace region=6 if A=="East"

replace region=7 if A=="London"

replace region=8 if A=="South East"

replace region=9 if A=="South West"

replace region=10 if A=="Wales"
```

Next, we label this variable to reflect the categories it represents.

Write the commands and compare with the do file in the online appendix

Note that since this census file refers to England and Wales, it does not contain any information on Scotland and Northern Ireland. Census data for Scotland and Northern Ireland are collected by different agencies and hence available separately. For this exercise we will exclude Scotland and Northern Ireland from the analysis. Finally, we save the file in Stata format with the name `temp`.

After the two datasets are merged, identify which cases are unmatched and why (hint: tabulate the variables `rregion2` and `_merge`).

Write the commands and compare with the do file in the online appendix

5.4 Descriptive Analysis of Poverty

We are now ready to analyse how poor and non-poor persons compare in terms of the variables we discussed at the beginning of this chapter: `rhgsex numkids numNotEmp femaleHoH rhhsize` (sex, number of children in the household, number of non-employed persons in the household, whether the head of household is female and household size). There are many ways to do these comparisons. One of the methods that would suit this situation is to cross-tabulate the variable `poor` with each of these variables. It is good data management practice to use loops for any repetitive action (as we did in Chapter 4), to reduce coding error:

```
foreach var in rhgsex numkids numNotEmp ///

  femaleHoH rhhsize {

  tabulate `var' poor, row nofreq chi2

}
```

The command `tabulate `var' poor, row nofreq chi2` produces two-way tables of each of these variables with the poverty status indicator, but outputs the row percentages without cell frequencies by specifying `row nofreq` as options. This informs us of the proportion of men and women who are poor and not poor. If these proportions are different, can we say that this is not merely due to chance? To test this we ask Stata to perform the Pearson chi-squared test of independence for the two variables by specifying the `chi2` option. For example, `tab rhgsex poor, row nofreq chi2` tests the null hypothesis that women and men are equally likely to be poor.

```
                 |          poor
  sex - hh grid  |        0          1 |      Total
-----------------+--------------------------+----------
          male   |     79.00      21.00 |     100.00
        female   |     75.92      24.08 |     100.00
-----------------+--------------------------+----------
         Total   |     77.41      22.59 |     100.00

        Pearson chi2(1) =   25.4561    Pr = 0.000
```

Figure 5.8   Stata output for cross-tabulation of sex and poverty status indicator

Figure 5.8 shows that a larger proportion of women are poor than men (24% versus 21%). The Pearson chi-squared test results show that poverty status and gender are not independent at the 1% level of significance (Pr < 0.01). In other words, it is highly unlikely that the observed distribution is due to chance.

We can now report the poverty rates across different regions of England and Wales:

```
tabstat poor, by(rregion2) format(%9.2f)
```

We can also examine whether regional deprivation rates are correlated with poverty status using the ratio of households living in social housing to all households in each region as a measure of deprivation: `pr_social_rented`.

While a chi-squared test is appropriate to test the independence of two categorical variables (see Chapter 3), and a Pearson correlation coefficient is appropriate to measure the degree of association between two continuous variables (see Chapter 6), neither of these are appropriate for a continuous and a categorical variable as is the case here. An appropriate method would be to estimate a logit or probit model with poverty status as the dependent variable and regional deprivation as the explanatory variable. We will discuss logit and probit estimations in Chapters 8 and 10. Note that since we may be more interested in understanding how all the different factors affect the risk of poverty, in addition to regional deprivation we would also include these variables as explanatory variables. In this chapter we will restrict the analysis to simply comparing the average regional deprivation scores for poor and non-poor. We find that there is no difference in the average deprivation scores across the two groups.

5.5 Combining Household- and Individual-Level Data in the PSID, SOEP and UKHLS

In Section 5.3.2 we learnt how to merge individual- and household-level BHPS data files. The key was identifying the unique household-level identifier and making sure this variable was present in both individual- and household-level files. This is the case for the UKHLS and SOEP data files. The unique person-level identifier in the SOEP is called `persnr` and the wave-specific household identifier is called `$hhnr` (see the SOEP documentation and the online Appendix A). Note that $ is the placeholder for the wave prefix just as `w` is in the BHPS. Similarly, in the UKHLS the unique person-level identifier is called `pidp` and the wave-specific household-level identifier is called `w_hidp`. As `$hhnr` and `w_hidp` are present in both the individual- and household-level files, we can use the same commands shown in Section 5.3.2 for the BHPS.

Matching files at other levels of analysis will require identification of the correct merging or linking variables. For a list of such variables for the BHPS see Table 8 in Taylor et al. (2010); and for the SOEP see Table 4.1 in Haisken-DeNew and Frick (2005).

The data structure for the PSID is quite different from the other surveys. The rest of this subsection is devoted to a discussion of how to merge individual- and household-level datasets in the PSID. Although the individual-level data are supplied as one single wide-format file (see Section 4.1), the 'family' files are supplied separately by year. The best way of combining the individual- and family-level files is to generate a long-format file for the household data, which can then be merged with the long-format individual-level file (see Section 4.4 to see how to do this).

First, we have to convert the household files into Stata format, select and rename the variables of interest, and generate the wave or year identifier (remember to give it the same name as the wave/year variable in the long-format individual-level file).

Note that while in datasets such as the BHPS, SOEP and UKHLS, the variable for the household identifier has the same name in different files. In the PSID the name of the variable differs across files. Hence, the household identifier has to be renamed in a way that is consistent across waves and with the individual file. The documentation clarifies the correspondence between the variables for the household identifiers (see also Table 5.6). In other words, all the household identifier variables in the family files (V3, V442, ...) have to be renamed to the same name, such as hid, in each of the separate year/wave files before they are combined into a long-format file. Once the yearly household files have been prepared, they can be appended into a long format, as specified in Chapter 4.

When converting the wide-format individual-level file to a long-format individual-level file (as shown in Section 4.4), the household identifiers first need to be renamed appropriately as we did with the Age variables in Section 4.4: rename ER30001 hid1968; rename ER30020 hid1969; and so on for the rest of the years.

Table 5.6   Family interview numbers in single-year family files and in the cross-year individual file

Year file	Family file	Individual
1968	V3	ER30001
1969	V442	ER30020
1970	V1102	ER30043
...	...	...
1993	V21602	ER30806
1994	ER2002	ER33101
1995	ER5002	ER33201
...	...	...

As in the BHPS, UKHLS and SOEP, the household identifier in the PSID changes from year to year. Thus, the long-format household-level file can be merged with the long-format individual-level file by using both the household and wave or year identifiers (see Figure 5.2).

The results of the merge command show that not all observations have been matched (check the variable _merge). You may recall that all people in the survey are assigned a 1968 family number (the variable ER3001), to be able to construct the personal identifier. However, those who were not part of the survey in 1968 have a 1968 family number, but no corresponding record in the family files. Furthermore, individuals who were once part of a responding family may move away and may no longer be associated with that family. In these cases the individual's interview number and all other variables in the cross-year individual file are coded as 0, since no data have been collected in that year about that individual.

Since the individual respondent file includes observations also for those waves when the individual was not interviewed, and since the same household identification number is often assigned to different households across waves, to identify people living in the same family we need to drop from the individual file those cases/rows containing missing observations. We can do this, for example, by dropping all observations where age is missing (note that this would not work if we used the variable sex, since, as we have seen in Chapter 4, this is included as one single variable). The merged data are now ready for analysis.

5.6 Converting Individual-Level Files into Household-Level files

In this section we will show how to convert individual-level files into household-level files. Suppose we were interested in carrying out the poverty analysis at the household level. For example, we might want to compute the proportion of female-headed households that are poor. Let us start with the BHPS dataset we have created and keep just two variables: femaleHoH and poor. We know that both these variables are invariant within a household, so we can keep one observation per household:

```
bysort rhid: keep if _n == 1
```

where _n is a Stata-generated observation counter variable. The above command asks Stata first to count the observations within each group identified by rhid and then keep the first observation of each group or household. Using the duplicates command we can check that the resulting dataset is indeed a household-level file.

In this example we do not care about which observation within a household is kept, so this will work fine. If we wanted to keep the observation of the oldest member in the household and the data were already sorted in ascending order by age within the household, then we would do the following:

```
bysort rhid: keep if _n ==_N
```

Remember that _N measures the total number of observations in the group and _n the number of the observation within the group. Thus, _n and _N are equal for the last observation of the group (the oldest person). However, if the data were not sorted by age, then we would do the following:

```
bysort rhid (rage): keep if _n==_N
```

Here the data are first sorted both by the household identifier (rhid) and then, within it, by age (rage). But as rage is within parentheses, it is ignored in the by-group operation, which is carried out only for groups specified by rhid.

5.7 Setting Up the Data in Wide Format

5.7.1 Merging Files into Wide Format

Up to now we have focused only on the data for 2008 (wave r). One of the advantages of using a longitudinal dataset is the ability to identify transitions into and out of different states, such as poverty. With cross-section data we can estimate the poverty rate for each year but not whether some people are persistently poor or if different people move in and out of poverty in each year. As always, to use longitudinal data we need to combine data from different waves. In Chapter 4, you saw how to combine separate wave-specific data files into a single long-format file and here you will see how to combine those files into a single wide-format file.

Let us concentrate on just two waves – wave q and wave r. Figure 5.9 is an illustration of matching data files of two waves into one wide-format file containing poverty statuses in waves q and r. By repeating some of the Stata commands used in the earlier sections we can create two datasets, PoorWave_q and PoorWave_r, containing the poverty status variables qpoor and rpoor. You can do these separately or by using a foreach loop as shown in Chapter 4.

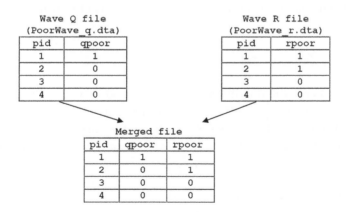

Figure 5.9   An illustration of matching files into a wide format

Write the commands and compare with the do file in the online appendix

Using the same principles of merging that we saw earlier, we can sort these datasets on the personal identifier, `pid`, and then merge them using it.

A glance at the values of the `_merge` variable created during this merging operation will show that there are quite a few individuals who are present in only one wave (see Figure 5.10).

```
. merge 1:1 pid using PoorWave_q

    Result                                # of obs.

    not matched                               2,416
        from master                             939    (_merge==1)
        from using                            1,477    (_merge==2)

    matched                                  19,238    (_merge==3)
```

Figure 5.10   Stata output of merging `PoorWave_r` and `PoorWave_q` files

Specifically, this table tells us that of the 20,715 adults and children who were enumerated (counted as being in the sample households) in 2007 (or wave q), 1,477 were not enumerated in 2008. This implies that 7% of the individuals in the 2007 sample households did not participate in the survey in 2008, either because they moved out of the household and are TSMs who are no longer living with an OSM or PSMs (see online appendix), or because they have moved and could not be located – or refused to participate, or died, and so on. The table also tells us that 939 additional individuals were enumerated in 2008; these are people such as new partners who moved into the 2007 households, adult children who moved back in with their parents, or children who were born or adopted. As any discussion of poverty transition requires that the same people appear in both datasets (but may be in different households), we drop cases that appear in only one dataset. The dataset is now ready for the analysis of transitions.

5.7.2 Poverty Transitions

If we want to know the distribution of different poverty transitions we need to create a variable that captures these transitions. One method is the one we used in Chapter 4 to create the change in marital status variable (mach). An alternative method is to concatenate the two poverty status variables using the command egen ... concat():

```
egen poorch = concat(qpoor rpoor) if ///
    qpoor<. & rpoor<.
```

This command concatenates or joins the variables specified within the parentheses to produce a new string variable. For example, if for a particular observation qpoor and rpoor have values of 0 and 1 respectively, then poorch will be equal to '01'. Note that '01' is a string value. Looking at the frequency distribution of poorch (Figure 5.11), we can see that 14% of the sample who were interviewed in both 2007 and 2008 (waves q and r) and provided household income information were in persistent poverty (the 11 combination), while an additional 8.5% (the 01 combination) moved into poverty in 2008 and 6% managed to get out of poverty in 2008.

```
. ta poorch

   poorch |      Freq.     Percent        Cum.
----------+-----------------------------------
       00 |     12,828       71.52       71.52
       01 |      1,521        8.48       80.00
       10 |      1,119        6.24       86.24
       11 |      2,468       13.76      100.00
----------+-----------------------------------
    Total |     17,936      100.00
```

Figure 5.11   Stata output for tabulation of poverty transitions

As mentioned in Section 3.6, it is a good housekeeping rule to delete unwanted temporary files and close the log file at the end of the program.

Write the commands and compare with the do file in the online appendix

5.8 Summary and Suggestions for Further Reading

In this chapter we have discussed how to link household- and individual-level data and how to compute household-level variables from individual-level data, including how to combine survey data with external data at the regional level, such as descriptive statistics from censuses.

Key points

- To link two datasets that contain information at the same or different levels of hierarchy use the command merge.
- Most of the household-level variables can be computed from the individual-level data in one single step using the command egen, combined with bysort.

- Use the Stata saved results to reduce the possibility of error in your computations.
- If you want to link survey data with data from external sources, such as the census aggregate statistics, make sure that the coding of the matching variable is exactly the same, and check the geographical coverage of the two datasets.

Suggestions for further reading

In this chapter we have used poverty analysis to illustrate Stata commands and techniques. The following suggestions are for those interested in poverty analysis:

- To learn more about poverty in the UK, including poverty measures commonly used, see www.poverty.org.uk/index.htm.
- A useful website to learn more about poverty and its measurement in the EU is www. eapn.eu/en.
- The World Bank with its emphasis on poverty reduction maintains a poverty analysis resource at http://go.worldbank.org/8GKDUJWK20. Specifically take a look at:

  o Coudouel, A., Hentschel, J.S. and Wodon, Q.T. (2002) Poverty Measurement and Analysis. In the *PRSP Sourcebook*. Washington, DC, The World Bank. Chapter 1. Available at: http://go.worldbank.org/0C60K5UK40.
  o Haughton, J. and Khandker, S.R. (2009) *The Handbook on Poverty and Inequality*. Washington, DC, The World Bank. Available at: http://go.worldbank. org/7JGPK76TM0.

- A key component of poverty measurement is the equivalence scale. There are a number of equivalence scales available, each making different assumptions. You can find discussions on the sensitivity of poverty measures to the choice of equivalence scales in:

  o Citro, C.F. and Michael, R.T. (1995) *Measuring Poverty: A New Approach*. Washington, DC, National Academy Press.
  o Creedy, J. and Sleeman, C. (2005) Adult Equivalence Scale, Inequality and Poverty. *New Zealand Economic Papers* 39(1): 51–81.
  o Lewbel, A. and Pendakur, K. (2006) Equivalence Scale. In *The New Palgrave Dictionary of Economics*, 2nd Edition. Basingstoke, Palgrave Macmillan. And in a useful note produced by the OECD available at www.oecd.org/eco/ growth/OECD-Note-EquivalenceScales.pdf.

IDENTIFYING HOUSEHOLD MEMBERS AND MATCHING INFORMATION OF SPOUSES AND PARTNERS

Aim

This chapter discusses how to identify spouses, partners, children, siblings and other household members. It also discusses how to combine information of the individual with that of other household members in order to analyse assortative matching, intergenerational mobility and similar types of research questions.

6.1 Introduction

An interesting research question is whether people choose to partner with individuals who are like them (positive assortative matching) or very different from them (negative assortative matching) in terms of some observable characteristics such as age, education, race or ethnicity, income, occupation. Such type of empirical analysis requires that the data of the respondent and their partner appear in the same row of observation. In Section 6.3 we show how to set up the data in this form when partner identifier variables are included in the data. Household survey datasets generally include identifiers of spouse, partners and parents, but not those of other relationships. Quite often, even though some identifiers are not available, it is still possible to identify them using information on relationships. In Section 6.2 we show how to do this for the BHPS, UKHLS, SOEP and PSID.

6.2 Identifying Household Members

6.2.1 Identifying Household Members in the BHPS

In the BHPS, identifiers of spouses, partners and parents are readily available. Each person in the household is assigned a person number that is unique within the household and the wave, wpno (again, here we use the general prefix w to mean any wave prefix – from a to r – in the case of the BHPS). The person number of spouse or partner, father and mother are recorded in the variables whgspn, whgfno and whgmno. The unique cross-wave identifiers for spouse or partner, father and mother are recorded in the variables wspid, wfpid and wmpid. These identifiers are included in the windall and windresp files. If any of these family members are not in the household, these variables are assigned a value of 0. Identifiers for other family members, such as children, siblings, grandparents, grandchildren, are not provided. In this section we show how to create such identifiers using the data files called wegoalt. These files show the relationship of every person (referred to as the 'ego') with every other person in the household (referred to as the 'alter'). It follows that this file consists of $n - 1$ rows of observation for each person in an n-person household and does not include individuals living in single-person households. The variable wrel together with wsex and wosex provide complete relationship information of the 'alter' to the 'ego' and can be used to create the identifiers. Figure 6.1 shows the structure of these files, using wave b as an example. The files contain some additional information about the residential status of the 'alter' in the last (wave a) and the following wave (wave c). This can be useful in identifying changes in household composition. To keep things simple we use data from one wave. We choose begoalt.

The file illustrated in Figure 6.1 contains the records for one household identified by bhid 12345. This is a three-person household (there are three groups of observations) consisting of one man and two women (from the variable bsex). The man (bpid = 1111) is legally married to one of the women in the household (bpid = 2222) and the other woman (bpid = 3333) is the daughter of this couple

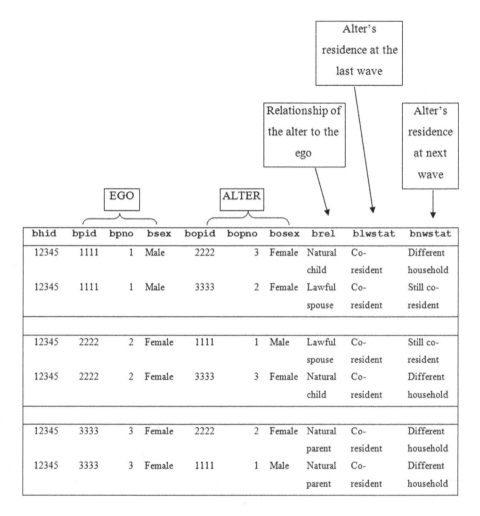

Figure 6.1 An illustration of a three-person household in the `begoalt` data file

(from the variable `brel`). They were all living in the same household at the last wave (from the variable `blwstat`) but by the next wave the daughter will move out (from the variable `bnwstat`).

To create any of the relationship identifiers we will have to use variables `brel`, `bsex` and `bosex`. The first step is to look at the coding frame of these variables (see Figure 6.2).

If we want to identify daughters, for example, we can use logical statements (as we did in Chapter 5) to create a variable that captures the unique cross-wave identifier of the individual's daughter in the household:

```
generate long daughter_pid = 0
replace daughter_pid = bopid if ///
   (brel == 4 & bosex == 2)
```

```
. label list bsex bosex brel
bsex:
                -9 missing or wild
                -8 inapplicable
                 1 male
                 2 female
bosex:
                -9 missing or wild
                -8 inapplicable
                 1 male
                 2 female
brel:
                -9 missing hh information
                 0 undefined
                 2 lawful spouse
                 3 live-in partner
                 4 natural child
                 5 adopted child
                 6 foster child
                 7 step/partner's-child
                 9 daughter/son-in-law
                10 natural brother/sister
                11 other brother/sister
                12 brother/sister-in-law
                13 natural parent
                14 other parent
                15 mother/father-in-law
                16 any grand parent
                17 any grand child
                18 any cousin
                19 any aunt/uncle
                20 any nephew/niece
                21 any other relative
                22 employee
                23 lodger/border
                24 unrelated sharer
                25 step parent
                26 employer
                27 landlady/lord
                28 half-sibling
                29 other child
                30 other
```

Figure 6.2   Value labels for brel, bsex and bosex

Sons will have a value of 0. As discussed in Section 3.1.3, if the variable that is being generated has more than seven digits, Stata will round the number down to seven digits and store the variable by default as float. But as person identifiers generally have quite a large number of digits (as in the case for pid) then the data type should be specified as long or double depending on the number of digits (see Figure 3.2).

A similar code can be used to create identifiers of other relationships. Create cross-wave identifiers of spouse or partner, brother, grandfather and grandmother and compare the identifier of spouse or partner with the one provided with bindall.

Write the commands and compare with the do file in the online appendix

6.2.2 Identifying Household Members in the UKHLS

As the UKHLS data are structured in a very similar manner to those of the BHPS, the data files and variables available for identifying household members are also either the same or similar. As in the BHPS, a set of relationship identifiers is available in the `w_indall` and `w_indresp` files. Table 6.1 compares the identifiers available in the BHPS with those available in the UKHLS.

The `w_egoalt` files in the UKHLS data are the equivalent to the `wegoalt` files in the BHPS. These are very similar in structure and content. The main differences are: first, in the BHPS the variable `wrel` shows the relationship of the 'alter' (identified by `whid` and `wopno` or by `wopid`) to the 'ego' (identified by `whid` and `wpno` or by `pid`), while in the UKHLS `w_relationship` shows the relationship of the 'ego' (identified by `w_hidp` and `w_pno` or by `pidp`) to the 'alter' (identified by `w_hidp` and `w_apno` or by `apidp`). Second, the variables `wlwstat` and `wnwstat` in the BHPS indicating the location of the 'alter' in the last and the next waves are different in the UKHLS. Third, the variables identifying the sex of the 'ego' and the 'alter' are `w_esex` and `w_asex` in the UKHLS, and `wsex` and `wosex` in the BHPS.

Table 6.1 Comparison of variables identifying spouse, partners, parents and grandparents in the BHPS and the UKHLS

	BHPS		UKHLS	
	Person number	Cross-wave identifier	Person number	Cross-wave identifier
Spouse or partner	whgspn	wsppid	w_ppno	w_ppid
Spouse			w_sppno	w_sppid
Natural, adoptive or step mother	whgmno	wmpid	w_mnspno	mnspid
Natural mother			w_mnpno	mpid
Natural, adoptive or step father	whgfno	wfpid	w_fnspno	fnspid
Natural father			w_fnpno	fpid
Grandmother			w_grmpno	
Grandfather			w_grfpno	

6.2.3 Identifying Household Members in the SOEP

The SOEP provides indicator variables for spouse and partner, parents and twins. The cross-wave identifier for spouse or partner is recorded in the variable `partnryr` (where `yr` refers to the two-digit interview year) and is available in the `$pgen` files ($ refers to the wave prefix). A value of 0 signifies that there is no spouse or partner present in the household. Another variable, `partzyr`, records the nature of the partnership (married versus cohabiting).

The unique cross-wave person identifiers of a sample member's father and mother are available in the `bioparen` file and are called `vnr` and `mnr`. Information on the children of any woman interviewed at least once since 1984 and of any man interviewed at least once since 2001 is stored in the `biobirth` and `bio-brthm` files, respectively. If the children are part of the SOEP sample, their unique cross-wave identifiers are also included in these files. Cross-wave person identifiers of those identified as twins, triplets or quadruplets are in the file `biotwin`.

To identify other family members we need to use the variable `$stell`, available in the `$pbrutto` file, which records the relationship of each household member to the head of the household. Figure 6.3 lists the value labels for the variable `astell` in the file `apbrutto` and shows the relationships that can be identified in wave 1 (or wave a).

```
. label list astell
astell:
               -3 [-3] Answer improbable
               -2 [-2] Does not apply
               -1 [-1] No Answer
                0 [0] Head Of Household
                1 [1] Spouse Of HH Head
                2 [2] Life Partner
                3 [3] Son, Daughter
                4 [4] Foster Child
                5 [5] Son, Daughter-In-Law
                6 [6] Father, Mother
                7 [7] Parent-In-Law
                8 [8] Brother, Sister,-In Law
                9 [9] Grandchild
               10 [10] Other Relative
               11 [11] Non-Relative
```

Figure 6.3   Value label for `astell`

It is clear that only certain types of relationships can be identified. We next create cross-wave identifiers of siblings for children of the household head in the first wave. It is not possible to do the same for children of any of the other household members.

The steps to create these sibling identifiers are outlined and illustrated in Table 6.2. First, we keep observations for children of the household head in the file `apbrutto` (Step 1):

```
keep if inlist(astell,3,4)
```

The command `keep if inlist(var,n1,n2,...,nk)` is a very useful command when you want to specify a condition with non-consecutive values of a variable. If these were consecutive then specifying a range would do. The command above asks Stata to keep only those observations for which values of the variable `astell` are either 3 or 4.

Table 6.2 Illustration of the steps to create sibling identifiers in the SOEP

Initial dataset								
whhnr	**persnr**	**wstell**						
1	1001	0						
1	1002	1						
1	1111	3						
1	2222	4						
1	3333	3						
Dataset after Step 1								
whhnr	**persnr**	**wstell**						
1	1111	3						
1	2222	4						
1	3333	5						
Dataset after Step 2								
whhnr	**persnr**	**x1**	**x2**	**x3**				
1	1111	1111						
1	2222		2222					
1	3333			3333				
Dataset after Step 3								
whhnr	**persnr**	**x1**	**x2**	**x3**	**sibid 1**	**sibid 2**	**sibid 3**	
1	1111	1111			1111	2222	3333	
1	2222		2222		1111	2222	3333	
1	3333			3333	1111	2222	3333	

(Continued)

Table 6.2   (Continued)

Dataset after Step 4							
whhnr	persnr	x1	x2	x3	sibid 1	sibid 2	sibid 3
1	1111	1111	.	.	.	2222	3333
1	2222	.	2222	.	1111	.	3333
1	3333	.	.	3333	1111	2222	.

Dataset after Step 5			
whhnr	persnr	sibid	num
1	1111	.	1
1	1111	2222	2
1	1111	3333	3
1	2222	.	1
1	2222	1111	2
1	2222	3333	3
1	3333	.	1
1	3333	1111	2
1	3333	2222	3

Dataset after Step 6			
whhnr	persnr	sibid	num
1	1111	2222	1
1	1111	3333	2
1	2222	1111	1
1	2222	3333	2
1	3333	1111	1
1	3333	2222	2

Dataset after Step 7			
whhnr	persnr	sibid1	sibid2	sibid3
1	1111	2222	3333	.
1	2222	1111	3333	.
1	3333	1111	2222	.

Next we count the number of children of each household head since this will be useful in the following steps:

```
bysort ahhnr: generate nkids=_N
```

```
. fre nkids
```

nkids

		Freq.	Percent	Valid	Cum.
Valid	1	1278	22.11	22.11	22.11
	2	2410	41.70	41.70	63.81
	3	1230	21.28	21.28	85.09
	4	488	8.44	8.44	93.53
	5	230	3.98	3.98	97.51
	6	72	1.25	1.25	98.75
	7	56	0.97	0.97	99.72
	8	16	0.28	0.28	100.00
	Total	5780	100.00	100.00	

Figure 6.4   Number of children of household head in SOEP wave a

For each child (or observation) we record the cross-wave identifier in separate temporary variables, sibid1, sibid2, ... To do this we have to repeat some commands for each child in the household. So, for increased efficiency we make use of the forvalues command (see Section 4.5). This is where having information on the number of children in the household is handy: we would like the command to be repeated for each child in the family, but the number of children varies across families. To make sure this command works for all families we should specify that the commands be repeated eight times, because this is the maximum number of children in any household in wave a (see Figure 6.4):

```
forvalues i=1/8 {
   bysort ahhnr: generate x`i'=persnr if _n==`i'
}
```

A better alternative is to automate this process. First we create a variable that calculates the maximum value of nkids and then define a local macro which equals this maximum value:

```
egen tempvar=max(nkids)
local nkids=tempvar
forvalues i=1/`nkids' {
```

```
    bysort ahhnr: generate x`i'=persnr if _n==`i'
}
```

The data now look like Step 2 of Table 6.2:

```
forvalues i=1/`nkids' {
  bysort ahhnr: egen sibid`i'=mean(x`i')
}
```

The data now look like Step 3 of Table 6.2. We need to remove sibling id when it is the same as the person's own id:

```
forvalues i=1/`nkids' {
  replace sibid`i'=. if persnr==sibid`i' ///
  & sibid`i'<.
}
```

The data now look like Step 4 of Table 6.2. Next, we will only keep household, person and sibling identifiers and reshape the data into long format:

```
keep ahhnr persnr sibid*
reshape long sibid, i(persnr) j(num)
```

The data now look like Step 5 in Table 6.2. Next, we drop all cases with missing values for sibid, drop the variable num and create a new variable with the same name that counts the number of siblings. After this step the data look like Step 6 of Table 6.2:

```
keep if sibid<.
drop num
bysort persnr: generate num=_n
```

Next, if we reshape the data into wide format (reshape wide sibid, i(persnr) j(num)), the data will look like Step 7 of Table 6.2 and are now ready for analysis.

6.2.4 Identifying Household Members in the PSID

Most of the information in the PSID is contained in the family files, which include data not only on the family, but also on the different members of the family, such as their income. These data can be matched to data from the respondent via the household identifier (see Chapter 5).

Household members in the PSID can be identified by the variables in the individual respondent file that identify the relationship of the respondent with the head of the household. Also in this case there is one variable for each interview year. It is also worth noting that the coding of these variables changes in 1983.

Because of the length of the study, the PSID includes multiple generations. It follows people when families split, or when children leave the family, thus leading to additional individual and family interviews. It also provides an additional file – called PID (Parents Identification) – that allows the identification of the parents, if they have ever been part of the survey. This file has been constructed using information collected from various sources about parents and children since 1993. The variables in this file contain the personal identification number of the natural and adoptive parents together with basic information about the source of the parental information.

The identification number of the individual in the individual respondent file is computed by combining the variables ER3001 (1968 Interview Number) and ER3002 (Person Number), while in the parents identification file it is computed by combining the variables PID1 (1968 Interview Number of Individual) and PID2 (Person Number of Individual). The two files can then be combined using the personal identification number of the respondent. We can then use the personal identification number of the parents to retrieve their data from the individual and family files.

6.2.5 Other Family Members

It is important to note here that, as the SOEP, BHPS and UKHLS are household surveys, an attempt is made to interview all household members but not all family members. Households are generally defined as individuals sharing the same residence and at least one meal, or some variant of this. Most surveys do not include non-residential family members in the samples. One exception is the UKHLS, which includes in the sample household members who are currently away at institutions but would otherwise be present in the household and may be interviewed by proxy.

Generally these surveys start with a sample of households and follow the individuals of these households over time. So, for example, children who move out of the parental home are followed, as well as their parents. However, parents or other family members who were not co-resident at the time of the first interview are generally not considered part of the sample and therefore not interviewed (since they are effectively part of a non-sampled household), unless they move back in with the sample members. Sometimes, questions are asked about relationships with some non-resident family members but generally not about the characteristics of such family members. For example, in the BHPS in some years respondents are asked how often they meet their children who are not living with them. This data feature means that certain research questions that require information for family members (co-resident or not) cannot be analysed. Let us take an example. Say we want to measure the degree of correlation between the labour market earnings or wages of parents and their children measured when they are 40 years old. First, we will have to identify the parents and children when they were living in the same household, which in some cases will be when the children were young. As we have already mentioned, in many surveys parents identification numbers are provided in separate fixed files (see Sections 6.2.2 and 6.2.3). Then the parents' wage information will have to be picked up when they are 40, children's wage information is picked up when they turn 40 some years later, and both need to be matched. For those individuals interviewed for the first time after their children had moved out, we may never be able to pick up this information. So, this intergenerational mobility-type of analysis using household surveys can be conducted on the previous subsample, after a long period of time. In other words, for this type of analysis we need large samples with long panel lives.

6.3 Matching Data of Respondents with Those of Their Spouses and Partners

In this section we are interested in analysing assortative matching: that is, we want to find out how partners match on different characteristics. In keeping with the rest of the chapter we use the bindresp file for this exercise, which also includes spouse and partner identifiers.

What can we learn from this data file? Quite a lot. Look at Table 6.3, which is an illustration of the bindresp file. It tells us that in the household identified by bhid = 1002 a 34-year-old man identified by his person number bpno = 4 lives with his partner, who is a 28-year-old woman identified by her person number bpno = 5. We know this because the spouse or partner identifier, bhg-spn, for each of them is the person number of the other.

We can also see that the man living in the household identified by bhid = 1005 and identified by person number bpno = 1 lives by himself, since bhg-spn is zero, which implies that a spouse or partner is not in the household. This could be because he is single. Or it could be that he has a spouse or partner (ascertained by bmastat, which provides information on marital status, not shown in Table 6.3) but is not currently living together with his spouse or partner.

In the household identified by bhid = 1006, the person identified by bpno = 1 is living with a partner whose person number is 3, but there is no corresponding entry for the partner; that is, there is no row of observation for bpno = 3 for that household. This is because, although the partner or spouse was present in the household and hence enumerated by the interviewer as living in the household, the partner was not interviewed and so is not present in this respondent file, bindresp. To verify this, you can look for the partner in bindall, which has information on all individuals enumerated in responding households, including non-respondents.

To analyse assortative matching patterns we need information (such as age, education or any other variable on which we want to analyse matching) of both partners in the same data row. This data structure is illustrated in Table 6.4.

Table 6.3 An illustration of spouse or partner information in the bindresp file

bhid	bpno	bhgspn	bhgsex	bage
1001	1	2	Male	28
1001	2	1	Male	22
1002	4	5	Male	34
1002	5	4	Female	28
1003	1	5	Female	26
1003	5	1	Male	26
1004	1	2	Male	57
1004	2	1	Female	47
1004	3	4	Male	29
1004	4	3	Female	22
1005	1	0	Male	49
1006	1	3	Male	22

Note that individuals without partners or whose partners were not interviewed (for example, individuals in households bhid = 1005 and bhid = 1006) are excluded from this dataset since we do not have information for both partners.

What is clear from Table 6.3 is that a couple within a household are not necessarily assigned person numbers 1 and 2, or even consecutive person numbers. Also, there can be more than one couple in each household. These issues make this matching exercise relatively complicated. The steps for this matching exercise are

Table 6.4 An illustration of the target dataset where each row contains information about one couple

bhid	bpno	bhgspn	bhgsex	bage	bhgsex_spouse	bage_spouse
1001	1	2	Male	28	Male	22
1002	4	5	Male	34	Female	28
1003	1	5	Female	26	Male	26
1004	1	2	Male	57	Female	47
1004	3	4	Male	29	Female	22

as follows. First of all, we will create two copies of this dataset. We will leave the first copy as it is (as in Table 6.3); this will be the respondent file:

```
use "$mydir/bindresp", clear

keep bhid bpno bhgspn bage bsex bqfachi

drop if bhgspn==0

sort bhid bpno

save respondent, replace
```

We will then create a second copy, which we will modify as in Table 6.5. This will be the spouse and partner file. We will rename all variables (except spouse or partner identifier bhgspn) such that the names signify that these observations belong to the spouse or partner. The trick is to rename bhgspn to bpno, after dropping the existing bpno variable:

```
use "$mydir/bindresp", clear

keep bhid bpno bhgspn bage bsex bqfachi

drop if bhgspn==0

drop bpno

rename bhgspn bpno

foreach var in bsex bage bqfachi {

   rename `var' `var'_partner

}
```

Table 6.5 is the resulting file.

Table 6.5   Transformation of bindresp for creating couple dataset

hid	bpno	bhgsex_partner	bage_partner
1001	2	Male	28
1001	1	Male	22
1002	5	Male	34
1002	4	Female	28
1003	5	Female	26
1003	1	Male	26
1004	2	Male	57
1004	1	Female	47
1004	4	Male	29
1004	3	Female	22
1005	0	Male	49
1006	1	Male	22

Finally, we merge the two copies of the data using bhid and bpno. In the second file, bpno is zero for all respondents without a spouse or partner in the household. If we try to match the two datasets using bhid and bpno we will get an error message saying that there are non-unique values in the dataset. So, we must remember to drop these cases before matching:

```
sort bhid bpno

merge 1:1 bhid bpno using respondent
```

The result of this matching exercise is shown in Figure 6.5.

```
Result                                # of obs.
-------------------------------------------------
not matched                               434
        from master                       217    (_merge==1)
        from using                        217    (_merge==2)
matched                                 6,048    (_merge==3)
-------------------------------------------------
```

Figure 6.5   Stata output of the result of matching respondent and spouse datasets

The 434 unmatched cases represent the 217 respondents with a spouse or partner who was not interviewed. Using the example of bhid = 1006 and bpno = 3 in Table 6.3, Table 6.6 illustrates the explanation for the 434 unmatched cases.

Table 6.6   Unmatched cases when matching respondent and spouse or partner data files

Master data (spouse or partner data)		Using data (respondent data)		
bhid	bpno	bhid	bpno	_merge
1006	3			1
		1006	1	2

The unmatched cases in the master file are respondents whose spouse or partner were not interviewed (like bpno = 1 in bhid = 1006 in Table 6.5). We will drop these unmatched cases. The data now look like those in Table 6.7. However, for each couple there are two rows of identical information. So, we will need to drop one of those observations.

Table 6.7   An illustration of the dataset where a respondent's data have been matched to those of their spouse or partner

bhid	bpno	bhgsex_partner	bage_partner	bhgsex	bage
1001	1	Male	22	Male	28
1001	2	Male	28	Male	22
1002	4	Female	28	Male	34
1002	5	Male	34	Female	28
1003	1	Male	26	Female	26
1003	5	Female	26	Male	26
1004	1	Female	47	Male	57
1004	2	Male	57	Female	47
1004	3	Female	22	Male	29
1004	4	Male	29	Female	22

But how do we uniquely identify each couple in households with more than one couple? We can do this by creating a unique couple identifier for each couple (see bcoupleID in Table 6.8) and then dropping one of the two observations for each value of this identifier. As we have seen quite often, in Stata there may be more than one way to achieve the same objective. Both the following commands will create such an identifier:

```
egen bcoupleID = rowmin(bpno bhgspn)
generate bcoupleID_alt = ///
    cond(bpno < bhgspn, bpno, bhgspn)
```

The first method uses the command egen with rowmin, which is one of Stata's egen commands that assigns the minimum value among the variables specified (bpno and bhgspn) to the new variable being generated. The second method uses the command cond(var1 < var2, a, b), which creates a variable that takes on value a (in our case bpno) if the logical condition before the first comma is true and b (in our case bhgspns) otherwise. So, the above command creates a unique couple identifier, bcoupleID, which is the minimum value of the person number of the respondent and their spouse or partner and so the same for each couple.

Next, we keep one observation for each couple using the commands bysort and keep.

Table 6.8   Unique couple identifier `bcoupleID`

bhid	bpno	bhgspn	bhgsex	bage	bcoupleID
1001	1	2	Male	28	1
1001	2	1	Male	22	1
1002	4	5	Male	34	4
1002	5	4	Female	28	4
1003	1	5	Female	26	1
1003	5	1	Male	26	1
1004	1	2	Male	57	1
1004	2	1	Female	47	1
1004	3	4	Male	29	3
1004	4	3	Female	22	3
1005	1	0	Male	49	.
1006	1	3	Male	22	1

Write the commands and compare with the do file in the online appendix

We could have used this unique couple identifier to match couple information directly, that is, without having to create two copies of the data, renaming variables, and so on. To see that, let us open the file `bindresp` again and create the couple identifier as before, and, also as before, drop unpartnered individuals.

Now we can use the observation counter variables to create the age variable of the spouse or partner. Note that Stata recognises `var[1]` as the value of the variable `var` for the first observation within the dataset. But if we type `bysort var2: gen var3 = var[1]`, then Stata recognises `var[1]` as the value of the variable `var` for the first observation within each group defined by `var2`. So, if we type

```
bysort bhid bcoupleID: generate bage_partner = ///
    cond(_n==2, bage[1], bage[2], .)
```

`bage[1]` and `bage[2]` are the first and the second observations within each group identified by `bhid bcoupleID`. In other words, the above command asks Stata to look at the two rows of observations for each couple uniquely identified by `bhid bcoupleID` and then compute `bage_partner`, which is assigned the value of `bage` of the first observation if the current observation is the second one and vice versa.

We can check that those without a spouse or partner in this dataset (these are the 217 individuals whose spouse or partner were not interviewed) have a missing value for `bage_partner`.

Write the commands and compare with the do file in the online appendix

In a similar way, we can create variables to depict the gender and educational qualification of the spouse or partner. As before, there will be two sets of observations for each couple and so we should drop one of those.

Write the commands and compare with the do file in the online appendix

6.4 Analysis: Assortative Matching

We can use graphs and compute descriptive statistics to identify the degree of assortative matching on age and educational qualification. For example, we can create a scatterplot of an individual's age against that of their partner or spouse with the command

```
scatter bage bage_partner, scheme(s1manual) ///
    saving(age_matching, replace)
```

This graph looks like the one in Figure 6.6 and is saved in the working directory with the name age.

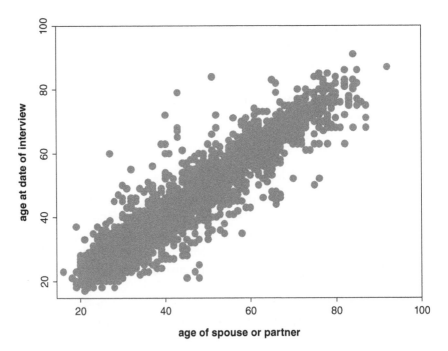

Figure 6.6   Scatterplot of respondent's age against that of their spouse or partner

Figure 6.6 shows that there is a positive association in the age of the two partners. We could add a regression line and check its slope (see Figure 6.7):

```
scatter bage bage_partner || lfit ///
   bage bage_partner, scheme(s1manual) ///
   saving("$dirresults\age_matching2", replace)
```

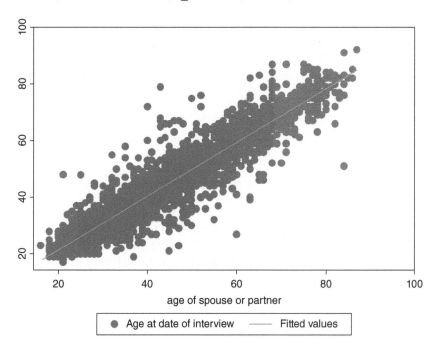

Figure 6.7   Scatterplot with fitted regression line of respondent's age against that of their spouse or partner

Alternatively, we can look at the degree of linear correlation between the ages of the two partners with the command

```
correlate bage bage_partner
```

Stata estimates the Pearson correlation coefficient between the age of the two partners as 0.937, which implies that people generally tend to partner with individuals who are near to their own age. Be careful about how you interpret this statistic. It will only measure the linear relationship between these two variables. In other words, if the estimated correlation coefficient is very low it does not rule out the possibility that the two variables are correlated, but this correlation may be non-linear. We can add a test of whether the correlation is statistically significant using the command pwcorr; see the Stata help for more details.

We could also look at the association between other characteristics of each couple, for example education, using the command tab.

Figure 6.8 shows that, while there is some degree of positive assortative matching on education, as evidenced by the proportion along the diagonal, it is not very high, except for those with no academic qualifications. However, it is worth noticing that the difference between some of these qualifications is very small. Hence, we could consider people matching with a partner one level up or down as an assortative match.

```
. tab bqfachi bqfachi_partner if bqfachi>0 & bqfachi_partner>0, cell nofreq
```

highest academic qualification	highest academic qualification of spouse or partner							Total
	higher de	1st degre	hnd,hnc,t	a level	o level	cse	none of t	
higher degree	0.36	0.47	0.25	0.21	0.36	0.04	0.07	1.76
1st degree	0.29	2.79	1.07	0.90	1.43	0.07	0.75	7.31
hnd,hnc,teaching	0.11	0.75	1.00	0.68	1.68	0.14	1.43	5.80
a level	0.14	1.15	0.97	3.33	4.37	0.75	3.40	14.12
o level	0.21	1.00	1.65	4.73	8.74	2.01	7.49	25.83
cse	0.04	0.04	0.14	0.90	1.90	0.68	1.07	4.77
none of these	0.14	0.32	1.15	3.26	7.95	1.15	26.44	40.42
Total	1.29	6.52	6.23	14.01	26.44	4.84	40.67	100.00

Figure 6.8   Frequency table showing the distribution of academic qualifications of couples

One of the reasons for positive assortative matching on education is that qualifications reflect social class or social standing (Maré 1991). So we could collapse these categories into those categories that reflect very different future lifetime earnings potential:

```
recode bqfachi (1/3=2 high) (4/6 = 1 low) ///

    (7=0 none) (-9/-1=.), gen(edu)
```

Similarly for the partner's education and repeating the analysis (see Figure 6.9). Now we find a much higher degree of positive assortative matching on education.

```
. tab edu edu_partner, cell nofreq
```

RECODE of bqfachi (highest academic qualificat ion)	RECODE of bqfachi_partner (highest academic qualification of spouse or partner)			Total
	none	low	high	
none	26.44	11.93	2.04	40.42
low	12.40	27.41	5.05	44.86
high	1.83	5.80	7.09	14.73
Total	40.67	45.15	14.19	100.00

Figure 6.9   Assortative matching on education among couples

Using similar techniques we can also identify same-sex couples. If the interest in assortative matching comes from an interest in understanding gender roles, gender attitudes in opposite-sex couples, then the analysis should be restricted to opposite-sex couples.

Write the commands and compare with the do file in the online appendix

6.5 Summary and Suggestions for Further Reading

In this chapter we have discussed how to identify different family members in each of the four household surveys, how to match information from particular pairs of household members (spouses and partners in the BHPS) and how to compute and interpret cross-tabulations, scatterplots and the Pearson correlation coefficient.

Key points

- Look in the data for identifiers of the household member you want to match. In some cases the identifiers are already included in the main data files.
- If identifiers are not provided, look for the data file specifying such relationships.
- To match information of two – or more – household members create two – or more – copies of the dataset, renaming the relevant variables to identify the different household members, and then use the command merge.

Suggestions for further reading

- For examples on the analysis of matching patterns between married and cohabiting couples see:
  - Jepsen, L.K. and Jepsen, C.A. (2002) An Empirical Analysis of the Matching Patterns of Same-Sex and Opposite-Sex Couples. *Demography* 39(3): 435–53.
  - Kan, M.Y. and Heath, A. (2006) The Political Values and Choices of Husbands and Wives. *Journal of Marriage and the Family* 68(1): 70–86.
  - Maré, D.C. (1991) Five Decades of Educational Assortative Mating. *American Sociological Review* 56(1): 15–32.

PART II

ANALYSIS OF CROSS-SECTION AND PANEL DATA

SAMPLE DESIGN, NON-RESPONSE AND WEIGHTS

The purpose of empirical analysis using data is to estimate different population parameters such as means, proportions, regression coefficients. This chapter discusses how to measure the quality of such estimators when the data are collected from a sample, and the standard techniques that are used to improve their quality.

7.1. Introduction

This chapter is divided into four main sections. First, the introductory section discusses the main concepts. Section 7.2 focuses on weights, Section 7.3 discusses standard errors and Section 7.4 focuses on model selection. Sections 7.2 to 7.4 have been structured such that each discuss, in order, the theory, survey-specific variables, relevant Stata commands and the application using BHPS data.

7.1.1 Key Concepts

In empirical research we often want to learn something about the population of interest based on information collected in surveys. The population characteristics that we want to know about, such as mean pay, the proportion of people who are employed, or the impact of an explanatory variable on a dependent variable (the regression coefficients), are referred to as population parameters. When such measures are based on a sample (such as the sample mean pay, the proportion of sample members who are employed and regression coefficients) and are used to estimate population parameters, they are referred to as estimators. The actual value of the estimator for any particular sample is known as the estimate. So, the sample mean pay is an estimator of the population mean pay and the actual value of the sample mean pay we observe is an estimate of the population mean pay. Since we do not know the true value of the population parameter, how do we judge the quality of this estimate? We do that by making use of what we know about the sampling distributions of the estimators.

We can draw a sample from the population using different sampling methods (see Section 7.1.3), which are referred to as a sampling plan or sample design. Given a specific sample design, different samples can be (hypothetically) drawn from the same population. Each of these samples will yield a different estimate of the population parameter. The distribution of all these values of the 'estimator' is known as the sampling distribution of that estimator under that particular sample design. Figure 7.1 shows the sampling distribution of an estimator of a population parameter under two different sampling designs, S_1 and S_2.

The difference between the mean, or expected value, of the sampling distribution of an estimator and the true value of the population parameter is referred to as bias. The bias shows on average how much we can expect the sample

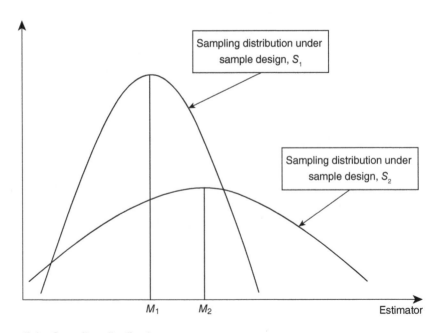

Figure 7.1   Sampling distributions

estimate to differ from the true population parameter. A zero-bias estimator, also known as an unbiased estimator, is often preferred. The problem is that we have only one sample and hence one value for the estimator. If the value of the estimator can vary over a wide range, then we may end up by chance with a value that is very different from the true value in the population. This variability is measured by the standard deviation of the sampling distribution, which is referred to as the standard error (SE) of the estimator. As you would expect, the smaller the standard error, the more precise the estimator.

Going back to Figure 7.1, let us assume that the true value of the population parameter is equal to M_2. It follows that the estimator under S_2 is an unbiased estimator of the population parameter but not the one under S_1. On the other hand, the standard error of the estimator under S_1 is smaller (and more precise) than that under S_2. So how do we decide which one is better? The mean square error (MSE) of an estimator of a population parameter under a particular sampling design is the sum of the bias squared and the standard error squared. The lower the mean square error, the better the estimator. Later we will discuss other sources of errors in estimating a population parameter. Each of these sources contributes to the bias and to the standard error. That part of the MSE that arises because of the sampling is often referred to as sampling error.

Computation of the sampling error requires knowledge of every sample that can be drawn using a specific sample design. But in reality we draw one sample only. How do we then calculate the MSE of an estimator? Most sample surveys are based on random samples, or probability samples, which have statistical properties that can be used to estimate the bias and standard error of the estimators, just based on the sample statistics. These will be discussed shortly in this chapter, but for further details on the estimations see Levy and Lemeshow (1999).

7.1.2 Sample Designs

When you read about different surveys, you will notice that almost all of them have a different sample design. Costs and benefits of different sample designs are taken into consideration when making this choice. In this section we discuss some of the most popular sample designs, specifically simple random sampling, cluster sampling and stratified sampling. Any basic book on sampling and statistics will start off with a discussion of simple random samples (SRSs) because this design serves as a benchmark for all sample designs.[1] As Levy and Lemeshow (1999: 47) explain, the SRS 'provides the foundation upon which statistical theory

---

[1]There are two types of SRSs, one where the population units are sampled without replacement (SRSWOR) and one where they are sampled with replacement (SRSWR). A population unit can appear only once in SRSWOR, as its name suggests, and it is the more popular.

of sampling is constructed'. In practice SRS design is not implemented very often because it has some problems.

SRS designs are very costly to implement, particularly in face-to-face surveys as the sample selected may consist of sample units scattered across the country, requiring interviewers to travel long distances. Instead, if some geographical regions were randomly selected and then some sample units within those regions were randomly selected, then interviewers would need to travel only to those specific regions. This is an example of a clustered sample. A second reason to use clustered sampling is related to access to a sampling frame. A sampling frame is the list of all population units from which a sample is to be drawn. Quite often, sampling frames are not available, but a list of groups of sampling units or clusters is available. For example, if we wanted to select a sample of school students in the UK but did not have a list of all school students, just a list of all schools in UK, we could randomly select a few schools and from their list of all students (in those selected schools) we could either select all students (one-stage cluster sampling) or randomly select some students from each selected school (multi-stage cluster sampling). The clusters selected at the first stage of sampling are referred to as primary sampling units (or PSUs).

When we estimate population parameters we generally want a good representation of key socio-demographic groups (by gender, age, ethnic group, region of residence) in the sample in order to study differences in outcomes such as education, earnings, life satisfaction. However, with an SRS design there is no way of ensuring that the sample contains reasonable proportions of people with relevant characteristics. In other words, every population unit, no matter what its characteristics, has the exact same chance of being selected into the sample. In an extreme case you may end up with a sample consisting only (or mostly) of one particular group, say, residents of Wales. This would be a rare event, but not impossible – like throwing a dice 100 times and getting a 6 each time.

Having a sample of people residing only in Wales is a problem if outcomes vary by region. To overcome this problem, we could divide the population into mutually exclusive and exhaustive units based on regions (referred to as strata) and draw separate samples from each stratum. For example, we could divide up the UK population into four strata – England, Scotland, Wales and Northern Ireland – and then draw a sample from each of the four strata. This would ensure we do not end up with a sample of people residing in Wales only. This sampling method is known as stratified sampling. Generally, censuses collect basic socio-demographic information across the entire population and are particularly useful when implementing stratified sampling designs.

Stratified sampling can be of two types: in the first type subsamples are selected from each stratum with the same selection probabilities; in the second type, subsamples are selected with different selection probabilities. Why does this matter? Suppose we want to estimate the mean pay in the UK based on a stratified sample. Also, suppose that the average pay varies across the different stratum (country). If the sample is a stratified sample with equal selection probability, then the sample mean is an unbiased estimator of the population mean. But if the sample is a stratified sample with unequal selection probability, the sample mean may be biased. Then why use such a sample design? A stratified sample with unequal selection probabilities may be preferred if we want to compare outcomes across groups of different population sizes. Take for example the case of the UK. According to the 2011 UK Census, 84% of the UK population resides in England while between 3% and 8% reside in the other three countries (see Table 7.1). If we were to select an equal probability stratified sample of size 10,000, then we would end up with relatively small sample sizes for Scotland, Wales and Northern Ireland (see Table 7.1). Under these circumstances it is advisable to have higher selection probabilities in the numerically smaller sized strata, so that we can conduct separate analyses by country. Sections 7.2 and 7.3 discuss how to deal with the generated bias.

Table 7.1   Distribution of 2011 UK population and a sample with equal selection probability across the four countries

	Population of usual residents in 2011	Percentage	Sample size
United Kingdom	63,182,000	100%	10,000
England	53,012,456	84%	8,390
Wales	3,063,456	5%	485
Scotland	5,295,000	8%	838
Northern Ireland	1,810,863	3%	287

7.1.3 Sampling Error

Sampling error refers to the errors in the estimation that arise from the fact that the estimates are based on a sample instead of the population. The sampling error has two components: sampling bias and sampling variance (see Section 7.1.1 and Figure 7.1). For the purposes of illustration, we will discuss sampling error in the context of the estimation of one specific population parameter, the population mean pay.

Under any sample design where the selection probability of every population unit is the same, the sample mean is an unbiased estimator of the population mean (Levy and Lemeshow 1999). As discussed in the last section, a sample design where all population units do not have the same selection probability, and those selected with different probabilities differ in terms of the population parameter of interest, may produce biased estimators.

Under the SRS design, the sample variance adjusted with a population correction factor is an unbiased estimator of the standard error. Suppose that N denotes population size, n is the sample size, X_i is the value of pay for the ith population unit, x_i the value of pay for the ith sample unit, s the sample standard deviation of pay and σ the population standard deviation of pay. The average computed from the sample

$$\left(\frac{\sum_{i=1}^{n} x_i}{n} \right)$$

is an unbiased estimator of the average in the whole population

$$\left(\frac{\sum_{i=1}^{N} X_i}{N} \right)$$

and

$$\sqrt{\frac{N-n}{N}} \left(\frac{s}{\sqrt{n}} \right)$$

is an unbiased estimator of σ under the SRS design. The population correction factor is $\sqrt{(N-n)/N}$ and as you can see it is almost one when the sample size is small compared with population size. Quite often this is the case and $s/\sqrt{n}$ is used as an estimator of the standard error. It follows that the standard error, or the precision of an estimator, increases with the sample size and with the degree of homogeneity of the population characteristic, in this example pay. The lower the sample size and the higher the variation of the variable of interest in the population, as measured by its standard deviation, the lower the precision of the estimator.

If you take an SRS and a clustered sample of the same size, in most cases the estimators based on the clustered sample will have higher standard errors than those based on the SRS. The standard errors will be higher the larger the cluster size and the more homogeneous the clusters in terms of the population characteristic. Quite often clusters are selected with a probability proportional to their size, generally measured by the number of population units within the cluster. This sample design is referred to as probability proportional to size (PPS) and increases the precision of the estimators. Estimators based on stratified samples generally have lower standard errors than an SRS of the same size. This difference increases with within-strata homogeneity of the population characteristic and decreases with across-strata homogeneity. Most statistical software assumes that the data come from an SRS and produces standard errors based on that assumption. So, if the sample we are using is clustered, or stratified, or both (as is often the case), then the estimated standard errors will be wrong (we will discuss how to correct for this in Sections 7.3.1 and 7.3.2).

7.1.4 Coverage and Non-Response Error

In addition to sampling errors, there are three other sources of errors while estimating a population parameter. According to Groves et al. (2004), there are four main sources of error: sampling, coverage, non-response and measurement. Each source contributes to the overall bias and standard error of estimators.

Coverage error arises when the sample is drawn from a sampling frame which does not cover the entire population of interest. For example, we may have coverage error if the population of interest is all adults living in the UK and the sampling frame used is a list of individuals with landline telephone numbers. Suppose we want to estimate the average pay in the UK using the sample mean of pay. If those without a landline are more likely to have lower pay and at the same time have no probability of being selected into the sample, then the estimate of mean pay based on the sample of people who have a landline is likely to be biased upwards.

After a sample is selected, information can be collected from sample members only if they participate in the survey. This can fail to happen if some sample members cannot be contacted, or if, when they are contacted, they refuse (or are unable) to participate. This generates non-response error. For a more detailed discussion of non-response and attrition see Section 2.6. If those not responding are more likely to have lower pay, our estimate of the average pay in the UK will be biased upward (Groves 2006). If respondents and non-respondents are not systematically different in terms of our variable of interest, then non-response only reduces the sample size, with consequences for the precision of our estimators but not for the bias. There is a large body of research, particularly in the field of survey methodology, which deals with non-response bias, reasons for non-response and methods to reduce this error (see Uhrig 2008; Lynn and Clarke 2006; Singer 2006; Groves and Couper 1998). See Uhrig (2008) and Lynn et al. (2012) for a discussion of non-response and attrition in the BHPS and UKHLS, respectively.

7.2 When and How to Use Weights

7.2.1 Weighted Estimators

If we can identify and measure, or observe (that is, if we have information on) factors that lead to biased estimates (as discussed in Section 7.1), we can produce weights based on these factors by giving smaller weights to the over-represented sample units and larger weights to the under-represented units. Sampling theories discuss how appropriately weighted estimators are unbiased estimators of population parameters (see Levy and Lemeshow 1999).

Let us use the example in the last section, where a sample was drawn from the population of the UK, but Scotland, Wales and Northern Ireland were over-sampled; that is, they had higher selection probabilities than the rest of the sample, which in this case is England. As we discussed, the unweighted sample mean pay may be a biased estimator of the average pay in the UK if the pay in Scotland, Wales and Northern Ireland is lower than that in England. The weighted sample mean pay, where the weights are the inverse of the regional selection probabilities (and so higher for residents of England but lower for all other regions), will be an unbiased estimator of the population mean pay. This weighed estimator belongs to a class of estimators called the Horvitz–Thompson estimators, which are unbiased estimators of the population parameters and 'can be computed for any sampling design so long as one can assess the probability, π_i, of any unit being included in the sample. This is often feasible even for very complex sampling schemes' (Levy and Lemeshow 1999: 339).

The two main sources of bias are unequal selection probability and non-response; most surveys provide sample design weights and non-response weights to correct for these biases. Sample design weights are the inverse of the selection probability. Non-response weights are generally computed as the inverse of the response probabilities estimated using a response model. There are various methods of computing non-response weights, see Elliot (1991) for a detailed discussion. To estimate response models, information on both respondents and non-respondents is required. Information collected by interviewers on the doorstep before the interview begins, as well as geographical information (including census aggregate statistics) that can be linked to the place of residence, are often used to estimate such models. In longitudinal datasets information about the person from the last wave is also used in models of wave-on-wave non-response. Before starting to use weights provided with the survey data, it is important to read the documentation to understand how these weights were constructed and what they reflect. For example, as we will explain below, the weights provided with BHPS data are composite weights correcting for both unequal selection probability and response propensity, while the UKHLS additionally includes design weights which only correct for unequal selection probability to allow advanced users to use these weights and adjust for non-response on their own.

Once we have identified the right set of weights to use, producing weighted estimates is quite simple in Stata – simply add the name of the weight variable along with the original Stata command as follows:

```
stata_command [pweight = weightvar]
```

Note that Stata allows four types of weights to be used in the analysis: probability or sampling weights (pweight), analytic weights (aweight), frequency weights (fweight) and importance weights (iweight). The types of weights we have discussed so far (design and non-response weights) are probability weights and as the observations in these datasets are individual observations and do not represent frequencies or means, we will need to specify the pweight option. To learn more about the other types of weights see the Stata help.

You will find that Stata does not allow the pweight option for some commands, such as summarize or tabulate. This is because these commands are intended to be used to describe the sample and not to estimate population parameters. As probability weights are used to compute unbiased population estimates, the `pweight` option is not allowed with these commands. See the Stata FAQs for further discussion of this issue. The alternative commands that can be used with the `pweight` option are `mean` and `proportion`.

7.2.2 Weights in the BHPS

As already mentioned in Chapter 2, the BHPS started in 1991 with an equal probability original 'Essex' sample of approximately 5,500 households which was representative of Great Britain south of the Caledonian Canal. In 1999 two additional regional boosts or oversamples of 1,500 households from Scotland and Wales were added and in 2001 an oversample of 2,000 households from Northern Ireland was added.[2] Like all surveys, the BHPS experienced non-response and attrition of its sample members. It provides cross-sectional and longitudinal weights for each wave and for different types of samples – adult respondents (16 years or older), youth respondents (11–15 years old), all household members enumerated in responding households, all responding households (for details on how these weights are computed see Chapter V in Taylor et al. 2010). The weights are provided within the main data files.

Cross-sectional weights correct for sample design as well as non-response in that wave, and when used they produce unbiased estimates of parameters of the GB and UK population of that year. These weights are truncated (to reduce the effect of weighting on variance), post-stratified and rescaled so that the weighted sum adds up to the sample size and not the population size. From wave 9 onwards, regional extension samples were added to the original BHPS sample. To allow analysis using these extension samples along with the original sample, additional weights are provided (see the online appendix for details on the appropriate cross-sectional weights to use).

At each wave, longitudinal weights are also provided, but these weights are only available for adult respondents who have responded at every wave including the current one, and for household members who were enumerated in responding households at every wave including the current wave. However, these weights are only available at the level of individuals and are not available at the level of households as there is no concept of a longitudinal household in the BHPS. These weights are the product of the wave 1 cross-sectional weights (in case of regional boosts this is the cross-sectional weight for the wave in which they were first sampled) and each subsequent wave-on-wave non-response weights. Longitudinal weights allow us to produce unbiased estimates of parameters of the 1991 population and their descendants surviving to the interview

---

[2]In 1997, it was decided that the UK component of the cross-national household panel survey ECHP will be included and surveyed along with the BHPS. This was continued until wave 11 (2001, see the online appendix for more details).

year. For example, if we produce the weighted mean pay reported by the sample of individuals who continuously responded from wave 1 until wave 12, by using the longitudinal respondent weight lwxrwght, we will get an unbiased estimate of the mean pay of the 1991 British population and their descendants who survived until 2002.

A list of the different weight variables along with a description of these weights are available in the online appendix (also see Chapter V in Taylor et al. 2010).

7.2.3 Weights in the SOEP

The SOEP started in 1984 with two samples of private households, one drawn from the native population and the other from households with a foreign-born household head (see also Chapter 2). In 1990 a sample of households with an East German citizen as household head was added. Further samples were added in 1994–95 (of immigrants), in 1998 (as a refresher sample), in 2001 (innovation sample) and in 2002 (an oversample of high-income population). Sampling probability differed across these samples and, like all surveys, SOEP experienced non-response and attrition of its sample members.

Cross-sectional and longitudinal weights for SOEP data are available in two separate wide-format files: individual weights are available in a file named phrf (which also includes the individual identifier persnr) and household weights are in a file named hhrf (which also includes the original household identifier, hhnr, and the current household identifier, hhnrakt). The cross-sectional individual-level weights are called $phrf and the cross-sectional household-level weights are called $hhrf, at wave $ (SOEP documentation uses $ instead of w in the BHPS as a placeholder for wave prefix). Those who did not participate in a particular wave will have a zero weight for that wave. In other words, there are no missing data in these files. If you want to use some of the subsamples A–F separately then you may need to multiply the standard cross-sectional weights with different factors (for details see Section 1.8 of Haisken-DeNew and Frick 2005). For example, if you want to use subsamples A to C for interview years 1995 to 1997 then the cross-sectional weights need to be multiplied by 1.053 (Haisken-DeNew and Frick 2005).

A larger set of longitudinal weights is available with SOEP data as compared with the BHPS. The variable $pbleib represents the inverse of the probability that a respondent at wave $ had also responded in the previous wave. Users can then compute the longitudinal weights between any two waves by multiplying the cross-sectional weight of the earlier wave by these wave-on-wave non-response weights for the intervening waves. For example, the longitudinal weight for a longitudinal sample of wave 4 (d) to wave 7 (f) respondents can be computed as the product of the cross-sectional weight of wave 4 and the wave-on-wave weights for waves 5, 6 and 7:

```
dphrf * epbleib * fpbleib * gpbleib
```

For further details on the computation and variety of weights available in the SOEP see Sections 5.3 and 5.4 in Haisken-DeNew and Frick (2005).

7.2.4 Weights in the PSID

As we mentioned in Chapter 2, the PSID started in 1968 with two independent samples: an equal probability sample of about 3,000 families, representative of the US resident population; and an oversample about 2,000 low-income families. In 1997 and 1999, two additional immigrant samples of 441 and 71 families were added; two-thirds of the core sample were also dropped in 1997; and the interview frequency changed from annual to every other year (see the online appendix for details on the PSID survey). Like all surveys, the PSID also experiences non-response and attrition of its sample members. Because of such characteristics, PSID data include weights which account for differential selection probability, non-response and attrition. The data provide longitudinal individual and family weights, and from 1997 onwards, cross-sectional individual weights. Heeringa et al. (2011) recommend using longitudinal family weights for cross-sectional family-level analysis.

All members of the 1968 sample of households and their descendants are defined as a PSID sample family member (or as having the 'PSID gene') and always have a non-zero cross-sectional and longitudinal weight when they respond to the survey. All others who join the households of these PSID sample family members are defined as PSID non-sample family members and receive zero longitudinal but positive cross-sectional weights. Cross-sectional weights are based on longitudinal weights, where both sample and non-sample members are assigned family-level weights using the 'fair shares' method (Heeringa et al. 2011). Cross-sectional weights are post-stratified on population characteristics using Current Population Survey (www.census.gov/cps/) data but not longitudinal weights. It should be noted that the longitudinal weights were adjusted for cumulative panel attrition in some years only: 1969, 1974, 1979, 1984, 1989, 1993, 1997, 2003, 2007. In the intervening years, the longitudinal weights are carried over. Longitudinal family weights are the average of the longitudinal weights of all family members. Split-off families receive the same longitudinal weight as the original family. For an overview of the cross-sectional weights see Heeringa et al. (2011); for longitudinal weights see Gouskova et al. (2008, 2009).

A quick method of identifying PSID weight variables is to search for 'weight' in the Web-based variable search facility at http://simba.isr.umich.edu/VS/s.aspx. Additional weights are available for specific questionnaires such as time diaries, child development supplement, and so on. All yearly user guides also provide a section on weights. These and additional technical papers on sample weights are available at http://psidonline.isr.umich.edu/Guide/documents.aspx.

7.2.5 Weights in the UKHLS

The UKHLS started in 2009 with a sample size of 30,000 households representative of the UK population. The sample also included an ethnic minority boost sample of 4,000 households drawn from areas of high ethnic minority concentration in Great Britain (see also Chapter 2). The sample of BHPS respondents surviving after the 18th wave was added to the UKHLS sample from the second wave onwards. There was no regional boost for Scotland or Wales, but the Northern Ireland sample was selected with twice the probability as the rest of the general sample.

Cross-sectional and longitudinal weights are provided with the UKHLS data for each wave (for details on the computation of these weights see Knies 2014). Both composite weights, which correct for sample design, non-response and attrition (as in the BHPS), as well as 'design' weights that only correct for the sample design (unequal selection probability), are provided. Weights are provided that allow analysis of the UKHLS and BHPS samples separately, as well as those that allow analysis combining both samples.

Different cross-sectional and longitudinal weights are available for use with different analysis samples – adult respondents, enumerated individuals, responding households, youth respondents, self-completion respondents, and so on. Note that longitudinal weights are not available for households as there is no concept of a longitudinal household in the UKHLS.

7.2.6 Producing Weighted Estimates Using the BHPS

As an example, we want to estimate the mean pay and the effect of education on pay in the UK in 2008. To do this we will use BHPS data collected in 2008 (that is, the 18th wave) and use cross-sectional respondent weights, xrwtuk1, to produce unbiased estimates. First, let us open the respondent data file of wave 18, rindresp, and keep the variables we will need for this exercise. To produce a weighted estimate of mean pay and its standard error we will use the command

```
mean paygu [pweight = xrwtuk1]
```

To see to what extent weighting affects the estimates, we compute the unweighted estimate and compare weighted and unweighted estimates. Remember to recode the data first so that all missing values are coded as system missings and, for convenience, drop the wave prefix.

Write the commands and compare with the do and log files in the online appendix

7.2.7 Why Don't We Always Use Weights?

If computing weighted statistics is so easy in Stata, why do we not always use weights? Using weights or not depends on the aim of the analysis. If we are using a non-random sample to compute descriptive statistics for the whole population, such as the proportion of single parents in the UK or gender pay gap in the UK, we should always use sample weights. However, in some cases we may want to provide descriptive statistics for the sample we are using in our analysis, for example to show that we do have a reasonable number of single parents in our sample. In this case we are interested in descriptive statistics for the sample – not for the population – and for this reason we should show non-weighted figures.

Using sample weights in regression models is common in some disciplines but not in others. This is a hotly debated topic among academics (DuMouchel and Duncan 1983; Pfeffermann 1993; Magee et al. 1998; Gelman 2007; Faiella 2010). One of the arguments in favour of using sample weights in regression analyses is that weighted regression coefficients correct for oversampling of certain subpopulations (for example, oversampling of ethnic minority groups in the UKHLS, oversampling of regions in the BHPS). If the aim of the regression analysis is to obtain population descriptive statistics and not causal effects then weighted estimation (where, as before, weights are the inverse of selection probabilities) is the best method. However, as Solon et al. (2013) point out, if the aim of the multivariate analysis is to estimate causal effects then the answer is less clear cut.

It has been shown that weighting in regression analyses is not necessary if the sampling probability is exogenous to the model and the model is correctly specified. For example, if there is oversampling of some ethnic minority groups and if the correctly specified model includes dummies for these ethnic groups, then unweighted estimates are consistent. Weighting will also produce consistent estimates but may produce less precise estimates (particularly if the error term was homoscedastic without weighting). But as models are rarely (if ever) correctly specified, Solon et al. (2013) suggest estimating the model using weights as well as without and reporting both sets of estimates. If weighted and unweighted estimates are very different then it is an indication that the model may not be correctly specified.

On the other hand, if the sampling is endogenous to the model, that is, if sampling is based on the dependent variable, then only weighted estimation produces consistent estimates of the causal effects. An example of endogenous sampling is if we want to estimate the causal effect of education on wages and high-wage persons are more likely to respond to the survey.

Finally, heteroscedasticity-robust standard errors should be estimated for weighted estimates of regression coefficients.

For a more complete discussion of when to use and not to use weights see Solon et al. (2013) and Cameron and Trivedi (2005: Chapter 24).

7.3 Estimating Standard Errors

7.3.1 Estimating Standard Errors in Stata

Statistical software like Stata produces standard errors of the estimators under the assumption that the data provided are from an SRS sample. As we are now aware, in practice, complex survey designs are used, which are either clustered or stratified, or both. So how do we produce unbiased estimates of standard errors of the estimates we are interested in? In Stata this can be implemented by using the svy set of commands. The first step is to tell Stata which variables reflect the cluster, strata and weight associated with each sample unit or observation. If the names of the cluster, strata and weight variables are psu, strata and weight, then the command is

```
svyset psu [pweight = weight], strata(strata)
```

Now all you need to do is type svy: followed by the Stata command and Stata will produce estimates and standard errors that take into account the weight and sample design. Note that once you specify the weight in the svyset command, there is no need to write [pweight = weight] in the command line.

7.3.2 Estimating Standard Errors Using the BHPS

Now we will use Stata svy set of commands and BHPS data from its 18th wave to estimate standard errors of mean pay and the effect of education on pay in the UK in 2008. Starting from the dataset we produced in Section 7.2.6, we will merge in information on the primary sampling unit and strata from the rhhsamp file. Table 7.2 lists the sampling design variables available with the different datasets, and the files in which these are stored. The names of these variables for the BHPS are wpsu and wstrata.

Table 7.2   Description of sampling information available in the PSID, BHPS, SOEP and UKHLS

	Strata	Primary sampling unit (PSU)	Available in
PSID	ER31996	ER31997	All files
BHPS	wstrata	wpsu	whhsamp
SOEP	strat1, strat2	sampoint	varianz
UKHLS	w_strata	w_psu	w_hhsamp, w_hhresp, w_indall, w_indresp, w_youth
	strata	psu	xwavedat

We start with the command `svyset`, followed by the commands to estimate the mean pay:

```
svyset psu [pweight = xrwtuk1], strata(strata)

svy: mean paygu
```

However, Stata does not output any standard errors. Recall that the Northern Ireland extension sample (identified in individual data files by `memorig = 7` and in household data files by `hhorig = 7`) has an SRS design and in the dataset all observations from this sample have a value of –8 (that is, BHPS missing value code) for `psu` and `strata`. The problem is not that the values are –8 for all these cases, but that there is one stratum with a single PSU (as mentioned in the note below the Stata output: 'Note: missing standard errors because of stratum with single sampling unit'). If there is just one PSU within a stratum, it is not possible to estimate the within-stratum variance.

A quick fix is to use the household identifier for the Northern Ireland sample as values of the `psu`, because an SRS design could also be viewed as a design in which each sample unit is sampled from its own separate cluster. The UKHLS also includes a Northern Ireland subsample with an SRS design. But in this survey this issue was recognised before the data were released and every household in the Northern Ireland subsample was assigned a unique value for `psu`. In the case of the BHPS, before using the `svyset` commands we need to assign values to the `psu` in Northern Ireland:

```
replace psu = hid if memorig == 7
```

If we compare the mean pay computed in Section 7.2.6 with those obtained using the `svy` command, we find that the estimates of mean pay remain the same, because both are weighted estimates using the same weights, but the estimates of standard errors change. The whole set of results is in the `log` file in the online appendix. The estimated standard error for mean pay rises from 23.04 to 24.75. In other words, by assuming the sample design to be an SRS we had underestimated the standard error of the mean pay. As discussed earlier, a clustered sample is most likely to produce estimates with larger standard errors than an SRS of the same size. The opposite is the case for stratified design. As the BHPS sample is both clustered and stratified, these results imply that the imprecision of the estimates introduced by using a clustered design was far greater than the increase in precision introduced by using a stratified design.

Note that the case for a single PSU stratum may also arise because of the type of analysis you are interested in. For example, if we are interested in the mean pay for men living in the East Midlands in 2008 we will end up with a subsample where there is a stratum with a single PSU. In such cases the above solution will not work. One alternative method to solve this problem is to reassign the single PSU in a stratum to an adjacent stratum and continue to do this until all strata have more than one PSU. Alternatively you can delete the single-unit stratum, but remember that this may bias your estimates. Stata allows a few other options: we can specify three types of singleunit options when we svyset the data. These options for singleunit (certainty, scaled, centered) specify different methods of computing the within-stratum variance for these single PSU strata. See the Stata manual for more details.

The svy option also allows analysis of subpopulations and testing the difference in estimates. For example, we could estimate the mean pay separately for the men and women:

```
svy: mean paygu, over(sex)
```

or use the subpop option:

```
svy, subpop(if sex == 1): mean paygu
svy, subpop(if sex == 2): mean paygu
```

Both methods yield the exact same estimates. We find that the estimate mean pay for women is much lower, £1,379.60 per month, than that of men, £2,260.50

```
. svy: mean paygu, over(Female)
(running mean on estimation sample)

Survey: Mean estimation

Number of strata =      121          Number of obs      =      7351
Number of PSUs   =     1069          Population size = 7826.64
                                     Design df          =       948

        male: Female = male
      female: Female = female
```

	Over	Mean	Linearized Std. Err.	[95% Conf. Interval]	
paygu					
	male	2260.484	39.13203	2183.689	2337.28
	female	1379.633	25.00279	1330.566	1428.7

```
. test [paygu]female = [paygu]male

Adjusted Wald test

 ( 1)   - [paygu]male + [paygu]female = 0

       F(  1,    948) =    405.97
              Prob > F =    0.0000
```

Figure 7.2 Testing gender differences in mean pay using the svy command

per month. We can also test whether this difference is statistically significant. To do this, we will have to use the value labels of the variable sex. The svy commands and their results are shown in Figure 7.2.

The test of the null hypothesis that there is no gender difference in pay shows that the probability of observing the estimated means is almost zero (Prob > F = 0.0000). In other words, the gender difference in pay is statistically significant.

7.4 Summary and Suggestions for Further Reading

In this chapter we have discussed some of the most commonly used sample designs, how they lead to estimators of different quality, and what techniques can be used to improve the quality of these estimators. We have discussed different sources of errors that may appear when using survey sample statistics to estimate population parameters, and methods to minimize the impact of these errors.

Key points

- The simple random sample (SRS) is the easiest to deal with and is often used as the benchmark to evaluate other sample designs.
- Clustered and stratified samples are generally cheaper than SRSs and do not require knowledge of the full list of all population units.
- Stratified samples ensure diversity in the sample, often reduce sampling error and are the best type of sampling design to allow analysis of small populations (by allowing oversampling from populations).
- Consider using sample weights to produce unbiased estimates when population units have unequal selection probabilities and when there is survey non-response, using the svy set of commands.

Suggestions for further reading

- For more details on sample design, weighting and non-response see:
  - Elliot, D. (1991) *Weighting for Non-Response: A Survey Researcher's Guide.* London, Office of Population Censuses and Surveys, Social Survey Decision.
  - Levy, P.S. and Lemeshow, S. (1999) *Sampling of Populations: Methods and Application.* New York, Wiley.

- o Solon, G., Haider, S.J. and Wooldridge, J. (2013) What Are We Weighting For? NBER Working Paper 18859. This gives useful examples that demonstrate the impact of using or not using weights.

- For more details on weights in the four surveys discussed in this book see:

PSID

- o Gouskova, E., Heeringa, S.G., McGonagle, K. and Schoeni, R.F. (2008) Panel Study of Income Dynamics Revised Longitudinal Weights 1993–2005. Survey Research Center, Institute for Social Research, University of Michigan.
- o Gouskova, E., Heeringa, S.G., McGonagle, K., Schoeni, R.F. and Stafford, F. (2009) Panel Study of Income Dynamics Construction and Evaluation of the Longitudinal Sample Weight 2007. Survey Research Center, Institute for Social Research, University of Michigan.
- o McGonagle, K., Schoeni, R.F., Sastry, N. and Freedman, V.A. (2012) The Panel Study of Income Dynamics: Overview, Recent Innovations, and Potential for Life Course Research. *Longitudinal and Life Course Studies* 3(2): 268–84.
- o Heeringa, S.G., Berglund, P.A., Khan, A., Lee, S. and Gouskova, E. (2011) PSID Cross-Sectional Individual Weights, 1997–2009. Survey Research Center, Institute for Social Research, University of Michigan.

SOEP

- o Haisken-DeNew, J.P. and Frick, J.R. (2005) Desktop Companion to the German Socio-Economic Panel (SOEP). Berlin. Available at: www.diw.de/documents/dokumentenarchiv/17/diw_01.c.38951.de/dtc.409713.pdf.

BHPS

- o Lynn, P. (2006) Quality Profile: British Household Panel Survey Waves 1 to 13: 1991–2003, Version 2.0.
- o Taylor, M.F., Brice, J., Buck, N. and Prentice-Lane, E. (2010) *British Household Panel Survey User Manual Volume A: Introduction, Technical Report and Appendices*. Colchester, University of Essex.

UKHLS

- o Knies, G. (2014) *Understanding Society: The UK Household Longitudinal Study: Wave 1-3, 2009–2013 User Manual*. Colchester, University of Essex.

$$\bigcirc\!\!\!\!8$$

ANALYSIS OF CROSS-SECTION DATA

Aim

This chapter discusses how to estimate models for continuous and for discrete dependent variables, how to compute different types of standard errors, linear and non-linear tests on the coefficients, how to obtain predictions, residuals, and their meaning. The techniques are illustrated using, as examples, models for wages, employment and life satisfaction, estimated using BHPS data for 2008.

8.1 Introduction

One of the main reasons we analyse data is to uncover correlations between two or more variables, for example wages and age if we want to analyse the impact of age/experience on wages; wages and sex if we want to compare wages of women with wages of men; life satisfaction and marriage if we want to analyse whether married people are happier than non-married ones. In general, we will use more than just one explanatory variable to explain variation in a dependent variable (wages or life satisfaction in the example above) across the sample.

An important distinction among estimation methods is related to the type of dependent variable used, which can be continuous or discrete. Continuous variables, such as weight, height or wages, have an infinite 'non-countable' set of outcomes; discrete variables, such as gender, employment status, qualification levels or occupation, have a finite – countable – set of outcomes (see Greene 2003).

Among discrete variables, we often distinguish between binary variables, which have only two values 0 or 1 (for example, employed or not; these are also called dummy variables), and multinomial variables, which have more than two values. A multinomial variable can be ordinal, such as the level of education (primary school, high school, college), where the different values have an intrinsic order; or categorical, such as marital status or employment status, for which the different outcomes cannot be ordered. We will deal with the estimation methods related to these four types of dependent variables separately.

There are more types of variables, which we do not deal with here, for example interval variables, or variables with a mass point at zero. In some cases we may want to rescale the original outcome in a different form, for example we may want to convert a continuous variable into categories or we may want to combine an ordered variable into a dummy one. For more details on other types of variables and associated estimation techniques see Long (1997) and Winkelmann and Boes (2006).

Since this chapter is about cross-section analysis, we focus on the last wave of the BHPS and use data only in the `rindresp.dta` file, which contains information about adult respondents interviewed in wave 18. As explained in the previous chapters, before doing any type of analysis, we need to open the dataset, drop the wave prefix r from the names of all the variables, and appropriately recode missing values.

Write the commands and compare with the do file in the online appendix

8.2 Continuous Dependent Variables

8.2.1 Correlation Coefficients Versus Regression Coefficients

Our first variable of interest – our dependent variable – is 'wage', which is a continuous variable. If we want to analyse how wages vary with age we can use the command `correlate`. For example, the command `correlate paygu age` shows a positive correlation of 0.1492, thus suggesting that on average older workers earn higher wages (the full set of results is in the `log` file in the online appendix). If we plot wages against age (`scatter paygu age`), however, the scatterplot shows a large variability. We can also use the `twoway` command to plot the fitted value against the scatterplot:

```
twoway (scatter paygu age) (lfit paygu age), ///
    scheme(s1manual)
```

The resulting graph looks like the one in Figure 8.1.

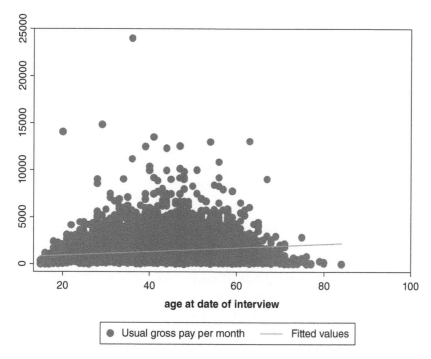

Figure 8.1   Scatterplot of wages against age

The correlation coefficient and the two-way scatterplot give us a first hint that there may be a link between wages and age. Figure 8.1 may also suggest that the relationship between wages and age is not linear. Indeed, the literature has suggested that wages do increase with age, but faster at the beginning of the working career and more slowly later on, and that the relationship between wages and age has a quadratic form (for a review see for example Grossbard 2006).

Other individual characteristics may play a role and may therefore have an indirect impact on this correlation coefficient. For example, one of the results in the literature is that people with higher education earn higher wages (Harmon et al. 2003). For example, if most workers with high levels of education are also older, while most of those with low levels of education are young, part of the correlation between wages and age may be due to the different levels of education of young and old workers. Hence, if we want to analyse the impact of age on wages, we should take into account other variables, such as education.

The easiest way to account for other variables (also called covariates) is to estimate multivariate regression models, in which we can include all explanatory variables that may be relevant to explain differences in wages. For example, among the explanatory variables it is common to include age and its square, a dummy for women, a dummy for married, and dummies for qualification levels or education (for a discussion of the main determinants of wages see Polachek 2006). Because in wave 18 of the BHPS we have an oversample of people living in Wales, Scotland and Northern Ireland (compared with England), and since wages are on average higher in England than in the rest of the UK, we should also include regional dummies among the explanatory variables. Although we could address the problem of unequal selection probability using weights (as explained in Chapter 7), the regional dummies pick up the impact on wages of region-specific characteristics that would otherwise not be included in the model. In summary, we want to estimate the following wage regression:

$$\text{Log wage}_i = \alpha_0 + \alpha_1 \text{Age}_i + \alpha_2 \text{Age}_i \text{ square} + \alpha_3 \text{Female dummy}_i + \\ \alpha_4 \text{Married dummy}_i + \alpha_5 \text{Qualification dummies}_i + \\ \alpha_6 \text{Region dummies}_i + \text{error term}_i \qquad (8.1)$$

The subscript i identifies individuals and the Greek letters (α_0, α_1, and so on) are the coefficients to be estimated. Since wage is a continuous variable (it does not matter that it can only have positive values), we can estimate Equation (8.1) by means of ordinary least squares (OLS). However, since the distribution of wages is generally skewed to the left, it is common practice to use the log of wages as the dependent variable. The distribution of log wages is generally closer to a normal distribution than that of wages. Furthermore, when using the log of wages, interpretations of the regression coefficients refer to the relative rather than the absolute change in wages. We can use the kdensity and twoway graphs to look at the distribution of wages and log wages.

Write the commands and compare with the do and log files in the online appendix

It is also clear from the graphs that a quadratic in age is likely to fit the log wage model better than a linear term only. Now we generate the variables needed for the regression model: age square, female, married, qualification and region dummies.

Write the commands and compare with the do file in the online appendix

We can estimate the wage regression using the command regress followed by the name of the dependent variable and the list of explanatory variables. The command regress estimates the model using OLS; that is, by minimising the sum of the square residuals (see Greene 2003). As an exercise, we can compare the results of a model estimating a wage equation when only age is included among the explanatory variables, with the results of a model including all explanatory variables given in Equation (8.1). The results of this exercise are shown in Figure 8.2. Remember that for each set of dummies we need to set one aside as reference group to avoid problems of perfect collinearity. For gender we only include a dummy for women (no dummy for men); for qualifications we omit Q6 (no or other qualifications); for regions we omit R7 (London); and so on. The choice of which dummy to omit does not change the overall model or results, just the interpretation (see below). Generally we omit the most populous category since interpretation of the coefficient in this case is in relation to the 'norm'. However, the specific research question may also dictate which categories should be excluded. For example, we may want to estimate whether acquiring certain types of qualifications (university degree, A levels, GCSEs or O levels) has an impact on wages. In this case the best reference category would be 'no qualifications' since we can estimate the impact of having a university degree (and so on) compared with having no qualifications.

```
. regress LnW age

      Source |       SS       df       MS              Number of obs =    7067
-------------+------------------------------           F(  1,  7065) =  233.95
       Model | 151.535381      1  151.535381           Prob > F      =  0.0000
    Residual | 4576.13267   7065  .647718708           R-squared     =  0.0321
-------------+------------------------------           Adj R-squared =  0.0319
       Total | 4727.66805   7066   .66907275           Root MSE      =  .80481


         LnW |     Coef.   Std. Err.      t    P>|t|     [95% Conf. Interval]
-------------+----------------------------------------------------------------
         age |  .0111543   .0007293    15.30   0.000     .0097247    .0125838
       _cons |  6.748847   .0302577   223.05   0.000     6.689533    6.808161


* Compare with:

. regress LnW age age2 Female Married Q1-Q5 R1-R6 R8-R12

      Source |       SS       df       MS              Number of obs =    6933
-------------+------------------------------           F( 20,  6912) =  217.90
       Model | 1763.50556     20  88.1752779           Prob > F      =  0.0000
    Residual | 2797.04324   6912   .40466482           R-squared     =  0.3867
-------------+------------------------------           Adj R-squared =  0.3849
       Total | 4560.54879   6932  .657897979           Root MSE      =  .63613


         LnW |     Coef.   Std. Err.      t    P>|t|     [95% Conf. Interval]
-------------+----------------------------------------------------------------
         age |  .1277878   .0036589    34.93   0.000     .1206152    .1349604
        age2 | -.0014583   .0000442   -33.01   0.000    -.0015449   -.0013717
      Female | -.5173127   .0153669   -33.66   0.000    -.5474366   -.4871888
     Married |  .0835274   .0188041     4.44   0.000     .0466656    .1203891
          Q1 |  .7055081   .0287987    24.50   0.000     .6490539    .7619623
          Q2 |  .5010076   .0358421    13.98   0.000     .4307461    .5712691
          Q3 |  .2901391   .0280411    10.35   0.000     .2351699    .3451084
          Q4 |  .1872705   .0272528     6.87   0.000     .1338467    .2406943
          Q5 |  .1165528   .0396332     2.94   0.003     .0388596     .194246
          R1 | -.2786627   .0589121    -4.73   0.000    -.3941486   -.1631768
          R2 | -.3066754   .0458084    -6.69   0.000    -.3964739   -.2168769
          R3 | -.2909338   .0483127    -6.02   0.000    -.3856416    -.196226
          R4 | -.3418577   .0491452    -6.96   0.000    -.4381973    -.245518
          R5 | -.3572488   .0496795    -7.19   0.000    -.4546359   -.2598618
          R6 |  -.258527   .0486662    -5.31   0.000    -.3539278   -.1631262
          R8 | -.2885082   .0444103    -6.50   0.000    -.3755661   -.2014503
          R9 | -.3170754   .0480772    -6.60   0.000    -.4113216   -.2228293
         R10 | -.3830289   .0413105    -9.27   0.000    -.4640102   -.3020475
         R11 | -.3182777   .0408353    -7.79   0.000    -.3983274    -.238228
         R12 | -.3309315   .0419792    -7.88   0.000    -.4132236   -.2486394
       _cons |  4.878964   .0780401    62.52   0.000     4.725981    5.031946
```

Figure 8.2   Results of the command regress

Note that the number of observations differs across the two models. This is because people with missing values in one or more of the explanatory variables are omitted from the estimation. Stata automatically excludes from the estimation sample all rows (observations) with at least one missing value. The estimation sample, which consists of all observations used for the estimation of the model, is stored in the variable e(sample); see Section 8.2.3 for further details on the post-estimation commands.

The two rows below the number of observations show the critical value and the probability of the F-test, a test that all coefficients, excluding the constant, are zero. If all coefficients were zero, then none of them would be helpful in explaining variation in the dependent variable. If this was the case, we could say that the model itself is not statistically significant. R^2 and the adjusted R^2 are reported as measures of the goodness of fit (see the Stata manual for more details).

The regression coefficients are an estimate of how much a unit increase in one of the explanatory variables increases (or decreases, if the coefficient is negative) the dependent variable. We often call these effects 'marginal effects'. For example, the first model in Figure 8.2 suggests that one extra year of age, on average, increases log wages by 0.0111543. Because the dependent variable is in logs, the interpretation can be in terms of percentages: one extra year of age increases wages by about 1.1%. The second model shows a much larger coefficient of 0.1277878. This second model includes a much larger number of explanatory variables, and the coefficient of each variable can then be interpreted as the change in wages due to a unit increase in the explanatory variable, holding constant the values of all other explanatory variables. The impact of age appears to be much larger when we take into account all other characteristics such as qualification, marital status, and so on. In the second model therefore the impact of age is net of the impact of the other covariates, including age square. The interpretation of the impact of age in the second model is non-linear and varies with age (0.128 times years of age minus 0.001 times years of age square).

The interpretation of marginal effects for explanatory variables that are dummies is essentially the same, but refers to moving from zero (the individual does not have that characteristic) to one (the individual has that characteristic), so that married people earn on average 8.7% higher wages than those who are not married, and women earn 40.4% less than men, keeping everything else constant. The coefficient of the Female dummy is rather large. One of the reasons why we find this large coefficient is that the dependent variable here is the log of monthly wages while our sample includes both full- and part-time workers. Since the proportion of part-timers is much larger among women than men, women's average monthly earnings would by default be lower even if their hourly wages were the same as men's. Most of the literature analysing the determinants of wages uses hourly wages and, often, excludes women. We can re-estimate the model after including a dummy for part-time workers.

Write the commands and compare with the do and log files in the online appendix

Going back to Figure 8.2, having the highest level of qualification (Q1, university degree or higher, as opposed to Q6, no or other qualifications, which is the reference group) increases monthly wages by 102.5%, while having qualification Q2 (teaching qualifications) increases wages by 65.0%, compared with having no qualifications (Q6).

Besides the regression coefficients, the results table also shows the standard errors, t-values, significance levels (p-values) and the 95% confidence intervals. The p-value (P>|t|) represents the probability of obtaining a t-statistic at least as high (or low if negative) as the observed t-statistic if the null hypothesis that the coefficient is zero is true. The coefficients are statistically significant when the probability P>|t| is smaller than a certain threshold (normally, when using large samples, we use 0.05 or 0.01 as threshold). If P>|t| is smaller than the threshold, we are confident that the coefficient is not zero and therefore the explanatory variable has an impact on the dependent variable. If the coefficient is not statistically significant (when P>|t| is larger than 0.05), then we would conclude that there is no evidence that the explanatory variable has an impact on the dependent variable. All the coefficients in Figure 8.2 are statistically significant.

Since the regression coefficients are meant to be an estimate of a parameter in the population (see Chapter 7), the confidence interval gives us the interval in which the value of the parameter in the population lies, with a 95% confidence. The confidence interval around the coefficient of the female dummy is [−0.547; −0.487], suggesting that on average monthly wages of women are between 48.7% and 54.7% lower than those of men. When the confidence interval includes both positive and negative values, the regression coefficient is not statistically different from zero at the 5% level because zero is included in the interval as a possible value of the coefficient.

Care should be taken when interpreting the coefficients since both the statistical significance and the magnitude should be considered. For example, if the dummy for those who are married is statistically significant but suggests that the difference between married and non-married people is 0.005%, we can consider its impact as minimal and not 'economically' significant. In other words, although statistically there is a difference, this is practically irrelevant.

8.2.2 Different Types of Standard Errors

The standard errors that Stata estimates by default are based on the assumption that the error terms ('error term$_i$' in Equation (8.1)) are independent and identically distributed (see Greene 2003). We can estimate standard errors that take into account error structures that may violate these assumptions by using the vce() option. The default option in Stata is vce(ols), which uses the standard variance estimator for OLS regression (see Greene 2003). To compute for example the Huber–White standard errors which account for heteroscedasticity (different variance across observations, see Section 8.2.4; and also Greene 2003; White 1980; Huber 1967), we can add the option vce(robust) at the end of the command. The command and its results are shown in Figure 8.3.

```
. regress LnW age age2 Female Married Q1-Q5 R1-R6 R8-R12, vce(robust)

Linear regression                                    Number of obs  =     6933
                                                     F( 20,  6912)  =   199.52
                                                     Prob > F       =   0.0000
                                                     R-squared      =   0.3867
                                                     Root MSE       =   .63613

-----------------------------------------------------------------------------
             |               Robust
        LnW  |    Coef.    Std. Err.      t    P>|t|    [95% Conf. Interval]
-------------+---------------------------------------------------------------
        age  |  .1277878   .0042482    30.08   0.000    .1194601    .1361156
       age2  | -.0014583   .0000519   -28.11   0.000    -.00156    -.0013566
     Female  | -.5173127   .0151984   -34.04   0.000   -.5471062   -.4875193
    Married  |  .0835274   .0177792     4.70   0.000    .0486747    .1183801
         Q1  |  .7055081   .0295252    23.90   0.000    .6476296    .7633866
         Q2  |  .5010076   .0362811    13.81   0.000    .4298855    .5721297
         Q3  |  .2901391   .0289532    10.02   0.000    .2333821    .3468962
         Q4  |  .1872705   .0287069     6.52   0.000    .1309963    .2435448
         Q5  |  .1165528   .0373302     3.12   0.002    .0433741    .1897315
         R1  | -.2786627   .0536325    -5.20   0.000   -.3837988   -.1735266
         R2  | -.3066754   .0464689    -6.60   0.000   -.3977687   -.2155822
         R3  | -.2909338   .0466247    -6.24   0.000   -.3823325   -.1995351
         R4  | -.3418577   .0483738    -7.07   0.000   -.4366852   -.2470301
         R5  | -.3572488   .0509676    -7.01   0.000    -.457161   -.2573366
         R6  |  -.258527   .0514016    -5.03   0.000    -.35929    -.157764
         R8  | -.2885082   .0464486    -6.21   0.000   -.3795616   -.1974547
         R9  | -.3170754   .0474077    -6.69   0.000   -.4100092   -.2241417
        R10  | -.3830289   .0417081    -9.18   0.000   -.4647895   -.3012682
        R11  | -.3182777    .040951    -7.77   0.000   -.3985543   -.2380012
        R12  | -.3309315    .041912    -7.90   0.000   -.4130919   -.2487711
       _cons |  4.878964    .089349    54.61   0.000    4.703812    5.054115
-----------------------------------------------------------------------------
```

Figure 8.3   Robust standard errors

How do the results change if we use robust standard errors? In this case, not much: all the explanatory variables remain statistically significant. Using the option robust does not change the regression coefficients; it only changes the standard errors and may therefore have an impact on the level of statistical significance, but not on the sign and magnitude of the coefficients. Robust standard errors are often slightly larger than non-robust ones and may reduce the level of statistical significance of the regression coefficients.

Additionally, the errors may be correlated and violate the assumption of independence. This may happen for example if one of our explanatory variables is aggregated, like the unemployment rate at the regional level. All people living in the same region will be affected by the same regional unemployment rate, thus generating correlation among the outcomes of all those who live in the same region. In this case we would prefer to estimate cluster-robust standard errors by using the option vce(cluster region), which accounts for the correlation of observations within the same region (see Froot 1989; Williams 2000), as well as correcting for heteroscedasticity. Note that here cluster is part of the command, while region is the name of the variable we want to cluster by. Other possible options for the estimation of the standard errors are bootstrap and jackknife methods (look at the Stata help for the commands vce(bootstrap) and vce(jackknife)).

8.2.3 Post-Estimation Commands

Stata has a number of commands that can be used after the estimation of a model. One of these is the command predict, followed by the name of a new variable. This command computes predictions, residuals and other statistics, after the estimation. The specific options available depend on the model estimated; common options are xb to compute linear predictions, stdp to compute the standard error of the prediction, residuals to obtain the residuals of the model. The command computes the requested statistic for all possible observations, even if they have not been used to compute the coefficients of the model, and can be used for in-sample and out-of-sample predictions (even using other datasets). The restriction if e(sample), for example predict newvar if e(sample), restricts the prediction to the sample that has been used for the estimation.

We can compute linear tests on the coefficients using the command test, which performs Wald tests (see also the command testparm, which is often used to perform tests on many coefficients). We use the command followed by the list of regression coefficients to test that the coefficients are (not statistically different from) zero. For example, test Female tests whether the coefficient of the female dummy is statistically different from zero, while test Q1 Q2 Q3 Q4 Q5 tests whether the education dummies are jointly statistically significant (that is, jointly different from zero). We can also test whether linear expressions are equal (test exp=exp[=...]). When estimating systems of equations using commands such as sureg or reg3 (not covered in this book, but see the Stata help for details) we can test that the coefficients of the variables (varlist) in a certain equation (eqno) are zero using the command test [eqno] [: varlist], or that the coefficients between equations are equal using the command test [eqno=eqno[=...]] [: varlist] (for more details see the Stata manual and Greene 2003).

When the test is rejected, the probability is lower than the specified threshold and the coefficient(s) is (are jointly) statistically significant. Figure 8.4 shows two examples.

```
. test Female

( 1)   Female = 0

       F(  1,   6912) = 1158.55
              Prob > F =    0.0000

. test Q1 Q2 Q3 Q4 Q5

( 1)   Q1 = 0
( 2)   Q2 = 0
( 3)   Q3 = 0
( 4)   Q4 = 0
( 5)   Q5 = 0

       F(  5,   6912) =   190.02
              Prob > F =    0.0000
```

Figure 8.4   Linear tests on the coefficients

The result of the first test in Figure 8.4 has a very large value of 1158.55 and a very low probability, which almost equals zero. This suggests that the female dummy is statistically different from zero and that, after controlling for the other characteristics we have included in the model, on average women are paid less than men. The result of the second test is also highly statistically significant and suggests that the education dummies are jointly statistically significant.

Besides Wald tests, we can perform likelihood ratio tests with the command lrtest, or Wald-type tests of non-linear hypotheses with the command testnl; see the Stata manual for more details.

Although, as we will see below, the estimation methods differ when we use discrete variables, the post-estimation commands are essentially the same, few command options may not be supported and few extra ones may become available. If in doubt, check the manual for details.

8.2.4 Diagnostics

One of the assumptions of OLS is the homogeneity of the variance of the residuals (homoscedasticity, see Verbeek 2008). This means that the variance of the residuals should be the same across observations. We can test for homoscedasticity by using the command rvfplot, yline(0) right after the estimation. The command plots the residuals against a straight line on zero, which should help to identify if there is any pattern in the residuals. We can also compute the Breusch–Pagan/Cook–Weisberg test for heteroscedasticity using the command estat hettest (see Breusch and Pagan 1979; Cook and Weisberg 1983). As we can see from the log files in the online appendix, in our case the null hypothesis of constant variance is rejected, thus suggesting heteroscedasticity of the residuals. Hence, in our estimations we should use robust standard errors (see Section 8.2.2).

Write the commands and compare with the do and log files in the online appendix

Multicollinearity is a problem that arises when the correlation among the explanatory variables is very high. When some of the explanatory variables are strongly correlated, there is a risk that the parameter estimate may be statistically identified on the basis of a very small pattern of difference between the measures. The estimates of the regression coefficient may become unstable (for example, the regression coefficients may change a lot when we include or exclude explanatory variables from the model) and the standard errors may become inflated. We can check for multicollinearity by computing the variance inflation factor (VIF) using the commands estat vif and collin (if the command collin is not already installed we will have to find it, see Section 3.1.1, and install it, Section 3.3). Both commands show the VIF together with levels of tolerance for each explanatory variable. Clear rules do not exist; however, some analysts exclude those explanatory variables for which the reciprocal of the VIF is smaller than the tolerance. As an alternative rule of thumb, we may consider removing the explanatory variables whose VIF is higher than 10 (or 30). As we can see from the log files in the online appendix, in our specific regression model it is only age and its square that present a VIF higher than 10. However, considerations related to economic theory (see Polachek 2006; Wooldridge 2009: Chapter 3) would prevent us from dropping these relevant explanatory variables from the model. In such cases we should think about the research problem, and if we find that many of the explanatory variables are highly correlated but should be included in the model, then we may consider aggregating these variables and creating an index. We can then include the index in the model rather than all the explanatory variables. In this way we are able to measure the effect of the combined variable but not the effect of the individual ones (Wooldridge 2009: 97). Also, if the explanatory variables that are highly correlated with each other are not correlated strongly with the variables of interest, then multicollinearity is not a serious problem for that specific analysis.

Another assumption of OLS is the normality of the residuals. Although this assumption is not necessary to obtain unbiased estimates of the regression coefficients, it is necessary for hypothesis testing and for the correct identification of whether the regression coefficients are statistically significant. In finite samples, under the assumption that the error term is normally distributed, the test statistics for the coefficients follow a t-distribution where the variance of the error distribution is not known. In large samples, and under certain conditions, the normality of the error term is not necessary for hypothesis testing (Greene 2003).

However, as Cameron and Trivedi (2010) point out, it is still common to use the *t*-distribution since it may provide a better approximation than the standard normal distribution. To check normality we first compute the residuals using the command `predict`. We can then plot the residuals against a normal distribution.

Write the commands and compare with the `do` and `log` files in the online appendix

The command `mvtest norm`, followed by a list of variables, computes a series of normality tests for univariate, bivariate and multivariate normality. If we use the option `stats(all)`, the command shows the Doornik and Hansen (2008) omnibus test; the Henze and Zirkler (1990) consistent test for normality; and the Mardia (1970) measures of multivariate kurtosis and skewness. The command shows the value of the test, the critical value of χ^2 and the associated probability. As we can see from the `log` files in the online appendix, in our case all probabilities are lower than 0.01: all tests reject the null hypothesis of normality. When the residuals are not normally distributed, we should not rely on the *t*-test to analyse whether a coefficient is statistically significant or not. There is no general rule, but one possible option to overcome this problem is to use the bootstrap option to improve estimation of the standard errors.

Write the commands and compare with the `do` and `log` files in the online appendix

8.2.5 Interaction Terms

Figure 8.3 suggests that monthly wages of married people are on average 8.7% higher than those of non-married people. This result is consistent with the literature (see for example Bardasi and Taylor 2008) and is often referred to as the 'marriage premium'. The literature has found that the marriage premium differs between men and women. If we want to analyse if in our dataset the marriage premium differs between men and women, we have two options. We can either run the model separately for men and women and compare the coefficients of the variable `Married` in the two models, or add an interaction term. The interaction is essentially the product of the two dummies `Married` and `Female`; this new term is then added as a further explanatory variable in the model. Figure 8.5 shows the command and its results.

The coefficient of the interaction term (`MarriedWoman`) is negative and statistically significant. Hence, while married men on average earn 30.0% more than non-married men, married women earn less than non-married ones. Remember, however, that the coefficient of the interaction term should be interpreted on top of the coefficient of the variable itself: married women do not earn 27.4% less than non-married women, they earn roughly ([exp(.262–.322)–1] × 100) 6%

```
. regress LnW age age2 Female Married MarriedWoman Q1-Q5 R1-R6 R8-R12, vce(robust)

Linear regression                                    Number of obs =      6933
                                                     F( 21,   6911) =    197.69
                                                     Prob > F       =    0.0000
                                                     R-squared      =    0.3950
                                                     Root MSE       =    .63186
```

LnW	Coef.	Robust Std. Err.	t	P>|t|	[95% Conf. Interval]	
age	.1276517	.0042391	30.11	0.000	.1193417	.1359617
age2	-.0014612	.0000517	-28.24	0.000	-.0015626	-.0013598
Female	-.2948867	.029477	-10.00	0.000	-.3526708	-.2371026
Married	.2621487	.0248542	10.55	0.000	.2134269	.3108706
MarriedWoman	-.3218283	.0342282	-9.40	0.000	-.388926	-.2547305
Q1	.7027223	.0292402	24.03	0.000	.6454025	.7600421
Q2	.4988589	.0360588	13.83	0.000	.4281726	.5695453
Q3	.2826265	.0285748	9.89	0.000	.226611	.3386419
Q4	.1857889	.0283883	6.54	0.000	.1301392	.2414387
Q5	.1159745	.0370145	3.13	0.002	.0434146	.1885344
R1	-.2761127	.0537536	-5.14	0.000	-.3814864	-.1707391
R2	-.2988173	.0464111	-6.44	0.000	-.3897972	-.2078373
R3	-.2868429	.0464893	-6.17	0.000	-.3779762	-.1957096
R4	-.3388793	.048426	-7.00	0.000	-.4338092	-.2439494
R5	-.3559591	.0508977	-6.99	0.000	-.4557343	-.2561839
R6	-.2522411	.0510619	-4.94	0.000	-.3523382	-.1521441
R8	-.2839727	.0463723	-6.12	0.000	-.3748766	-.1930688
R9	-.3158565	.0473003	-6.68	0.000	-.4085796	-.2231334
R10	-.38301	.0416297	-9.20	0.000	-.464617	-.301403
R11	-.3159382	.0409452	-7.72	0.000	-.3962034	-.235673
R12	-.3337361	.0419031	-7.96	0.000	-.415879	-.2515932
_cons	4.764389	.089859	53.02	0.000	4.588238	4.94054

Figure 8.5   Including interaction terms

less than non-married ones. At this point we can also test whether the sum of the two coefficients is zero.

Note that when we include an interaction term we allow the coefficient of the first interacted variable (in this case Married) to change depending on the value of the second interacted variable (in this case Female). Hence, while we allow the coefficient of the marital status variable to differ between men and women, the coefficients of all other variables are assumed to be the same for both men and women. When we estimate separate models for men and women, we allow the coefficients of all variables to differ by sex, thus possibly obtaining different results.

Write the commands and compare with the do and log files in the online appendix

8.3 Using Weights in Regression Models

In Chapter 7 we discussed how to produce weighted estimates and how to account for the complex survey design to produce correct standard errors. How do the results of the wage model estimated in Section 8.2 differ if we take into account weights and survey design?

Although the weights that we can use to correct for non-response are already included in the individual respondent file we are using (rindresp), the data necessary to identify the strata and the primary sample unit are related to the household residence and can be found only in the household-level file rhhsamp. Hence, to be able to estimate models that take into account the survey design we need to merge data from the rindresp and rhhsamp files. The variables we need from the rhhsamp file are rpsu for the primary sample unit and rstrata for the strata. We use the household identifier (rhid) to link the two data files (remember that in the previous sections we dropped the prefix from the household identifier in the individual respondent file).

Write the commands and compare with the do file in the online appendix

To estimate the wage model using weights we use the command regress and specify that the weights (xwtuk1) are probability weights ([pweight = xwtuk1]):

```
regress LnW age age2 Female Married Q1-Q5 ///
    R1-R6 R8-R12 [pweight = xwtuk1]
```

If we also want to take into account the complex survey design, we first use the command svyset to define the characteristics of the survey design, and then svy: regress ... to estimate our model. As mentioned in Chapter 7, to avoid problems with the different survey design for Northern Ireland, before the command svyset we need to assign to the variable identifying the primary sample unit in Northern Ireland a value equal to the household identifier:

```
replace psu = hid if memorig == 7
svyset psu [pweight = xrwtuk1], strata(strata)
svy: regress LnW age age2 Female Married Q1-Q5 ///
    R1-R6 R8-R12
```

As the BHPS includes regional boosts and our wage model includes region dummies, we can see this as a case of exogenous sampling for which weighting is not necessary. However, if for example the probability of non-response is related to wages, we may have a case of endogenous sampling where weighting is necessary (see Section 7.2.7). In Table 8.1 we report one unweighted regression models: one excluding, and one including, the regional dummies (column 1). and two weighted models: one without accounting for survey design (column 2) and one accounting for survey design (column 3)

Table 8.1   Weighted and unweighted regressions

	(1)	(2)	(3)
Age	0.128*	0.131*	0.131*
	(0.004)	(0.006)	(0.006)
Age-squared	−0.001*	−0.001*	−0.001*
	(0.000)	(0.000)	(0.000)
Dummy for women	−0.517*	−0.550*	−0.550*
	(0.015)	(0.021)	(0.021)
Whether married or cohabiting	0.084*	0.042	0.042
	(0.019)	(0.024)	(0.023)
First degree or higher	0.706*	0.703*	0.703*
	(0.029)	(0.041)	(0.044)
HND, HNC, equivalent	0.501*	0.500*	0.500*
	(0.036)	(0.052)	(0.052)
A level or equivalent	0.290*	0.308*	0.308*
	(0.028)	(0.040)	(0.041)
O level or equivalent	0.187*	0.189*	0.189*
	(0.027)	(0.040)	(0.042)
CSE	0.117*	0.116+	0.116+
	(0.040)	(0.048)	(0.052)
Intercept	4.879*	4.823*	4.823*
	(0.078)	(0.117)	(0.127)
Region dummies	Yes	Yes	Yes
Weights	No	Yes	Yes
Survey design	No	No	Yes
R^2	0.387	0.387	0.387
Observations	6933	6769	7449

Standard errors in parentheses; + significant at 5%; * significant at 1%.

The weighted and unweighted estimates are quite similar except for the gender pay penalty (the coefficient of the dummy for women) and the marriage wage premium (the coefficient of the marital status dummy).

The difference between the weighted and unweighted estimates of the marriage wage premium can be explained if, for example, the marriage wage premium is different across regions (see Solon et al. 2013). If this is the case, then the coefficients

of the marital status dummy in the weighted and unweighted models are estimates of the average marriage wage premium across UK regions where each model
applies different weights to the region-specific marriage wage premiums. Note,
however, that, as Solon et al. (2013) explain, neither model may correctly represent
the UK average marriage wage premium (the weighted estimates will do so only in
the unlikely case where the within-group variances of marital status are the same).
Hence, in the presence of such heterogeneous effects, it may be better to estimate
region-specific marriage wage premiums and region-specific gender pay penalties
instead of UK average ones. In this case we are not interested in regional differences
in these variables and the UK-wide model will do.

The estimates of standard errors confirm that weighted estimates generally
inflate standard errors and are therefore slightly less precise.

Results of the models estimated taking into account both sample weights and
the survey design appear in the third column of Table 8.1. Comparing columns
(2) and (3) we can see that the estimates that take into account the survey design
are exactly the same as those that do not account for it, but accounting for survey design does change the standard errors (as expected; see the discussion
about robust standard errors in Section 8.2.2 and also Chapter 7).

8.4 Binary Dependent Variables

8.4.1. Linear and Non-Linear Models

In some cases the variable of interest may be non-continuous. For example, we
may want to analyse what characteristics are associated with employment; in
this case the dependent variable may be a dummy (y_i) which is one if the person
is employed and zero if they are not. In particular, employment includes both
people who are in a paid job and those who are self-employed; we classify all
other cases as not employed (in some cases we may want to consider those on
maternity leave as employed).

Whether a person is employed may depend on individual and household
characteristics:

$$y_i^* = \beta_1 \text{Age}_i + \beta_2 \text{Age}_i \text{ square} + \beta_3 \text{Married dummy}_i +$$
$$\beta_4 \text{Qualification dummies}_i + \beta_5 \text{Region dummies}_i + \qquad (8.2)$$
$$\text{error term}_i$$

where i identifies individuals, and the variable y_i^* (often referred to as the 'latent
variable') identifies the individual propensity to be in employment. This propensity is unobservable, but we assume it depends on the variables on the right-
hand side of the equation. The individual is therefore observed to be employed

$(y_i = 1)$ when the propensity to be employed y_i^* crosses the threshold (zero in this case). Since women's labour supply decisions are more complex than those of men (by often including periods of inactivity due to fertility decisions), for simplicity in this model we focus on men only.

There are different econometric methods to estimate the coefficients of this model. For example, we could ignore the fact that the dependent variable is a dummy and estimate the model using OLS; this model is known as a linear probability model (LPM). Although the LPM is not uncommon, it is widely criticised by some researchers. The LPM has problems of heteroscedasticity, which can be taken care of by estimating robust standard errors, and it cannot ensure that the predicted values for the dependent variable (that is, the probability of being employed) will lie between zero and one (see for example Wooldridge 2009).

Alternative estimation methods are the logit and probit models. In this case the probability that the dependent variable is equal to one, given the explanatory variables, is

$$\text{Prob}(Y = 1 \mid X) = \text{F}(X\beta) \tag{8.3}$$

where $F(.)$ is often called the 'index function'; it has to be chosen so that the probability that the dependent variable is equal to one lies between zero and one. Cumulative distribution functions satisfy this criterion. The most common choices for $F(.)$ are the cumulative distribution function of a standard normal distribution, and the cumulative distribution function of a logistic distribution. In the first case, what we estimate is called the probit model; in the second case it is the logit model. These models are estimated using maximum likelihood techniques, as specified in Greene (2003). When using cross-section data, the results of probit and logit models are often very similar.

After creating the relevant variables we can estimate an LPM model using the command `regress`; a probit model using the command `probit`; and a logit model using the command `logit`. All three commands have the same syntax: the name of the command is followed by the dependent variable and the list of explanatory variables. Remember to exclude women from the sample, for example by using the sub-command `if`.

Write the commands and compare with the `do` and `log` files in the online appendix

Also remember that the commands `logit` and `probit` compare all zeros with all non-zero outcomes. Hence, if the dependent variable has values 0, 1, 2, 3, Stata interprets the zero as a negative outcome (the event did not happen) and all other values as a positive outcome (the event did happen) but with no distinctions between the different non-zero values. Hence, a probit or logit model estimate on a variable that has value 1, 2, 3 and no zeros will give an error message.

We can now compare the results of the three (LPM, probit and logit) models. The three commands and their results are shown in Figure 8.6.

```
. regress Employed age age2 Married Q1-Q5 R1-R6 R8-R12 if Female == 0

      Source |       SS       df       MS              Number of obs =     5940
-------------+------------------------------           F( 19,  5920) =   211.92
       Model |  558.396592    19  29.3892943           Prob > F      =   0.0000
    Residual |  821.003408  5920  .138683008           R-squared     =   0.4048
-------------+------------------------------           Adj R-squared =   0.4029
       Total |      1379.4  5939  .232261323           Root MSE      =    .3724


------------------------------------------------------------------------------
    Employed |     Coef.   Std. Err.      t    P>|t|     [95% Conf. Interval]
-------------+----------------------------------------------------------------
         age |   .0458287   .001493     30.70   0.000     .0429018    .0487556
        age2 |  -.0005592   .0000148   -37.87   0.000    -.0005882   -.0005303
     Married |   .1201092   .0120352     9.98   0.000     .0965158    .1437025
          Q1 |   .1993653   .0166232    11.99   0.000     .1667778    .2319528
...[output omitted]...
         R12 |  -.0797261   .0272793    -2.92   0.003    -.1332034   -.0262487
       _cons |   -.242146   .0411605    -5.88   0.000    -.3228355   -.1614565
------------------------------------------------------------------------------

. probit Employed age age2 Married Q1-Q5 R1-R6 R8-R12 if Female == 0

Iteration 0:   log likelihood = -3903.5171
...[output omitted]...
Iteration 4:   log likelihood = -2338.5193

Probit regression                               Number of obs   =      5940
                                                LR chi2(19)     =   3130.00
                                                Prob > chi2     =    0.0000
Log likelihood = -2338.5193                     Pseudo R2       =    0.4009


------------------------------------------------------------------------------
    Employed |     Coef.   Std. Err.      z    P>|z|     [95% Conf. Interval]
-------------+----------------------------------------------------------------
         age |   .2200136   .0075631    29.09   0.000     .2051902    .234837
        age2 |  -.0027216   .0000835   -32.58   0.000    -.0028853   -.0025578
     Married |   .4931326   .051643      9.55   0.000     .3919141    .5943511
          Q1 |   .7584157   .0735767    10.31   0.000     .614208     .9026235
...[output omitted]...
         R12 |  -.3415943   .1217306    -2.81   0.005    -.5801819   -.1030068
       _cons |  -3.651224   .1887046   -19.35   0.000    -4.021079    -3.28137
------------------------------------------------------------------------------
Note: 16 failures and 0 successes completely determined.

. logit Employed age age2 Married Q1-Q5 R1-R6 R8-R12 if Female == 0

Iteration 0:   log likelihood = -3903.5171
...[output omitted]...
Iteration 4:   log likelihood = -2325.0082

Logistic regression                             Number of obs   =      5940
                                                LR chi2(19)     =   3157.02
                                                Prob > chi2     =    0.0000
Log likelihood = -2325.0082                     Pseudo R2       =    0.4044


------------------------------------------------------------------------------
    Employed |     Coef.   Std. Err.      z    P>|z|     [95% Conf. Interval]
-------------+----------------------------------------------------------------
         age |   .3930998   .014043     27.99   0.000     .3655761    .4206235
        age2 |  -.0048742   .0001584   -30.77   0.000    -.0051847   -.0045637
     Married |   .8708715   .0930483     9.36   0.000     .6885002    1.053243
          Q1 |   1.270692   .1327634     9.57   0.000     1.01048     1.530903
...[output omitted]...
         R12 |  -.6153422   .2193408    -2.81   0.005    -1.045242   -.1854421
       _cons |  -6.496169   .3398631   -19.11   0.000    -7.162289    -5.83005
------------------------------------------------------------------------------
```

Figure 8.6   Estimation models for binary dependent variables

The sign and the statistical significance of the coefficients are consistent across the three models. The LPM model suggests that older men are more likely to have a job, although the square term in age suggests that the relationship is non-linear; married men are 12 percentage points more likely to have a job than those who are not married; and the probability of having a job is higher, the higher the level of education. The coefficients of the probit and logit models are very different from the coefficients of the LPM. This is because probit and logit are not linear models. In this case the coefficients are indicative of the direction of the relationship between dependent and explanatory variables, but, unlike the case of linear models (OLS or LPM), we cannot use the coefficients to infer directly the change in the probability of the dependent variable for a unit increase in the explanatory variable (see for example Long 1997). It would be incorrect to read the coefficient of the probit model as suggesting that married men are 49 percentage points more likely to have a job than those who are not married. To be able to interpret the results in this way, rather than the coefficients, for probit and logit models we often compute the marginal effects after the estimation command.

8.4.2 Coefficients, Marginal Effects, Odds Ratios

In a general model of the type $Y = F(\alpha + \beta X)$, the marginal effect of X on Y can be computed by taking the partial derivative with respect to X:

$$\frac{\partial Y}{\partial X} = \frac{\partial F(\alpha + \beta X)}{\partial X} = \beta F'(\alpha + \beta X) \tag{8.4}$$

where F' is the derivative of F with respect to X. Equation (8.4) is the change in Y due to an infinitesimal change in X. While in linear models the partial derivative equals β and is the same for all values of X, this is not the case in non-linear models. Because of the non-linearity, marginal effects vary over the distribution of the explanatory variable; hence, we have to decide at which point of the distribution we want to compute the marginal effects (this uncertainty is one of the reasons why some researchers prefer LPMs to non-linear models). The most common choices are to estimate the marginal effect at the mean, or to estimate the marginal effect at each observation and then take the average.

We can estimate the marginal effects using the command mfx (in all versions of Stata) or margins (from Stata 11 onwards) after estimation of the probit or logit model. By default, the command mfx computes the marginal effects at the means of the explanatory variables, while the command margins computes the average of the marginal effects. Both mfx and margins can also be used to estimate marginal effects for a particular type of respondent (look at the Stata manual for more information).

It is important to notice that for variables that are not continuous, such as the number of children or a dummy for whether married, it is not appropriate to compute marginal effects since for these variables an infinitesimal change has no meaning. In the case of variables such as dummies we are interested in estimating the change in the dependent variable when the explanatory variable moves from zero to one. The command `margins` computes the impact of a discrete change in the variables that are not continuous, provided that we have correctly identified them in the estimation using the factor notation (i.). For all other variables, even those that are discrete, the command `margins` still computes the effect of an infinitesimal change. Look at the `log` file in the online appendix to see how the results change when we account for the discrete change in the dummy variables.

Write the commands and compare with the `do` and `log` files in the online appendix

```
. probit Employed age age2 i.Married i.Q1-Q5 i.R1-R6 i.R8-R12 if Female == 0

...[output omitted]...

Probit regression                             Number of obs    =      5940
                                              LR chi2(19)      =   3130.00
                                              Prob > chi2      =    0.0000
Log likelihood = -2338.5193                   Pseudo R2        =    0.4009


------------------------------------------------------------------------------
   Employed |      Coef.   Std. Err.      z    P>|z|     [95% Conf. Interval]
------------+-----------------------------------------------------------------
        age |   .2200136   .0075631    29.09   0.000     .2051902    .234837
       age2 |  -.0027216   .0000835   -32.58   0.000    -.0028853   -.0025578
  1.Married |   .4931326    .051643     9.55   0.000     .3919141   .5943511
       1.Q1 |   .7584157   .0735767    10.31   0.000      .614208   .9026235
       1.Q2 |   .5049339   .0898357     5.62   0.000     .3288591   .6810087
       1.Q3 |   .3788537   .0617057     6.14   0.000     .2579127   .4997948
...[output omitted]...
      1.R11 |  -.1216355   .1211537    -1.00   0.315    -.3590923   .1158213
      1.R12 |  -.3415943   .1217306    -2.81   0.005    -.5801819  -.1030068
       _cons |  -3.651224   .1887046   -19.35   0.000    -4.021079   -3.28137
------------------------------------------------------------------------------

Note: 16 failures and 0 successes completely determined.

. margins, dydx(age age2 Married Q1 Q2 Q3 Q4 Q5 R1 R2 R3 R4 R5 R6 R8 R9 R10 R11 R12)

Average marginal effects                      Number of obs    =      5940
Model VCE     : OIM

Expression    : Pr(Employed), predict()
dy/dx w.r.t.  : age age2 1.Married 1.Q1 1.Q2 1.Q3 1.Q4 1.Q5 1.R1 1.R2 1.R3 1.R4 1.R5 1.R6
                1.R8 1.R9 1.R10 1.R11 1.R12


------------------------------------------------------------------------------
            |            Delta-method
            |      dy/dx   Std. Err.      z    P>|z|     [95% Conf. Interval]
------------+-----------------------------------------------------------------
        age |   .0487101   .0013236    36.80   0.000     .0461159   .0513044
       age2 |  -.0006025   .0000135   -44.55   0.000    -.0006291   -.000576
  1.Married |   .1161915   .0126079     9.22   0.000     .0914805   .1409025
       1.Q1 |   .1533711   .0130198    11.78   0.000     .1278528   .1788895
       1.Q2 |   .1019713   .0162217     6.29   0.000     .0701774   .1337652
       1.Q3 |   .0809203   .0125951     6.42   0.000     .0562344   .1056063
...[output omitted]...
      1.R11 |  -.0273432   .0276284    -0.99   0.322    -.0814938   .0268074
      1.R12 |  -.0793679   .0294466    -2.70   0.007    -.1370823  -.0216536
------------------------------------------------------------------------------

Note: dy/dx for factor levels is the discrete change from the base level.
```

Figure 8.7   Marginal effects

Figure 8.7 shows the regression coefficients and the marginal effects for the probit model.

The marginal effects of the probit model in Figure 8.7 suggest that married men are 11.6 percentage points more likely than non-married men to have a job, while the marginal effects of the logit model (see the `log` file in the online appendix) suggest a probability of 11.5 percentage points. Both are similar to the results of the LPM: 12.0 percentage points. It is also worthwhile to look at the difference between the value of the coefficients and the value of the marginal effects: for the logit, for example, the marginal effect for the married dummy is around 0.11, while the coefficient is 0.87!

In the command `margin` we have used the option `dydx(varlist)` to estimate the marginal effect for a list of variables (see for example Figure 8.7). Other options are possible, for example `eyex(varlist)` to estimate elasticities; `dyex(varlist)` and `eydx(varlist)` to estimate semi-elasticities ($d(y)/d(\ln x)$ and $d(\ln y)/d(x)$); check the Stata manual for more options.

Instead of showing marginal effects, some authors prefer to show odds ratios, which are computed by adding the option `or` at the end of the `logit` command. Odds ratios are the ratio of the odds that the event (the person has a job, our dependent variable) occurs in one group (for example, married people) to the odds that the event occurs in the other group (non-married people), where the odds are the ratio of the probability that the event will happen ($prob_1$ or $prob_2$ below) to the probability that the event will not happen (($1 - prob_1$) and ($1 - prob_2$)), as follows:

$$\frac{prob_1/(1-prob_1)}{prob_2/(1-prob_2)} = \frac{prob_1(1-prob_2)}{prob_2(1-prob_1)} \tag{8.5}$$

When the odds ratio is higher than one, the explanatory variable has a positive impact on the dependent variable; when the odds ratio is lower than one, the impact is negative. If the odds ratios of the variable `Married` is 2.39 (see the `log` file in the online appendix) it means that for those who are married the odds of having a job are 2.39 times higher than for someone who is not married (this, however, does not mean that a married person is over twice as likely to be employed than someone who is not married). The statistical significance in the results table refers now to the probability that the odds ratio is different than one (see also the confidence intervals in the last two columns of the table of results), where one would indicate that there are no differences between married and non-married people.

Note that for logit models the odds ratio is the exponential value of the coefficient and is constant across all values of the explanatory variables. This is one of the reasons why we may prefer to show odds ratios instead of marginal effects. It is not possible to compute odds ratios when using the command `probit`, since in probit models the odds ratios are not constant.

8.4.3 Different Types of Standard Errors and Other Post-Estimation Commands

Similar to the case of linear regression, in logit and probit models also we can compute robust standard errors using the option vce(robust), or use the cluster, bootstrap and jackknife options. The predict and test set of commands works in essentially the same way in both linear and non-linear models, with only minor variations; check the Stata manual for details.

8.5 Multiple Outcomes

In some cases the variable of interest may have three or more possible outcomes. This is the case for example for variables such as education level (primary, secondary, college, university, postgrad) or labour market status (employed, unemployed, inactive). While education levels have an intrinsic order between categories, labour force statuses do not have an intrinsic order. Typically, we use multinomial ordered probit or logit models for variables such as education, and unordered models for variables such as labour market status. Although it is possible to use unordered models for variables such as education, it is often best to exploit the further information related to the ordering of the dependent variable. In this case we can include the (ordering) restriction in the estimation of the model to make the results more precise. Ordered models should not be used for unordered variables since the restriction imposed would be arbitrary.

8.5.1 Ordered Outcomes

An increasing literature nowadays is interested in the determinants of happiness and life satisfaction (see Layard 2005; Frey 2008). Life satisfaction is generally measured by answers to questions such as 'How dissatisfied or satisfied are you with your life overall?' Respondents are asked to answer using a x-point scale. In the BHPS, for example, the scale ranges from 1 to 7, where 1 stands for 'not satisfied at all', 4 stands for 'not satisfied nor dissatisfied' and 7 stands for 'completely satisfied'.

If we want to analyse the impact of unemployment on life satisfaction, for example, we can estimate a model of the type

$$yit^* = \eta_0 \text{Unemployed dummy}_i + \eta_1 \text{Age}_i + \eta_2 \text{Age}_i^2 + \eta_3 \text{Married} \\ \text{dummy}_i + \eta_4 \text{Female dummy}_i + \eta_5 \text{Qualification} \\ \text{dummies}_i + \eta_6 \text{Region dummies}_i + \text{error term}_i$$

(8.6)

where i identifies individuals, and 'Unemployed dummy$_i$' is a dummy that is one for those who are currently unemployed and zero for those who are either employed or self-employed (for simplicity we exclude those who are inactive). The variable y_{it}^* is the latent variable for life satisfaction (y_{it}) and the underlying satisfaction score, y_{it}^*, is a continuous variable. However, because respondents are asked to choose from seven points in an ordered scale, they will choose the position in the scale that is closest to their score, so that

$$y_i = 1 \quad \text{if} \quad y_i^* \le 0$$

$$y_i = 2 \quad \text{if} \quad 0 < y_i^* \le \mu_1$$

$$y_i = 3 \quad \text{if} \quad \mu_1 < y_i^* \le \mu_2$$

and so on until

$$y_i = 7 \quad \text{if} \quad y_i^* > \mu_6$$

What we observe is only the ordinal variable ranging from 1 to 7, although what we want to estimate is the probability of observing one of the seven outcomes. This also implies that we will be estimating not only the coefficients of the independent variables, but also the cut-off points $(\mu_1, \mu_2, ..., \mu_6)$.

To estimate models in which the dependent variable has an ordered outcome we can use the command `ologit` or `oprobit`. If we assume that 'error term$_i$' follows a standard normal distribution we can use the ordered probit (`oprobit`); if we assume that 'error term$_{it}$' follows a logistic distribution we can use the ordered logit (`ologit`). The syntax of the `ologit` and `oprobit` commands – and post-estimation commands – is the same as the syntax of `logit` and `probit`.

Is there any impact on life satisfaction of being currently unemployed? After preparing the data for analysis, we estimate the ordered probit and logit models, and compute the respective marginal effects.

Write the commands and compare with the do file in the online appendix

The results of the ordered logit model are shown in Figure 8.8. The bottom of the results table shows the estimated values of the cut-off points, their standard errors and confidence intervals. Here, /cut1 is the estimated cut-off point to distinguish between those whose level of satisfaction is one and those for whom it is two, when all the explanatory variables are set to zero, which means that the cut-off point refers to the reference groups (the dummies left out from the model: men, non-married, and so on). People with values of -7.18 or less on the latent variable would reply that their level of satisfaction is 1; those with values between -7.18 and -5.96 would reply that their level of satisfaction is 2. Those with values between -1.75 and $+0.46$ would have a level of satisfaction of 6;

and those with values higher than 0.46 would have a level of satisfaction of 7. As the confidence intervals of the cut-off points do not include zero, the cut-off points are statistically significant and hence the existing number of cut-off points is valid. Unemployment decreases the latent variable (the level of satisfaction) suggesting that, other things equal, on average unemployed people are less happy than those who have a job. Once again, from the log files in the online appendix we can see that the marginal effects of the ordered logit and probit models are very similar to each other.

```
. ologit lfsato Unemployed Female age age2 Married Q1-Q5 R1-R6 R8-R12

Iteration 0:    log likelihood = -10995.744
Iteration 1:    log likelihood =  -10830.66
Iteration 2:    log likelihood = -10829.924
Iteration 3:    log likelihood = -10829.924

Ordered logistic regression                         Number of obs    =        7539
                                                    LR chi2(21)      =      331.64
                                                    Prob > chi2      =      0.0000
Log likelihood = -10829.924                         Pseudo R2        =      0.0151
```

lfsato	Coef.	Std. Err.	z	P>|z|	[95% Conf. Interval]	
Unemployed	-.906787	.1010913	-8.97	0.000	-1.104922	-.7086517
Female	.0275715	.0422807	0.65	0.514	-.0552972	.1104402
age	-.1210327	.0105657	-11.46	0.000	-.1417411	-.1003243
age2	.001421	.0001244	11.43	0.000	.0011773	.0016648
Married	.5973508	.0519144	11.51	0.000	.4956005	.6991012
Q1	.0286538	.0783082	0.37	0.714	-.1248275	.1821352
Q2	.0608814	.0976928	0.62	0.533	-.130593	.2523558
Q3	-.1553702	.076443	-2.03	0.042	-.3051958	-.0055446
Q4	-.1099204	.0745972	-1.47	0.141	-.2561282	.0362875
Q5	.0705086	.1093574	0.64	0.519	-.143828	.2848452
R1	-.0257945	.1615143	-0.16	0.873	-.3423567	.2907677
R2	.0535556	.1237301	0.43	0.665	-.1889508	.296062
R3	.0460722	.1300642	0.35	0.723	-.208849	.3009934
R4	-.0804732	.1323305	-0.61	0.543	-.3398362	.1788899
R5	-.1618233	.1336837	-1.21	0.226	-.4238385	.1001919
R6	.0309667	.130612	0.24	0.813	-.225028	.2869614
R8	-.165474	.1195626	-1.38	0.166	-.3998124	.0688643
R9	.0339182	.1293218	0.26	0.793	-.2195479	.2873842
R10	.0300755	.1114063	0.27	0.787	-.1882768	.2484278
R11	.0212467	.1103427	0.19	0.847	-.1950211	.2375145
R12	.2563722	.1161253	2.21	0.027	.0287708	.4839736
/cut1	-7.18087	.2766762			-7.723145	-6.638594
/cut2	-5.963278	.2469502			-6.447291	-5.479265
/cut3	-4.596357	.2364244			-5.05974	-4.132973
/cut4	-3.358247	.2331987			-3.815308	-2.901186
/cut5	-1.752493	.2311702			-2.205579	-1.299408
/cut6	.4595112	.2312727			.006225	.9127974

Figure 8.8   Impact of unemployment on life satisfaction

Also for the case of multinomial ordered outcomes we can assume linearity and therefore estimate our models using OLS with the command regress. The critical assumption here is that the difference between the various outcomes is constant across the outcomes. Hence, people would see the difference between a level of satisfaction of 7 (extremely satisfied) and of 6 (very satisfied) exactly the same as the difference between a level of satisfaction of 4 (not satisfied nor dissatisfied) and 3 (moderately unsatisfied). This linearity assumption is relaxed in the probit and logit models. One advantage of using linear models is the ease of interpretation as the marginal effects correspond to the estimated coefficients and are constant over the whole distribution (see Section 8.4.2).

One thing to note here is that when we compute marginal effects we need to specify which of the values in the scale we are interested in, using the options `predict` and `outcome`. For example, the post-estimation command `margins..., predict(outcome(2))` computes the impact of the variables on the probability that the level of satisfaction of the individual is 2. To have a complete picture, in this case we would have to show the marginal effects for each possible value of the dependent variable. From the `log` file in the online appendix we can see how much the marginal effects differ across the different outcomes (more on this in Section 8.5.2). Showing all these marginal effects is cumbersome when we have seven distinct outcomes, such as in the case of life satisfaction, and is one of the reasons why some researchers prefer to use LPMs.

8.5.2 Unordered Outcomes

Some variables of interest have more than two possible outcomes which cannot be ordered. In this case the most appropriate estimation techniques are unordered models, which can be estimated using the multinomial logit and multinomial probit model commands: `mlogit` and `mprobit`. We use `mprobit` if we assume that 'error term$_i$' follows a standard normal distribution, and `mlogit` if we assume a logistic distribution. With few exceptions, discussed below, the syntax of the `mlogit` and `mprobit` commands – and post-estimation commands – is the same as the syntax of `logit` and `probit`.

In both these models the variables vary across individuals but not across alternatives. Another type of model that allows for variables to vary across alternatives is the conditional logit model (McFadden 1974). The command to estimate this model is `asclogit`, while the command for the probit version – also called conditional probit model or alternative-specific multinomial probit model – is `asmprobit`.

In the previous sections we mentioned that the differences between logit and probit models are minor. In the case of multinomial and conditional logit models the econometric estimation relies on the assumption of independence of irrelevant alternatives, which means that the odds that one of the alternatives is chosen are determined without reference to the other possible alternatives. In other words, the choice between alternative 1 and alternative 2 does not depend on whether alternative 3 is also available and does not depend on the characteristics of alternative 3. This is a restrictive assumption if some of the alternatives are similar to each other; for example, 1. not participating in the labour market, 2. working in job A in firm A, 3. working in job A in firm B (for details see, among others, Long 1997). The econometric estimation of the multinomial (sometimes called conditional) probit model does not rely on the assumption of independence of irrelevant alternatives, which in this case may be a reason to prefer the probit to the logit model (see Wooldridge 2002).

If, for example, we want to analyse the impact of gender on the labour market status of the individual we can estimate a model of the type

$$y_i^* = \gamma_1 \text{Age}_i + \gamma_2 \text{Age}_i^2 + \gamma_3 \text{Married dummy}_i + \gamma_4 \text{Female} \\ \text{dummy}_i + \gamma_5 \text{Qualification dummies}_i + \gamma_6 \text{Region} \\ \text{dummies}_i + \text{error term}_{it} \tag{8.7}$$

where the possible outcomes of y_i^* are: employed, unemployed and inactive. The probability that we observe individual i in state q (employed, unemployed or inactive) is the probability that $y_{iq} > y_{ij}$ for each $j \neq q$.

Is there any impact of being a woman on the probability of being inactive? After preparing the data for analysis, we estimate the multinomial probit and logit models and compute the respective marginal effects for each of these three possible outcomes.

Write the commands and compare with the do file in the online appendix

As we have seen in the case of ordered outcomes, because there are multiple unordered outcomes, one of the outcomes will be used as reference. By default, Stata uses as reference the group with most observations; however, we can use the option `baseoutcome(n)` if we want the nth outcome (for example, employed) to be the reference. Similarly, the marginal effects should be computed for all other outcomes (and interpreted as a comparison with the reference outcome); this can be done using the option `predict(outcome())` when using the command `margins`. Figure 8.9 shows the results of the command `mprobit`; the results of the command `mlogit` are in the online appendix.

The command `mprobit` shows the estimated coefficients for all possible outcomes with the exception of the base category. We can then compute the marginal effects related to all outcomes, for all or few explanatory variables. The interpretation is similar to that of (multinomial) probit models: the first set of marginal effects suggests that women are about 11.4 percentage points less likely to have a job than men; they are also 1.9 percentage points less likely to

```
. mprobit LMS i.Female age age2 i.Married i.Q1-Q5 i.R1-R6 i.R8-R12, baseoutcome(1)
...[output omitted]...

. margins, dydx(Female Married) predict(outcome(1))

Average marginal effects                         Number of obs   =      13168
Model VCE    : OIM

Expression    : Pr(LMS==Has Job), predict(outcome(1))
dy/dx w.r.t. : 1.Female 1.Married

------------------------------------------------------------------------------
             |            Delta-method
             |    dy/dx    Std. Err.     z     P>|z|     [95% Conf. Interval]
-------------+----------------------------------------------------------------
    1.Female |  -.1136267   .0067122   -16.93   0.000    -.1267824    -.100471
   1.Married |   .0653132   .0083569     7.82   0.000     .0489339    .0816925
------------------------------------------------------------------------------
Note: dy/dx for factor levels is the discrete change from the base level.

. margins, dydx(Female Married) predict(outcome(2))

Average marginal effects                         Number of obs   =      13168
Model VCE    : OIM

Expression    : Pr(LMS==Unemployed), predict(outcome(2))
dy/dx w.r.t. : 1.Female 1.Married

------------------------------------------------------------------------------
             |            Delta-method
             |    dy/dx    Std. Err.     z     P>|z|     [95% Conf. Interval]
-------------+----------------------------------------------------------------
    1.Female |  -.0194471   .0031772    -6.12   0.000    -.0256743   -.0132199
   1.Married |  -.0236401   .0039879    -5.93   0.000    -.0314562    -.015824
------------------------------------------------------------------------------
Note: dy/dx for factor levels is the discrete change from the base level.

. margins, dydx(Female Married) predict(outcome(3))

Average marginal effects                         Number of obs   =      13168
Model VCE    : OIM

Expression    : Pr(LMS==Inactive), predict(outcome(3))
dy/dx w.r.t. : 1.Female 1.Married

------------------------------------------------------------------------------
             |            Delta-method
             |    dy/dx    Std. Err.     z     P>|z|     [95% Conf. Interval]
-------------+----------------------------------------------------------------
    1.Female |   .1330738   .0064137    20.75   0.000     .1205031    .1456444
   1.Married |  -.0416731   .0079388    -5.25   0.000    -.0572329   -.0261133
------------------------------------------------------------------------------
Note: dy/dx for factor levels is the discrete change from the base level.
```

Figure 8.9   Marginal effects of the unordered multinomial probit

be unemployed, and therefore 13.3 percentage points more likely to be inactive (the sum of the three different probabilities should be zero).

8.6 Heckman Selection Models

Missing data are a serious problem in estimating population parameters. There are different types of missing data, including data censoring and sample selection (see Wooldridge 2009). In this book we have discussed two of the most common types of missing data: sample selection on observables and selection on unobservables. When sample selection is on the basis of observable factors which can explain why some population units (individuals) are more likely to be included in the sample (either because of sample design or non-response), weighted estimations are sometimes preferred (see Chapter 7 and Section 8.3). As we have seen in Chapter 7, sample weights are computed as the inverse of the selection probability. If there is oversampling (or more generally different selection probabilities) the selection probabilities are known, because they have been set by design. In the case of non-response the selection probability is estimated on the basis of observed factors such as sex, age or employment status. However, when selection is on the basis of unobserved factors these weighting methods are not appropriate. Heckman (1979) has suggested a two-stage model to compute consistent estimators of population parameters when the units of observations are selected into the sample on the basis of unobserved factors.

One classic example is that of women's decision to participate in the labour market. While most men participate in the labour market, not all women do. Suppose that, as is the case in most societies, women are expected to contribute to a higher share of child-rearing activities than men, and that child care is expensive. Also it may be the case that women derive positive utility from raising their own children. It is possible that women who expect to earn wages high enough to cover child care costs and compensate for the loss of utility from not raising their children are more likely to participate in the labour market than women who expect to earn lower wages.

The sample of working women is therefore likely to consist of a (possibly random) sample of women without children but a (possibly highly) selected sample of skilled women with children (with expected high wages). If some of those factors that determine the skill level of women, such as motivation, effort, diligence, are not observed, and if these factors also have an influence on wages and the probability of participating in the labour market, the estimated coefficients of a wage model will be driven by these highly skilled women. The main problem here is that we cannot observe wages of those women who do not participate in the labour market.

Heckman (1979) suggests modelling the probability that a woman participates in the labour market (P) jointly with wages (W) of those who do participate:

$$P = \begin{cases} 1 & \text{if } X + Z\gamma + \vartheta \geq 0 \\ 0 & \text{otherwise} \end{cases} \tag{8.8}$$

$$W = \begin{cases} X\beta + \varepsilon & \text{if } P = 1 \\ \text{missing} & \text{if } P = 0 \end{cases} \tag{8.9}$$

where W measures wages and P is a binary variable which takes on the value 1 if a woman participates in the labour market and 0 otherwise, X includes those factors (variables) that explain wages, while Z includes those factors that explain labour market participation but not wages. Note that all those factors that do explain wages (X) also tend to explain the probability to participate in the labour market, so that Z includes all the variables in X, plus some additional ones.

The model also assumes that the error term in the selection equation (ϑ) is normally distributed with mean 0 and variance equal to 1, while the error term in the main regression equation (ε) is normally distributed with mean 0 and variance equal to σ. The correlation between the two error terms is equal to ρ. If ρ is different than zero, a standard regression that does not take into account the self-selection (in our case self-selection of women into the labour market) would lead to biased coefficient estimates, while the Heckman selection model would lead to consistent and efficient estimates for all parameters. When ρ is zero we can think of the self-selection as a random process (those women who do participate in the labour market are a random sample of all women); a standard regression model would be appropriate in this case.

To implement the two-stage Heckman selection method we estimate Equation (8.8) using a probit model. From the estimated coefficients we compute the 'inverse Mills ratio' (IMR; see below for more details) which we then use as an additional regression in Equation (8.9). Equation (8.9) is then estimated by OLS. The coefficients of the wage model estimated using this method are consistent estimators of population parameters under the assumption that ε and ϑ are distributed as bivariate normal distributions. As an alternative, Equations (8.8) and (8.9) can be estimated simultaneously using the maximum likelihood estimator (MLE).

Although it is not necessary, it is common practice to include in Equation (8.8) variables that are excluded from Equation (8.9) and that therefore act as instruments (see Section 8.7 for a short discussion of instruments). In the case of female labour market participation a commonly used instrument is the presence – or sometimes the number – of (young) dependent children in the household.

To estimate a Heckman selection model in Stata we use the command `heckman` followed by the dependent variable and the list of explanatory variables in the main model (for example, the wages model). The selection equation (the probability to participate in the labour market) is specified using the option `select(...)`; the dependent and explanatory variables for the selection equation are listed within the parentheses. In our case,

```
heckman LnW age age2 Married PartTime Q1-Q5 ///
   R1-R6 R8-R12 ///
   if Female == 1 & age >= 23 & age < 60, ///
   select(work = age age2 Married ///
```

```
Heckman selection model                          Number of obs    =      4070
(regression model with sample selection)         Censored obs     =      1109
                                                 Uncensored obs   =      2961

                                                 Wald chi2(20)    =   1964.13
Log pseudolikelihood = -4141.001                 Prob > chi2      =    0.0000
```

	Coef.	Robust Std. Err.	z	P>|z|	[95% Conf. Interval]	
LnW						
age	.0403529	.0086761	4.65	0.000	.0233481	.0573577
age2	-.0004184	.0001098	-3.81	0.000	-.0006336	-.0002032
Married	.0024247	.0226891	0.11	0.915	-.042045	.0468945
PartTime	-.8655154	.0261085	-33.15	0.000	-.9166872	-.8143436
Q1	.6578638	.0775116	8.49	0.000	.5059439	.8097836
Q2	.4070711	.0708434	5.75	0.000	.2682205	.5459217
Q3	.3259123	.0665929	4.89	0.000	.1953927	.4564319
Q4	.1424577	.0645076	2.21	0.027	.0160252	.2688903
Q5	.0500665	.0579052	0.86	0.387	-.0634256	.1635587
R1	-.2640085	.064835	-4.07	0.000	-.3910828	-.1369342
R2	-.2902065	.0599824	-4.84	0.000	-.4077699	-.1726431
R3	-.267454	.0608267	-4.40	0.000	-.3866721	-.1482359
R4	-.2974514	.0627542	-4.74	0.000	-.4204474	-.1744555
R5	-.3463974	.064679	-5.36	0.000	-.473166	-.2196288
R6	-.2837482	.0628418	-4.52	0.000	-.406916	-.1605805
R8	-.236092	.0597249	-3.95	0.000	-.3531508	-.1190333
R9	-.3094822	.0606722	-5.10	0.000	-.4283976	-.1905668
R10	-.3404277	.0536754	-6.34	0.000	-.4456296	-.2352258
R11	-.2519995	.0524406	-4.81	0.000	-.3547811	-.1492179
R12	-.2943966	.0547654	-5.38	0.000	-.4017349	-.1870583
_cons	6.551172	.2358671	27.77	0.000	6.088881	7.013463
Works						
age	.1331478	.0193818	6.87	0.000	.0951602	.1711355
age2	-.0017987	.00024	-7.50	0.000	-.002269	-.0013283
Married	.2626056	.0504373	5.21	0.000	.1637503	.3614609
Q1	1.057794	.0814626	12.99	0.000	.8981305	1.217458
Q2	.7456624	.0967417	7.71	0.000	.5560521	.9352727
Q3	.7535347	.0738803	10.20	0.000	.608732	.8983375
Q4	.7120935	.0667925	10.66	0.000	.5811826	.8430043
Q5	.3771014	.0979621	3.85	0.000	.1850992	.5691036
R1	.0031586	.1745308	0.02	0.986	-.3389155	.3452326
R2	-.0098349	.1418904	-0.07	0.945	-.2879349	.2682651
R3	.0506498	.1472185	0.34	0.731	-.2378932	.3391928
R4	-.0931455	.1483827	-0.63	0.530	-.3839703	.1976793
R5	.0815787	.1554687	0.52	0.600	-.2231344	.3862918
R6	-.0388129	.1461277	-0.27	0.791	-.325218	.2475922
R8	.2012568	.1429861	1.41	0.159	-.0789907	.4815043
R9	.1001348	.1551209	0.65	0.519	-.2038965	.4041661
R10	-.0642644	.1285866	-0.50	0.617	-.3162894	.1877606
R11	.044923	.1307084	0.34	0.731	-.2112608	.3011068
R12	-.1190685	.127693	-0.93	0.351	-.3693422	.1312051
nchild	-.301542	.0315292	-9.56	0.000	-.363338	-.239746
_cons	-2.182475	.3803974	-5.74	0.000	-2.928041	-1.43691
/athrho	-.4847439	.2963721	-1.64	0.102	-1.065623	.0961349
/lnsigma	-.6879872	.0559823	-12.29	0.000	-.7977106	-.5782639
rho	-.4500348	.2363475			-.7878063	.0958398
sigma	.5025866	.028136			.4503589	.5608713
lambda	-.2261815	.1308381			-.4826193	.0302564

```
Wald test of indep. eqns. (rho = 0): chi2(1) =   2.68   Prob > chi2 = 0.1019
```

Figure 8.10   Maximum likelihood estimates of Heckman selection wage model for women

```
    Q1-Q5 R1-R6 R8-R12 rnchild) ///
  first mills(MR) vce(robust)
```

Normally Stata shows only the results of the main (wage) model; the option `first` can be used to show also the estimates of the selection (probit) equation. With the option `mills` a new variable is created (called in our case MR) which contains the IMR for each observation. Similar to the other estimation commands we have discussed in this chapter, the option `vce` can be used to estimate various types of standard errors.

The dependent variable in the selection equation (`work`) is a dummy variable which takes on the value 1 if a woman participates in the labour market and 0 otherwise. In the BHPS, respondents are asked if they worked last week, and, if they did, a value of 1 is recorded in the variable `jbhas`. Those who say they did not work last week are asked whether they have a job; if they answer yes, a value of 1 is recorded in the variable `jboff`. Our variable `work` has a value of 1 if either `jbhas` or `jboff` is 1, and 0 otherwise. This way of identifying whether the respondent has a job is sometimes preferred to the use of the variable `jbstat`, which is the employment status directly reported by the respondent.

The instrument in the equation above is the number of children in the household (`nchild`). The results of this command are shown in Figure 8.10.

The top panel of the results table in Figure 8.10 shows the coefficients of the wage model computed after taking into account the possible self-selection of women in the labour market. The results of this wage equation show the correlation between the explanatory and dependent variables that we would have if all women participated in the labour market (including those who would earn very low wages if they did participate). In this case, for example, women with the highest level of education (Q1) would earn on average 93% more than those with no education (Q6, the reference group), while there would be no difference in wages between married and non-married women.

The second panel of the results table in Figure 8.10 shows the coefficients of the selection equation and suggests that the number of children in the household has a negative correlation with the woman's probability of participating in the labour market. Education seems to be one of the main drivers of self-selection into the labour market.

Stata does not estimate ρ and σ directly, but via transformations; these are reported at the bottom of the table as `/athrho` and `/lnsigma`. The estimated coefficients of ρ and σ are also reported. The estimated coefficient for ρ in our case is -0.45, but with a confidence interval that includes the value 0. Remember that ρ is the correlation between the error terms of the wage model and of the selection equation. The Wald test that the two equations are independent ($\rho = 0$) at the bottom of the table is 2.68 and is not rejected, thus suggesting that self-selecting into the labour market may not be a relevant issue. We would therefore expect the results of the Heckman selection model not to differ significantly from those of a standard wage regression assuming random selection in the labour market.

The Mills ratio mentioned above is a parameter that corrects the wage equation from the unobserved factors that have an effect on the self-selection. A Mills ratio equal to 0 would indicate the absence of self-selection. The Mills ratio is computed as the product of ρ and σ and is reported at the bottom of the table (lambda) with an estimate of the standard error and the confidence interval. Also for the case of lambda the confidence interval crosses the zero line and suggests no statistical significance.

It is useful to compare the coefficient estimated with a Heckman selection model to those estimated by OLS. In this case, since the selection does not seem relevant, we would expect the coefficients of the OLS and Heckman models to

```
Linear regression                              Number of obs =     2961
                                               F( 20,  2940) =   152.79
                                               Prob > F      =   0.0000
                                               R-squared     =   0.5441
                                               Root MSE      =   .48272
```

LnW	Coef.	Robust Std. Err.	t	P>|t|	[95% Conf. Interval]	
age	.046388	.0073095	6.35	0.000	.0320557	.0607202
age2	-.0005002	.0000907	-5.52	0.000	-.000678	-.0003225
Married	.0192148	.0196193	0.98	0.327	-.0192541	.0576837
PartTime	-.8878366	.0211297	-42.02	0.000	-.9292671	-.8464062
Q1	.7766111	.0350035	22.19	0.000	.7079773	.8452449
Q2	.4979393	.0455754	10.93	0.000	.4085763	.5873023
Q3	.4191105	.0362539	11.56	0.000	.348025	.490196
Q4	.2296972	.0345773	6.64	0.000	.1618991	.2974953
Q5	.1030482	.0469546	2.19	0.028	.010981	.1951154
R1	-.2620804	.0630697	-4.16	0.000	-.3857457	-.1384151
R2	-.2914039	.0588672	-4.95	0.000	-.4068289	-.1759788
R3	-.2600921	.059621	-4.36	0.000	-.3769952	-.1431889
R4	-.3089352	.0612434	-5.04	0.000	-.4290194	-.1888509
R5	-.3379509	.0630519	-5.36	0.000	-.4615813	-.2143205
R6	-.2849778	.0617957	-4.61	0.000	-.406145	-.1638106
R8	-.217186	.0576624	-3.77	0.000	-.3302488	-.1041233
R9	-.2992388	.05913	-5.06	0.000	-.4151792	-.1832985
R10	-.3480776	.0524864	-6.63	0.000	-.4509914	-.2451637
R11	-.2463581	.0513369	-4.80	0.000	-.347018	-.1456981
R12	-.3125936	.0533044	-5.86	0.000	-.4171114	-.2080758
_cons	6.268379	.1489524	42.08	0.000	5.976317	6.56044

Figure 8.11   OLS estimates of a linear wage model for employed women

be very similar. Nevertheless the results do show some changes in the coefficients, especially for the education dummies, which have smaller regression coefficients in the Heckman model. This may be due to highly motivated workers (or, in general, workers who are better paid because of some other unobserved characteristic) being more likely to participate in the labour market. Indeed, education is an important factor in the selection equation.

Remember, however, that the two regressions have different interpretations. The OLS regression in Figure 8.11 is based on 2,961 observations and shows the actual differences that are observed in the labour market, where we observe that those women with the highest level of qualification do earn on average (exp[0.78]–1)*100= 118% higher wages than those with no qualifications. The Heckman model, on the other hand (see Figure 8.10), is based on 4,070 observations and has to be interpreted as a prediction of what the difference in earnings would be if all women, including those who do not want to participate in the labour market, were working. In this case, we would predict the difference in earning between a woman with the highest level of education and a woman with the lowest to be on average about (exp[0.66] –1)*100 = 93%. This is, however, not what we currently observe in the labour market, since not all women work.

The default in Stata is to estimate the Heckman selection model using maximum likelihood. Sometimes it may be difficult to find the value of the coefficients that maximise the likelihood function (the model may not converge). In these cases it may help to specify feasible initial values. One option is to estimate the main equation using OLS and then use these coefficients as the initial values. Hence, we would use the `regress` command, save the estimated coefficients (`e(b)`) in a matrix, say `intB` using the command `matrix intB = e(b)`, and estimate the model by maximum likelihood using these as initial values with the option `from(intB)`. As a last resort, the option `two-step` requires Stata to use the two-stage estimation method instead of the maximum likelihood.

From Stata 13 we can estimate Heckman selection models in which the main dependent variable is binary (for example, working in a certain occupation) rather than continuous (such as wages) using the command `heckprobit`.

8.7 Endogeneity

Even when they are the results of a regression model, the correlations between dependent and explanatory variables do not necessarily imply causality (that is, the dependent variable is directly influenced by the explanatory variable). Some of the explanatory variables may be endogenous. This means that we do not know if it is X that influences Y; Y that influences X; or whether there is a third factor that influences both X and Y.

A classic example is the endogeneity of years of education in the wage regression (see Harmon et al. 2003). It is plausible that unobserved factors such as ability have an influence both on the level of education and on wages. More able people are more likely to reach higher levels of education and more likely to obtain higher wages, independently of their level of education. In this case it is not education that directly influences wages, but some other unobserved factors (omitted variables) that affect both wages and education in the same direction and therefore lead to the positive correlation between wages and education. If this is the case, the explanatory endogenous variable (years of education) is correlated with the error term and OLS estimations would be inconsistent. This type of endogeneity is due to unobserved common factors. Another type of endogeneity is due to two-way causation. For example, employers may reward job tenure of their employees with higher wages; at the same time, people tend to remain in jobs that pay higher wages, thus increasing their job tenure.

In the case of endogeneity we can use a two-stage least squares estimator, provided that we can find good (valid) instruments. Instruments are variables that do not belong in the model (wage equation in this case) since they are not correlated with the dependent variable, but are correlated with the endogenous explanatory variables (years of education or job tenure). Furthermore, good instruments should not be correlated with the error term in the main (wage) model (as this is the problem that affects the endogenous variable). There is a vast literature on endogeneity and valid instruments, which we cannot summarise here. For further information see the special issue of the *Journal of Econometrics* (2007, issue 139), Verbeek (2008), Wooldridge (2009) and more recently Imbens (2014).

In simple terms, to test for endogeneity we can follow four steps: (1) We regress the variable which might be endogenous on all instruments (including the other non-endogenous explanatory variables) and check that the instruments are good predictors for the dependent variable in this model. (2) We compute the residuals of the model. (3) We include the residuals in the original equation. If the regression coefficient of the residuals is statistically significant, then the variable is endogenous. (4) We estimate the model in Stata using the `ivregress` or `ivreg2` commands.

We can test that the instruments are good predictors for the endogenous variable by regressing the set of instruments on the endogenous variable or by using the set of tests (like the Stock–Yogo test) reported by Stata. It is more difficult to test that the instruments are uncorrelated with the dependent variable in the main model. One option is the Sargan test provided by Stata. The post-estimation commands for `ivregress` include exogeneity tests for the variable that we think may be endogenous (`estat endogenous`); tests to determine weak instruments (`estat firststage`); and tests for over-identifying restrictions (`estat overid`). Look at the Stata help for more details.

8.8 Summary and Suggestions for Further Reading

In this chapter we have discussed how to estimate models for continuous and for discrete dependent variables, how to compute different types of standard errors, linear and non-linear tests on the coefficients, how to obtain predictions, residuals, and their meaning.

Key points

- If the dependent variable is continuous, use the command `regress`.
- If the dependent variable is not continuous, use probit or logit models, and consider using a linear probability model.
- The regression coefficients of probit and logit models are not directly interpretable: compute marginal effects or odds ratios.
- If you suspect that your analysis is based on a non-random sample of the population and the selection is based on observed factors, use appropriate weights; if the selection is based on unobserved factors, consider estimating a Heckman selection model. Remember, however, that the Heckman selection model has a different interpretation than the standard regression model.

Suggestions for further reading

- For a clear and complete description of categorical and limited dependent variables and the models commonly used for these types of variables, see Long, J.S. (1997) *Regression Models for Categorical and Limited Dependent Variables*. London, Sage.
- Winkelmann and Boes cover a wide range of estimation techniques that are often used when using cross-section micro-data: Winkelmann, R. and Boes, S. (2006) *Analysis of Microdata*. Heidelberg, Springer.
- There is a vast literature on endogeneity:

  o In their Chapter 4, Angrist and Pischke offer a good discussion of endogeneity issues and how the literature has used different types of instrumental variables in the context of the impact of schooling on wages: Angrist, J.D. and Pischke, J.-S. (2009) *Mostly Harmless Econometrics – An Empiricist's Companion*. Princeton, NJ, Princeton University Press.

  o For a more statistically oriented discussion of instrumental variables, see Imbens, G.W. (2014) Instrumental Variables: An Econometrician's Perspective. NBER Working Paper 19983.

  o For a historical perspective on endogeneity and a discussion of the various techniques that have been used in the labour economics literature to make causal inference, see van der Klaauw, B. (2014) From Micro Data to Causality: Forty Years of Empirical Labor Economics. IZA Discussion Paper No. 8047.

- For an extensive summary of the literature surrounding the Mincer equation and on the different factors that affect individual wages, see Grossbard, S. (ed.) (2006) *Jacob Mincer – A Pioneer of Modern Labor Economics*. Berlin, Springer.
- You can also find some rather entertaining introductions to the findings of the literature on happiness, coming from different disciplines:

  o Layard R. (2005) *Happiness – Lessons from a New Science*. London , Penguin.
  o Powdthavee, N. (2011) *The Happiness Equation*. London, Icon Books.

9

ANALYSIS OF PANEL DATA FOR CONTINUOUS DEPENDENT VARIABLES

Aim

This chapter discusses estimation methods for panel data where the dependent variable is continuous. It shows how to estimate pooled models and how to account for individual unobserved heterogeneity; how to compute different types of standard errors, linear and non-linear tests for model selection; and how to obtain predictions, residuals, etc. The techniques are illustrated using as examples wage equations estimated using BHPS data for the period 1991–2008.

9.1 Introduction

The most important characteristic of panel data is that we have repeated observations per individual. Following individuals over time allows us to better disentangle causality and to better control for unobserved individual heterogeneity (that is, differences across individuals that do not change over time and which are not observed by the researcher, such as ability, motivation or perseverance). Various estimation techniques have been developed for panel data; econometrically, these estimation techniques are the same for balanced and unbalanced panels. Hence, when doing analysis we normally use unbalanced panels, which allows us to use a much larger number of observations and to increase efficiency.

In this chapter we focus on the marriage wage premium: wage differentials between married and non-married people. Typically, the literature finds that married people have on average higher wages than non-married people. It is possible that marriage makes people more productive, for example the division of household chores between partners may free up more time to work in the labour market. However, it is also possible that those who get married have specific characteristics, such as motivation or reliability, which are not measured in the data but are likely to affect both wages and the probability of getting married (see Bardasi and Taylor 2008). If we have only one observation per person, we cannot disentangle this type of endogeneity problem, unless we have good instruments. An advantage of using panel data to analyse the marriage wage premium is that we can observe the trajectory of wages and marital status over time, and how individual wages change – or not – following a change in marital status.

9.2 Modelling Unobserved Individual Heterogeneity

9.2.1 Pooled Estimations

For our model we can go back to the wage equation that we used in Chapter 8, namely Equation (8.1). With longitudinal data we now have two subscripts: i, which identifies individuals; and t, which identifies time (waves of interviews). Hence, each observation refers to a certain wave for a certain individual:

$$
\begin{aligned}
\text{Log wage}_{it} = {} & \beta_0 + \beta_1 \text{Age}_{it} + \beta_2 \text{Age}_{it}\text{ square} + \beta_3 \text{Female dummy}_{it} + \\
& \beta_4 \text{Married dummy}_{it} + \beta_5 \text{Qualification dummies}_{it} + \\
& \beta_6 \text{Region dummies}_{it} + \beta_7 \text{Year dummies}_{it} + \text{error term}_{it}
\end{aligned}
\tag{9.1}
$$

Note the inclusion of year dummies in this equation. There are many practical reasons to include year dummies among the explanatory variables. For example, nominal wages tend to increase over time even though real wages might not (for example, because of inflation), so that it would not be appropriate to compare wages in 1991 with wages in 2008. One solution is to compute real wages by deflating nominal wages using indices of inflation. The problem is that there are different indices that may lead to different results and the choice between them may sometimes be arbitrary. Furthermore, nominal wages may also increase because of other factors that are specific to a certain year but are not related to inflation. Year dummies would capture most of these unspecified factors. Since interviews in the BHPS have been carried out over few months (most of them between October and December), we may consider adding dummies for the month of the interview if we suspect seasonal or monthly factors may have an influence on our analysis. For the purpose of this exercise we do not include dummies for the month of the interview.

In a similar way to the time dummies, as already mentioned in Chapter 8, the region dummies should pick up most region-specific characteristics.

Since for the purpose of this chapter we are interested in the marriage wage premium, we focus here on the dummy variable for whether married. As usual, we start by opening the dataset saved at the end of Chapter 4 and by checking that all variables needed for the analysis have been created. If not, we need to create the necessary variables.

Write the commands and compare with the do file in the online appendix

It is also good practice to double-check that the variables we have created have the expected values. For example, a tabulation of employment status when wage data are not missing shows that the wage variable we are using in this exercise (paygu) is missing for self-employed people (information on labour earnings of self-employed are in the variable jspayg). Hence, the self-employed are automatically excluded from this analysis.

If we assume that 'error term$_{it}$' in Equation (9.1) is a random error term, with mean 0 and constant variance, we can estimate the wage equation using OLS even if we have multiple observations per individual (pooled model). We can estimate this model using the regress command. Remember, however, that observations referring to the same person are likely to be correlated; hence, we should specify that the standard errors are clustered by individual (using the variable pid).

Write the commands and compare with the do file in the online appendix

The model in Equation (9.1) has one single component in the error term (error term$_{it}$).[1] Although, for example, the time dummies and the region dummies allow us to have different intercepts for years and regions, all respondents living in a certain region in a certain year will have the same intercept. The advantage of panel data is that we can rewrite the error term to include an individual-specific, time-invariant component, which allows us to take into account individual unobserved heterogeneity.

9.2.2 Individual Unobserved Heterogeneity

When we have panel data we can rewrite the model in Equation (9.1) to include individual heterogeneity as in Equation (9.2) below. In this equation we assume that 'error term$_{it}$' includes a time-invariant individual component:

---

[1]Some authors distinguish between one- and two-way error component models. Technically, the year dummies would be considered as the second component. This does not have any implications for the models discussed here, but see Baltagi (2009) for more details. Here we use the term 'component' in a general way.

error term$_{it}$ = α_i + u_{it}; we assume that u_{it} is normally distributed, with mean 0 and constant variance. Also note that the term α_i does not have a t subscript, so that, in a similar way to the year dummies, it captures those individual-specific, time-invariant factors that are not otherwise captured by the other time-varying individual characteristics included in the model (such as marital status). Such characteristics may include for example motivation, reliability or ability, if we are prepared to assume that these characteristics are constant over people's lives. In general, all time-invariant individual characteristics, such as sex or ethnicity, may be collinear with the individual unobserved heterogeneity (α_i) and dropped from the models if we use certain estimation techniques (more details below).

After modelling the individual unobserved heterogeneity, Equation (9.1) becomes:

$$\text{Log wage}_{it} = \beta_0 + \beta_1 \text{Age}_{it} + \beta_2 \text{Age}_{it} \text{ square} + \beta_3 \text{Female dummy}_{it} +$$
$$\beta_4 \text{Married dummy}_{it} + \beta_5 \text{Qualification dummies}_{it} + \qquad (9.2)$$
$$\beta_6 \text{Region dummies}_{it} + \beta_7 \text{Year dummies}_{it} + \alpha_i + u_{it}$$

Depending on the assumptions that we are prepared to make about α_i, we can estimate the parameters of Equation (9.2) using different types of estimators. A common approach is to interpret the α_i as individual-specific dummies (compare with the pooled model, Equation (9.1), which restricts α_i to be the same across all individuals) and estimate the model by OLS; this is often called the least squares dummy variables (LSDV) estimator. In this case the individual effects are essentially additional explanatory dummy variables in the model, which may or may not be correlated with some of the other explanatory variables.

When the number of individuals is large, and especially when it is much larger than the number of waves, the model may become too cumbersome to estimate (this is called the 'incidental parameter problem', see Verbeek 2008). It can be shown that we can obtain exactly the same estimator for the β coefficients by transforming the model using the 'within transformation' (see Baltagi 2009 or Hsiao 2003) and then estimating the transformed model by OLS:

Original model: $y_{it} = \alpha_i + \beta x_{it} + u_{it}$ (9.3)

Within transformation: $(y_{it} - y_{i\cdot}) = \beta(x_{it} - x_{i\cdot}) + (u_{it} - u_{i\cdot})$ (9.4)

where $y_{i\cdot}$, $x_{i\cdot}$ and $u_{i\cdot}$ are the means of y_{it}, x_{it} and u_{it} over time, respectively. Since the average of α_i is exactly α_i, the individual-specific, time-invariant effects drop out of the equation. This transformation allows us to estimate the model without having to include dummies for each individual, which is unmanageable in most household datasets. This is called the within-estimator, or fixed effects estimator. Note that in this case only those individuals whose status changes over the period of analysis (only those for whom x_{it} is different than $x_{i\cdot}$) contribute to the estimation of the regression coefficient. Furthermore, all those variables that do not vary over the observation time (such as gender or ethnicity) drop out of the model. This means that models estimated by fixed effects will not be useful if we want to isolate the impact of explanatory variables that do not vary over time.

An alternative transformation consists of taking first differences (the value of the variable at time t minus its value at the previous period):

Original model: $y_{it} = \alpha_i + \beta x_{it} + u_{it}$ (9.5)

First difference: $(y_{it} - y_{i\,t-1}) = \beta(x_{it} - x_{it-1}) + (u_{it} - u_{it-1})$ (9.6)

Also in this case, since α_i does not vary over time, it drops out of the equation. The OLS estimator of this transformed model produces consistent estimates of the β coefficients and is called the first difference estimator. Note that in this case only respondents with consecutive observations contribute to the estimation of the regression coefficients: data for a respondent who only answers at every other wave are not used in the first difference estimator (but they are used by the fixed effects estimator). Without going into further detail (but for the econometrics behind it see Baltagi 2009 or Hsiao 2003) we can note that the conditions for consistency of the first difference estimator are slightly weaker than for the fixed effects estimator, although the fixed effects estimator tends to be more efficient. For consistency the first difference estimator requires the first difference of the error term $(u_{it} - u_{it-1})$ to be uncorrelated and homoscedastic; however, if the error term (u_{it}) is uncorrelated and homoscedastic, then the fixed effects estimator is more efficient. In general, if the fixed effects and first difference estimators give very different results, then the assumption that the error term is uncorrelated and homoscedastic may be problematic (see Verbeek 2008). However, if there are only two observations per individual, then the fixed effects and first different estimators are identical (see Wooldridge 2002).

A common alternative to the fixed effects and first difference estimators is the random effects estimator. In a random effects model we assume that the term α_i comes from an IID (Independent and Identically Distributed) distribution with mean 0 and constant variance, and that α_i is uncorrelated with the other explanatory variables. In the random effects model α_i is estimated as part of the error term and picks up all the correlation that is attributed to time. This model can be consistently estimated by OLS, fixed effects, first difference and random effects methods. Because of the structure of the error term, the pooled OLS estimator is consistent, but the estimated standard errors are incorrect unless robust standard errors are estimated. The random effects model (sometimes also called the multilevel model) is generally estimated by generalised least squares (GLS), which accounts for variation both within individuals and between them, or using maximum likelihood (ML) techniques. As these estimation methods take into account the individual-specific, time-invariant term, α_i in the error term, the random effects estimator is more efficient than all estimators in the class of estimators consistent under the same conditions (including pooled OLS, fixed effects and first difference estimators).

In Stata the command to estimate fixed and random effects models is xtreg followed by the name of the dependent variable and the list of explanatory variables, with the options fe (for the fixed effects estimator), re (for the random effects estimator estimated using GLS) or mle (for the random effects estimator estimated using ML). Other options, such as be for random effects estimated using the between regression estimator, or pa for the population-averaged estimator, are available; check the Stata manual and Baltagi (2009) or Hsiao (2003) for more details.

To estimate a model using the first difference method we need first to compute the first difference of all (dependent and explanatory) variables, and then estimate this differenced model with OLS. As an alternative, we can estimate the model by using the command regress followed by the dependent and explanatory variables preced.ed by the time-series operator D. which computes first differences directly (see Chapter 4). In this case we have to use the option nocons since the constant should be differenced out. We can also estimate cluster-robust standard errors by specifying the option vce(cluster pid) (see Cameron and Trivedi 2005).

Write the commands and compare with the do and log files in the online appendix

We have summarised the results of the different estimators in Table 9.1; the full set of results are in the log files in the online appendix. We discuss how to produce output tables similar to Table 9.1 in Chapter 14.

Table 9.1   Results of panel estimation of the wage equation

	(1) OLS	(2) Fixed Effects	(3) First Difference	(4) Random Effects GLS	(5) Random Effects ML
Age	0.129*	0.104*	0.133*	0.132*	0.132*
	(0.002)	(0.005)	(0.005)	(0.001)	(0.001)
Age square	−0.001*	−0.001*	−0.002*	−0.002*	−0.002*
	(0.000)	(0.000)	(0.000)	(0.000)	(0.000)
Female	−0.595*			−0.574*	−0.574*
	(0.009)			(0.009)	(0.009)
Married	0.084*	0.037*	0.003	0.059*	0.060*
	(0.010)	(0.006)	(0.006)	(0.005)	(0.005)
Higher degree	0.856*	1.055*	0.714*	0.920*	0.918*
	(0.028)	(0.030)	(0.042)	(0.020)	(0.019)
First degree	0.773*	1.037*	0.641*	0.920*	0.918*
	(0.018)	(0.023)	(0.030)	(0.013)	(0.013)
HND, HNC, teaching qualif.	0.580*	0.613*	0.373*	0.578*	0.577*
	(0.020)	(0.026)	(0.032)	(0.015)	(0.015)
A level	0.383*	0.466*	0.284*	0.420*	0.419*
	(0.016)	(0.021)	(0.026)	(0.012)	(0.012)

	(1) OLS	(2) Fixed Effects	(3) First Difference	(4) Random Effects GLS	(5) Random Effects ML
O level	0.255*	0.038	0.075*	0.149*	0.150*
	(0.015)	(0.021)	(0.025)	(0.011)	(0.011)
CSE	0.147*	0.184*	0.065	0.192*	0.192*
	(0.023)	(0.035)	(0.043)	(0.018)	(0.018)
F-test that all	1.00	14.33			
$u_i = 0$	(assumed)				
Probability		0.000			
corr(u_i,		−0.304		0.00	
Xb)				(assumed)	
Hausman test (difference in coeff. not systematic)				955.43	
Probability				0.000	
R^2	0.423	0.351	0.031		
Observations	118,152	118,152	91,923	118,152	118,152

Standard errors in parentheses; + significant at 5%; * significant at 1%.
Other explanatory variables: region and year dummies.

Table 9.1 shows that while some of the coefficients are relatively similar across estimators, others are rather different. For example, according to the OLS estimator, marriage increases wages by 8.7%. When we include individual fixed effects in the model to account for individual unobserved heterogeneity and estimate the model using fixed effects, the impact of marriage on wages decreases to only 3.8%. The impact of marriage is 6% to 6.1% based on the random effects estimates; the results of the two random effects estimators (see columns (4) and (5) of Table 9.1) are very similar. The first difference estimates of the coefficients are extremely small and not statistically significant. As expected, a coefficient for the female dummy is estimated when using the OLS and random effects methods, but not when using the fixed effects (and first difference) methods. This is because this dummy is a time-invariant individual characteristic, which drops out from the model when we compute the within (fixed effects) and the first difference transformations. Hence, when we use the fixed effects estimator we can only identify the impact of variables that change over time. The random effects estimator, instead, estimates a regression coefficient for all variables, even those that are time invariant.

Most people complete their education by the time they enter the labour market. But as a handful of people do change their level of education after they have entered the labour market, the dummies for the level of education do not drop out of the estimation. However, this means that the coefficients of these variables are identified by a very small number of observations (individuals) and may not be very reliable. We could restrict the sample to slightly older people (for example, by keeping in the models only people aged 23 or over rather than people aged 16 or over) who are likely to have completed full-time education, and drop the qualification dummies from the models. Here we would then consider the level of education as part of the individual time-invariant characteristics, included in α_i.

Note that a constant term is reported for the model estimated using fixed effects. This is because Stata estimates the model after placing a constraint that the sum of all individual fixed effects, α_i, is zero (see discussion of this issue in Stata FAQ online).

How do we choose among the different estimators? Surely we cannot base our choice on R^2, which is not even provided for the model estimated using random effects. We have to keep in mind that each of these estimation methods requires different assumptions to produce consistent estimates of the model, which we can test. The choice of the estimation method relies on which of these assumptions are satisfied.

9.2.3 Choosing the Right Estimator

If we use OLS we restrict all α_i to be equal to zero. In the `log` file of the online appendix we can see that in the top left part of the output of the fixed effects estimator (`xtreg , fe`), Stata provides an 'F test that all u_i = 0', which we have also reported in Table 9.1. The value of the test is 14.33 and the associated probability is 0.000. This means that the hypothesis is rejected, that the α_i are not zero and should therefore be included in the model by means of fixed or random effects estimators. Another method to test whether the α_i are equal to zero is by performing the Breusch and Pagan Lagrangian multiplier test after estimating the model using the random effects estimator using the command `xttest0`. In summary, the pooled OLS estimator is either not consistent (if the α_i are correlated with the explanatory variables) or it is consistent but not efficient (if the α_i are not correlated with the explanatory variables).

How do we choose between fixed and random effects? If the α_i are uncorrelated with the explanatory variables, then both fixed and random effects estimators produce consistent estimates but the random effects estimator is often preferred because it is more efficient than the fixed effects estimator. If the α_i are correlated with some of the explanatory variables, the random effects estimator is inconsistent and the fixed effects estimator should be preferred. Rather than a direct test on the correlation between the α_i and the explanatory variables, we use the Hausman test to analyse whether the results of the random effects estimator are systematically different than the results of the fixed effects estimator. If they are, it means that the random effects estimator is inconsistent and the fixed effects estimator, which is more robust, should be preferred (see, for example, Verbeek 2008).

We can implement the Hausman test in a few steps: (1) Estimate the fixed effects model and save the results using the command `estimates store` followed by the name of the new results. (2) Estimate the random effects model and save the results using the command `estimates store` in a further result.

(3) Compare the two estimators using the command hausman followed by the name of the results with the results of the fixed effects model, and by the name of the results with the results of the random effects model. For example, hausman Model_FE Model_RE.

Write the commands and compare with the do and log files in the online appendix

The Hausman test is a general test used to compare two different estimators; the comparison of fixed and random effects is only one of the possible uses of this test (see Hausman 1978). We can use the same command to compare different types of estimators, but we need to remember that the first variable should be the estimator which is consistent even when the hypothesis (in this case correlation between α_i and the explanatory variables) is incorrect, while the second variable should be the estimator which is more efficient if the hypothesis is correct, but inconsistent if the hypothesis is incorrect. The full set of results is in the log file in the online appendix. In Table 9.1 we have reported only the result of the test, which is 955.43 and has a probability of 0.000. This means that the hypothesis is rejected; the difference between the coefficients of the random and fixed effects estimators is systematic. This suggests that there is a correlation between the α_i and some of the explanatory variables; the random effects estimator is inconsistent, and the fixed effects one should be preferred.

We may prefer to use a random effects model if we are interested in the impact of variables that are time invariant, such as gender, ethnicity or country of birth, which would be dropped when using a fixed effects estimator (see Table 9.1). Section 9.4 discusses how the coefficients of time-invariant factors can be consistently estimated when the assumption of no correlation between α_i and the explanatory variables is relaxed.

9.3 A Note on Multilevel Models

A commonly used estimation technique is multilevel analysis. This type of analysis is usually used to investigate datasets that are hierarchical and in which some of the observations are nested within groups, such as the analysis of pupils, nested within schools. In these hierarchical models the pupils are considered as the lowest level and the school is at the higher level (some researchers identify more than two hierarchies and therefore levels). The basic idea is that pupils going to the same school share a common environment and that both the characteristics of the pupil and the environment (in this case the school) contribute to the outcome of interest (for example, pupil's grades). For an introduction to multilevel models we refer to Hox (2002).

Panel data can be seen as types of multilevel data, in which the multiple observations over time which refer to the same individual (lower level) are nested within individuals (individuals are the higher level). For example, if we have five waves of data (interviews) for each person, these five interviews are nested within the data for that person.

Without going into too much detail, the random effects model we discussed in Section 9.2 is equivalent to a random intercept multilevel model. Within the multilevel framework, random effects models also give us the possibility to decompose the 'random effects' into different 'random coefficients', which, in panel data, can be used to explore growth curve patterns as discussed in detail, for example, in Rabe-Hesketh and Skrondal (2012).

For linear dependent variables, multilevel random intercept models can be estimated in Stata using the command `xtmixed` (or `mixed` from Stata 13). For the case of non-linear models (see Chapter 10) the corresponding command for mixed effects logistic regression is `xtmelogit` (or `meqrlogit` from Stata 13), while the command `gllamm` fits generalised linear latent and mixed models (for more details see Rabe-Hesketh and Skrondal 2012).

9.4 Further Estimators

Going back to the models estimated in Section 9.2, one of the drawbacks of the fixed effects estimator is that we cannot estimate the impact of time-invariant characteristics such as gender or ethnicity. If the analysis of ethnicity is the aim of our research, we may want to use a random effects estimator, even if the Hausman test suggests that there is a correlation between individual-specific effects and some of the explanatory variables (and the random effects estimator is inconsistent). Mundlak (1978) suggests a method to estimate such a model consistently.

We can relax the assumption of independence between the observable time-varying characteristics and u_{it} by including in the model the individual mean of the time-varying covariates. Mundlak (1978) models the dependence between u_{it} (Equation (9.2)) and the other explanatory variables by assuming that the regression function of u_{it} is linear in the means of all the time-varying covariates. In practice, this is equivalent to a model in which we include the mean of the time-varying covariates among the explanatory variables and which we estimate using a random effects estimator (see also Wooldridge 2010). An example of a correlated random effects estimation is in the `do` and `log` files in the online appendix.

Although panel data can go some way to reduce problems of endogeneity, especially when endogeneity is due to omitted variables that are time invariant, we may still need to use instrumental variables if, for example, we have omitted variables that vary over time. Provided that we can find good instruments, Stata provides an instrumental variable estimator also for the case of panel data; look at the commands xtivreg and xtivreg2. These commands allow the estimation of a fixed effects model (using the fe option); of a first difference estimator (using the fd option); of GLS random effects model (using the re option); and others.

When multiple observations are available per individual, as in the case of panel data, we may want to estimate dynamic models in which the lag of the dependent variable appears among the explanatory variables:

$$y_{it} = X_{it}'\beta + \gamma y_{it-1} + \alpha_i + u_{it} \qquad (9.7)$$

In this case y_{it-1} depends on α_i irrespective of the estimator we choose; the estimators described in Section 9.2 will be inconsistent (see Verbeek 2008). Instrumental variable estimators have been suggested for these types of models, where the instruments are further lags of y_{it} and additional moment conditions (for details see Anderson and Hsiao 1981, 1982; Arellano and Bond 1991). For this situation Stata provides the command xtabond, which fits the estimator suggested by Arellano and Bond (1991); the commands xtdpd and xtdpdsys fit the estimators based on Arellano and Bover (1995) suggested by Blundell and Bond (1998); look at the Stata manual for more details.

9.5 Different Types of Standard Errors and Other Post-Estimation Commands

Similar to what we have seen in Chapter 8, the command xtreg also allows the computation of different types of standard errors using the vce() option, which allows robust, clustered standard errors, as well as standard errors computed via bootstrap or jackknife methods. The different estimators (fixed effects, random effects, between estimator) may allow only some of these options; check the Stata manual for details.

The predict set of commands works in essentially the same way as in the case of cross-section data; in this case, however, we have more options. For example, the option xb computes the linear prediction ($\alpha_0 + \beta x_{it}$ where α_0 is the overall constant); the option stdp computes the standard error of the linear prediction, excluding the variance due to uncertainty about the estimate of the fixed effects (α_i). The option xbu computes the prediction of $\alpha_0 + \alpha_i + \beta x_{it}$, that is the prediction including the fixed or random component. We can also compute both parts of the residuals: the option u computes the fixed or random effects (α_i), while e refers to the error term (u_{it}); ue computes the prediction of $\alpha_i + u_{it}$.

Similar to the case of cross-section data, we can compute linear and non-linear estimates (lincom and nlcom); Wald tests for linear and non-linear hypotheses (test and testnl); likelihood ratio tests (lrtest); and marginal effects after non-linear models (margins). Additional post-estimation commands are available; among these, xttest0 computes the Breusch–Pagan Lagrange Multiplier test for random effects.

9.6 Storing Text in Local Macros

All models in Table 9.1 include the same set of explanatory variables. We can either type the name of all variables every time we write the command, or save the list of explanatory variables in a local macro. To do this, first we define the content of our local macro, then we use it in the regression:

```
local ExplVariables = ///
   "age Female Married Q1 Q2 Q3 Q4 Q5 Q6"
xtreg LnW `ExplVariables', fe
```

Note that when we define the local macro, all the content which is within quotation marks has to be written in one single line. In other words, the three forward slashes cannot be used within the quotation marks because Stata would not recognise them.

9.7 Summary and Suggestions for Further Reading

In Chapter 8 we discussed various estimation methods that are commonly used in the case of cross-section data. In this chapter we have extended the discussion to estimation methods for panel data with continuous dependent variables. We have discussed how to account for individual unobserved heterogeneity, how to compute different types of standard errors, and how to obtain predictions and residuals. Models for panel data in the case of binary and multinomial dependent variables are discussed in Chapter 10.

Key points

- The most commonly used estimators for (static) panel data models are fixed effects and random effects. Correlated random effects models are also gaining popularity.
- Use a Hausman test to compare fixed and random effects estimators.
- Specific estimators are needed to solve endogeneity problems in dynamic models.

Suggestions for further reading

- To refresh the econometrics of panel data you can find a gentle introduction and the main intuition behind the econometric methods in: Verbeek, M. (2008) *A Guide to Modern Econometrics*. Chichester, Wiley.
- The books by Baltagi and Hsiao give more details of the econometrics behind panel data model estimation, including proofs and derivations:

   o Baltagi, B.H. (2009) *Econometric Analysis of Panel Data*. Chichester, Wiley.
   o Hsiao, C. (2003) *Analysis of Panel Data*. Cambridge, Cambridge University Press.

- For more details on multilevel models and growth curves see the following:

   o For a general introduction on techniques for multilevel analysis see for example Hox, J. (2002) *Multilevel Analysis, Techniques and Applications*. London, Lawrence Erlbaum Associates.
   o For those interested in social and personality psychology, a useful introduction focusing on applications specific to this discipline can be found in Nezlek, J.B. (2008) An Introduction to Multilevel Modeling for *Social and Personality Psychology*. *Social and Personality Psychology Compass* 2(2): 842–60.
   o For more practical discussions on the techniques and how to apply them in Stata, see Rabe-Hesketh S. and Skrondal A. (2012) *Multilevel and Longitudinal Modeling using Stata*. College Station, TX, Stata Press.

- In Chapter 5 of the book by Angrist and Pischke you will find a good discussion of panel data models including some estimators not discussed in this chapter (for example, difference in difference estimators): Angrist, J.D. and Pischke, J.-S. (2009) *Mostly Harmless Econometrics – An Empiricist's Companion*. Princeton, NJ, Princeton University Press.

$$\bigodot 10$$

ANALYSIS OF PANEL DATA FOR DISCRETE DEPENDENT VARIABLES

Aim

This chapter discusses estimation methods for panel data where the dependent variable is discrete. It also shows how to compute relevant test and predictions. The techniques are illustrated using as examples models of employment choices and life satisfaction using BHPS data for various waves.

10.1 Introduction

As we have seen in Chapter 8, estimation methods for continuous dependent variables are not appropriate when the dependent variable is discrete. In this chapter we discuss various estimation methods that can be used for binary and multinomial ordered dependent variables, and the conditions (in addition to the ones considered for panel data methods for continuous dependent variables) that need to be satisfied for these methods to yield consistent estimates.

10.2 Panel Data Methods for Binary Dependent Variables

10.2.1 Modelling Unobserved Heterogeneity

In Chapter 8, Section 8.4, we discussed how to estimate models with binary dependent variables. In the example in Equation (8.2) the dependent variable was a dummy which has value 1 for people who are employed and 0 for those who are not employed (unemployed or out of the labour force). In the case of panel data we rewrite Equation (8.2) after including a time dimension as

$$y_{it}{}^* = \beta_1 \text{Age}_{it} + \beta_2 \text{Age}_{it} \text{ square} + \beta_3 \text{Married dummy}_{it} +$$
$$\beta_4 \text{Qualification dummies}_{it} + \beta_5 \text{Region dummies}_{it} + \qquad (10.1)$$
$$\text{error term}_{it}$$

where we observe a value of 1 if $y_{it}{}^* > 0$ and a value of 0 otherwise.

Similar to Section 8.4, y_{it} is the observed employment status and $y_{it}{}^*$ is the employment propensity for individual i at time t. The explanatory variables are also measured at different points in time, although not all variables are time varying. In a similar way to Chapter 9, we can model unobserved heterogeneity by specifying that the error term includes two components: an unobserved individual effect, α_i, that does not change over time and a time-varying part, u_{it}, so that error term$_{it} = \alpha_i + u_{it}$.

To estimate this model we combine data from the last six waves of the BHPS in long form using a similar method as in Chapter 4. We also create the dependent and explanatory variables specified in Equation (10.1).

Write the commands and compare with the do file in the online appendix

The employment decision for women is often more complicated than that of men because it is more likely to be affected by fertility decisions (see also the discussion in Section 8.6). So, for the purpose of this exercise, we restrict the analysis to men only. We can restrict the analysis to men only either by dropping all women from the dataset, or by adding 'if Female = 0' at the end of the estimation command. Deleting women from the dataset may not always be the best solution. If at some point we want to compare estimates for men with those for women it is best to use the if statement in the estimation command; this also makes the do file much more general. On the other hand, if we are estimating a large number of models, it may be more efficient to drop these cases at the beginning rather than typing 'if Female = 0' many times.

Write the commands and compare with the do file in the online appendix

To keep the analysis similar to the one discussed in Chapter 8 and to allow comparison of estimates across different models, here we estimate models similar to the ones in Chapter 8. As we mentioned in Chapter 9, since a small number of people change their education level during their working career, researchers often restrict the estimation sample to older people, who most likely have completed their education (for example, aged 23 and over). This means that education changes for very few individuals in the data and can be treated like a time-invariant variable.

10.2.2 Pooled Estimations

If we assume that the error term is independent of the explanatory variables (and that the other standard conditions for consistency of OLS estimators in cross-sectional analysis hold) and there is no individual effect, so that either $\alpha_i = 0$ or α_i is the same for all individuals, we can consistently estimate the parameters of the model specified in Equation (10.1) using a pooled model. We use a probit model if we assume the error term to be distributed as a standard normal distribution, a logit model if we assume the error term to be distributed as a standard logistic distribution, or an LPM if we assume a linear distribution. Since we have repeated observations for each individual, the error terms are correlated across observations for the same individual. We specify the vce(cluster pid) option to compute standard errors robust to this correlation and any heteroscedasticity, if present. We use the command margins after the pooled probit and logit esti-mates to produce average marginal effects of the explanatory variables.

Interaction terms can be included in the models without having to generate new variables if we use the factor variable specification. Hence, instead of using age age2 as explanatory variables we use c.age##c.age, where c. is used to specify that age is a continuous variable. In a linear model the marginal effects are the same as the coefficients. One implication of including polynomials of explanatory variables is that it is not possible to interpret the marginal effects from the coefficients even in pooled LPM (in this case the impact of the variable age has to be combined with the impact of the square of the variable age). In this case we need to use the command margins to produce total marginal effects of the interacted variables, even for linear models. Note, however, that the estimation of these marginal effects may require a long time.

Since we estimate the same model using different estimators, it is more effi-cient to store the list of explanatory variables in a local macro as we did in Section 9.6. We call this local macro vlist:

```
local vlist c.age##c.age i.Married ///
    ib6.qfachi ib7.region2
regress Employed `vlist', vce(cluster pid)
margins, dydx(*)
```

```
probit Employed `vlist', vce(cluster pid)
margins, dydx(*)
logit Employed `vlist', vce(cluster pid)
margins, dydx(*)
```

Figure 10.1 reports the average marginal effects estimated using pooled LPM, pooled probit and pooled logit models. Notice that as age and age squared are specified in the form c.age##c.age, the command margins produces marginal effects for age rather than for age and age squared separately. The results in Figure 10.1 suggest that the probability of having a job is higher for older men, and partnered men are around 12 percentage points more likely to have a job than those who are not in a partnership. People who hold a first degree or higher have a higher probability of 18 percentage points of having a job than those with no qualifications in the OLS models, but 13 percentage points to 14 percentage points in the logit and probit models. The difference is likely to do with the different (linearity) assumptions of these two models.

In Sections 10.2.3 to 10.2.5 we discuss panel data methods and compare the marginal effects estimated using all these models in Section 10.2.6. We start with a discussion of the random effects estimator. This is the one which requires most assumptions for consistency; however, if all the assumptions are met, the random effects estimator is also the most efficient one. We then sequentially relax the assumptions required by the random effects estimator and discuss more robust estimators, such as the fixed effects one.

10.2.3 Random Effects Estimators

If the same conditions specified in Section 10.2.1 hold, but the individual-specific effects (α_i) are non-zero or are different for all or some individuals, the pooled logit, probit and LPM estimators discussed in Section 10.2.1 are usually inconsistent (Greene and Hensher 2010). As already discussed in Chapter 9, if the individual effects are not correlated with the explanatory variables, the random effects probit, random effects logit and fixed effects logit estimators are all consistent (and more efficient than the corresponding fixed effects models). In Stata the commands to estimate these random effects models are:

```
xtreg Employed `vlist', re
xtprobit Employed `vlist', re
xtlogit Employed `vlist', re
```

Remember to xtset the data before using the xtset of commands.

The technical note in the Stata manual for xtlogit warns us that the random effects logit model is estimated using a method known as quadrature and that its accuracy depends to some extent on the number of integration points used. The suggestion here is to use the command quadchk to check the accuracy

```
local vlist c.age##c.age i.Married ib6.qfachi ib7.region2


regress Employed `vlist', vce(cluster pid)
... [output omitted] ...
margins, dydx(*)
... [output omitted] ...
```

		Delta-method					
		dy/dx	Std. Err.	z	P>|z|	[95% Conf. Interval]	
age		-.0066125	.0002518	-26.26	0.000	-.0071059	-.006119
1.Married		.1243932	.0090452	13.75	0.000	.1066649	.1421216
qfachi							
1st degree		.0268292	.0174785	1.53	0.125	-.007428	.0610864
hnd, hnc, teaching		-.0122428	.0200328	-0.61	0.541	-.0515063	.0270208
a level		-.0546138	.0174002	-3.14	0.002	-.0887175	-.0205101
o level		-.039106	.0173034	-2.26	0.024	-.07302	-.005192
none of these		-.1560469	.0191383	-8.15	0.000	-.1935573	-.1185365

```
... [output omitted] ...
```

Note: dy/dx for factor levels is the discrete change from the base level.

```
probit  Employed `vlist', vce(cluster pid)
... [output omitted] ...
margins, dydx(*)
... [output omitted] ...
```

		Delta-method					
		dy/dx	Std. Err.	z	P>|z|	[95% Conf. Interval]	
age		-.0034245	.0002487	-13.77	0.000	-.003912	-.002937
1.Married		.1201933	.0095102	12.64	0.000	.1015538	.1388329
qfachi							
1st degree		.0295376	.0179835	1.64	0.100	-.0057093	.0647846
hnd, hnc, teaching		.0006217	.0202531	0.03	0.976	-.0390736	.040317
a level		-.0410177	.0170014	-2.41	0.016	-.0743399	-.0076956
o level		-.0224742	.0170798	-1.32	0.188	-.05595	.0110016
none of these		-.1285039	.0190305	-6.75	0.000	-.1658031	-.0912048

Note: dy/dx for factor levels is the discrete change from the base level.

```
logit  Employed `vlist', vce(cluster pid)
... [output omitted] ...
margins, dydx(*)
... [output omitted] ...
```

		Delta-method					
		dy/dx	Std. Err.	z	P>|z|	[95% Conf. Interval]	
age		-.0031841	.0002426	-13.12	0.000	-.0036596	-.0027086
1.Married		.1194992	.0094842	12.60	0.000	.1009105	.1380879
qfachi							
1st degree		.0180684	.0178869	1.01	0.312	-.0169892	.053126
hnd, hnc, teaching		-.0073222	.0202759	-0.36	0.718	-.0470623	.0324178
a level		-.0489841	.0167023	-2.93	0.003	-.0817201	-.0162482
o level		-.0246753	.0167739	-1.47	0.141	-.0575515	.0082008
none of these		-.1317158	.0188667	-6.98	0.000	-.1686939	-.0947377

```
... [output omitted] ...
```

Note: dy/dx for factor levels is the discrete change from the base level.

Figure 10.1   Average marginal effects on the probability of being employed

of the estimation method. This command estimates the models again using different integration points (fewer and more integration points than what we have specified in the xtlogit command). If the results differ when different numbers of integration points are used, the quadrature method with that specific number of integration points used is not accurate.

How much change should we be concerned about? According to Stata:

As a rule of thumb, if the coefficients do not change by more than a relative difference of 10^{-4} (0.01%), the choice of quadrature points does not significantly affect the outcome, and the results may be confidently interpreted. However, if the results do change appreciably – greater than a relative difference of 10^{-2} (1%) – then you should question whether the model can be reliably fit using the chosen quadrature method and the number of integration points. (StataCorp 2013b: 11)

It is a good idea to add the option nooutput, so that the iteration log and output of the refitted models are not shown.

```
. quadchk, nooutput

Refitting model intpoints() =  8
Refitting model intpoints() = 16

                        Quadrature check

                  Fitted       Comparison      Comparison
                  quadrature   quadrature      quadrature
                  12 points    8 points        16 points
------------------------------------------------------------
Log               -9889.0729   -9905.2029      -9910.804
likelihood                     -16.129938      -21.731051     Difference
                                .00163109       .00219748     Relative difference
------------------------------------------------------------
Employed:          1.0712286    1.2311395       1.0488609
   age                          .15991093      -.02236764     Difference
                                .14927806      -.02088036     Relative difference
------------------------------------------------------------
Employed:         -.01322034   -.01517454      -.01295896
c.age#c.age                    -.0019542        .00026139     Difference
                                .14781726      -.01977169     Relative difference
------------------------------------------------------------
Employed:          1.4830381    1.5624925       1.5108048
1.Married                       .07945447       .02776675     Difference
                                .05357547       .01872288     Relative difference
------------------------------------------------------------
Employed:          3.6263566    4.015829        3.7556053
   1.Q1                         .38947242       .12924874     Difference
                                .10740047       .03564149     Relative difference
------------------------------------------------------------
...[output omitted]...
------------------------------------------------------------
Employed:         -.66415795   -.73083234      -.67424841
   1.R11                       -.06667439      -.01009046     Difference
                                .10038935       .01519286     Relative difference
------------------------------------------------------------
Employed:         -.97814878   -1.0476822      -.99271831
   1.R12                       -.06953338      -.01456954     Difference
                                .07108671       .01489501     Relative difference
------------------------------------------------------------
Employed:         -17.329643   -19.730431      -17.012158
   _cons                       -2.4007883       .31748473     Difference
                                .13853651      -.01832033     Relative difference
------------------------------------------------------------
lnsig2u:           3.0275874    3.2987196       2.9991716
   _cons                        .27113215      -.02841588     Difference
                                .08955386      -.00938565     Relative difference
------------------------------------------------------------
```

Figure 10.2   Excerpt from results of quadchk using less than 50 integration points

We can see from Figure 10.2 that the relative difference between the results using different integration points is greater than the acceptable range for many of the variables. Hence, we should estimate the model again after increasing the number of integration points using the option `intpoints()`, before using the `quadchk` command again. For example, we can try with 50 integration points:

```
xtlogit Employed `vlist', re intpoints(50)
quadchk, nooutput
```

The results of the command `quadchk` now show that the relative differences are in the acceptable range for all the parameters. The result of the likelihood ratio tests for the null hypothesis that the unobserved heterogeneity is zero is shown below the tables of results, and as they are statistically significant we reject the hypothesis. Since the individual effects are different across individuals the pooled estimates are inconsistent (see Cameron and Trivedi 2005: 787).

We can now compute the average marginal effects. In the case of cross-section data, the command `margins, dydx(age)` computes the marginal effects as the average (across all observations) of the change in the predicted value of the dependent variable when age changes by one unit. In the case of panel data, the marginal effects are computed by additionally setting the unobserved heterogeneity at its average value for all observations.

Write the commands and compare with the do and log files in the online appendix

10.2.4 Fixed Effects Estimators

If the assumption that the individual fixed effects are not correlated with the explanatory variables does not hold, the random effects estimator discussed in Section 10.2.3 is inconsistent.

In the case of continuous dependent variables (Chapter 9), we can consistently estimate the parameters using fixed effects and first difference methods, which eliminate the unobserved heterogeneity: the distribution of the transformed models (see Equations (9.3) and (9.4)) is independent of the unobserved heterogeneity. In the case of the logistic distribution, a particular conditional distribution of the dependent variable has been found to have the same property of independence of the unobserved heterogeneity:

$$\text{Prob} \left(y_{i1}, y_{i2}, ..., y_{iT} \mid x_i, n_i, \theta_i\right) = \text{Prob} \left(y_{i1}, y_{i2}, ..., y_{iT} \mid x_i, n_i\right) \tag{10.2}$$

where $n_i = \sum y_{it}$.

We can therefore estimate a fixed effects logit model by maximum likelihood (see Wooldridge 2002; Greene and Hensher 2010). A similar conditional distribution does not exist for the standard normal distribution. Hence, we have no way to estimate a fixed effects probit model.

The fixed effects logit estimator can be estimated in Stata using the command xtlogit. The results of this command are given in Figure 10.3.

Write the commands and compare with the do and log files in the online appendix

Figure 10.3 shows that xtlogit produces some notes of warning (these are not error messages). The first note specifies that the data include multiple positive outcomes. This is the case when the dependent variable does not change over time, for example if some people are employed in all the waves we observe. Those observations where the dependent variable does not change are not used for the estimation of the fixed effects logit model. The second note specifies that

```
. xtlogit Employed c.age##c.age Married Q1-Q5 R1-R6 R8-R12, fe
note: multiple positive outcomes within groups encountered.
note: 7130 groups (30832 obs) dropped because of all positive or
      all negative outcomes.
note: R12 omitted because of no within-group variance.

Iteration 0:   log likelihood =   -2680.58
...

Conditional fixed-effects logistic regression    Number of obs     =      7486
Group variable: pid                               Number of groups  =      1463

                                                  Obs per group: min =         2
                                                                 avg =       5.1
                                                                 max =         6

                                                  LR chi2(18)       =   1103.35
Log likelihood  = -2265.8525                      Prob > chi2       =    0.0000

-------------------------------------------------------------------------------
    Employed |      Coef.   Std. Err.      z    P>|z|     [95% Conf. Interval]
-------------+-----------------------------------------------------------------
         age |   .9038244   .0492833    18.34   0.000     .8072309    1.000418
             |
 c.age#c.age |  -.0124403     .00056   -22.22   0.000    -.0135378   -.0113427
             |
     Married |   .1434521   .1787123     0.80   0.422    -.2068175    .4937218
          Q1 |   4.918604   .8591001     5.73   0.000     3.234799    6.602409
          Q2 |   3.026077   .9714984     3.11   0.002     1.121975    4.930179
          Q3 |   1.599133   .7128868     2.24   0.025     .2019006    2.996365
          Q4 |  -.3864567   .6815959    -0.57   0.571    -1.72236     .9494468
          Q5 |  -.7382407   1.063637    -0.69   0.488    -2.82293     1.346449
          R1 |  -.5165676   1.128736    -0.46   0.647    -2.728849    1.695714
          R2 |  -.9780104    .826784    -1.18   0.237    -2.598477    .6424565
          R3 |   -1.45619   .9938738    -1.47   0.143    -3.404147    .4917666
          R4 |   .0936151   .7931879     0.12   0.906    -1.461005    1.648235
          R5 |  -1.816572   .8202692    -2.21   0.027    -3.42427    -.2088738
          R6 |  -1.014925   .7231036    -1.40   0.160    -2.432182    .4023323
          R8 |   .6846618   .7008862     0.98   0.329    -.6890498    2.058373
          R9 |  -.2659209   .7392506    -0.36   0.719    -1.714826    1.182984
         R10 |  -.4788559   .9167955    -0.52   0.601    -2.275742     1.31803
         R11 |  -1.043017   .8134066    -1.28   0.200    -2.637265    .5512305
         R12 |          0  (omitted)
-------------------------------------------------------------------------------
```

Figure 10.3   Fixed effects logit estimation results

we have 7,130 individuals for whom this is the case, amounting to 30,832 person-wave observations. The third note specifies that in the data almost nobody moves in and out of Northern Ireland (the R12 dummy) and hence the R12 dummy is perfectly collinear with (some of) the other explanatory variables and therefore dropped from the estimation model. We can directly check that the number of observations for which the employment status does not change is 7,130 and that nobody moves in and out of Northern Ireland (the variable R12 does not change over time).

Write the commands and compare with the do and log files in the online appendix

The fixed effects logit model is also called conditional logistic regression for matched case–control groups. Although we use the xtlogit command to estimate the fixed effects logit model and the command clogit to estimate the conditional logit model, these are essentially the same method, and computationally xtlogit and clogit give the same results. Compare the results of the xtlogit and clogit commands.

Write the commands and compare with the do and log files in the online appendix

Note that the model that economists refer to as the conditional logit model (McFadden 1974) is different from the command we have just discussed, and is estimated using the Stata command asclogit (see Section 8.5.2).

Next, we may want to estimate the marginal effects. However, in this case, Stata issues an error message ('default predict option not appropriate with margins') saying that the marginal effects cannot be computed. For the fixed effects logit model we can only compute average marginal effects for the special case where the unobserved heterogeneity is zero. This can be specified as margins, dydx(age) predict(pu0). However, these marginal effects are of little value. Check the discussion on the Stata website. Hence, instead of computing marginal effects, we may prefer for the fixed effects logit model to report odds ratios, by specifying the option or.

10.2.5 Mundlak Correction

If we want to estimate a probit model but do not want to assume that the unobserved heterogeneity is not correlated with the explanatory variables, we can use the method suggested by Mundlak (1978) to produce consistent estimates of the parameter (see also Section 9.3). This method can be used to consistently estimate the parameters of random effects model where we want to relax the assumption that the explanatory variables are correlated with the unobserved heterogeneity.

For the case of balanced panels, Mundlak (1978) has shown that a model including the mean of the time-varying covariates estimated by random effects is consistent even when there is a correlation between the unobserved heterogeneity and the explanatory variables. Wooldridge (2010) shows that these models can be extended to the case of unbalanced panels if we include in the model time dummies and their means. The model becomes

$$y_{it}^* = \alpha_0 + \beta_1 \text{Age}_{it} + \beta_2 \text{Age}_{it} \text{ square} + \beta_3 \text{Married dummy}_{it} + \\ \beta_4 \text{Qualification dummies}_{it} + \beta_5 \text{Region dummies}_{it} + \\ \beta_6 \text{Wave dummies}_{it} + \alpha_i + \varepsilon_{it} \qquad (10.3)$$

where

$$\alpha_i = \alpha_0 + \alpha_1 (\text{Mean of time-varying explanatory} \\ \text{variables}) + \theta_i \qquad (10.4)$$

where θ_i is normally distributed and independent of the explanatory variables and ε_{it} is the error term for each i and t. The random effects estimator for this model is a consistent estimator of the parameters of the original model.

To implement this method in Stata, we first need to create the mean values of the time-varying explanatory variables and then estimate a random effects probit model including these mean values among the explanatory variables.

Write the commands and compare with the do file in the online appendix

10.2.6 Comparing Different Models

In Table 10.1 we report the marginal effects for the variable `Married`, obtained using different estimators. These marginal effects suggest that married men are more likely to be employed than non-married ones. In the random effects probit estimator with Mundlak correction, however, the marginal effects are not statistically significant, thus suggesting no differences in the probability of being employed between married and non-married men. Similarly, from all the fixed effects estimators we cannot conclude that married men are more likely to be employed than non-married men.

The large differences between the pooled and the random effects estimators are an indication that the pooled models may be misspecified and that the individual effects are not constant across individuals; this is also confirmed by the tests we discussed in Section 10.2.4. Given that the marginal effect of marital status becomes statistically insignificant in the fixed effects estimators, it is possible that the positive effect of marital status on employment in the other models

Table 10.1   Average marginal effects of being married on the probability of having a job

Average marginal effect	Married dummy	Number of observations
Pooled LPM	0.124* (0.0091)	38,318
Pooled probit	0.120* (0.0095)	38,318
Pooled logit	0.119* (0.0095)	38,318
Random effects LPM	0.067* (0.0060)	38,318
Random effects probit	0.818* (0.0674)	38,318
Random effects logit	1.483* (0.1193)	38,318
Random effects probit with Mundlak correction	0.099 (0.0959)	38,318
Fixed effects LPM	0.009 (0.008)	38,318
Odds ratio		
Multinomial fixed effects logit	1.154 (0.206)	7,486
Conditional fixed effects logit	1.154 (0.206)	7,486

Standard errors in parentheses; * significant at 1%.

may be due to selection: unobserved individual traits which increase both the marriageability and employability of individuals may be driving this difference.

In comparing different types of estimators, particularly non-linear ones, where marginal effects vary over the distribution of the explanatory variables, it is sometimes useful to predict outcomes for different values of the explanatory variable instead of estimating average marginal effects. We can use margins (see Sections 8.4 and 8.5) and marginsplot (see Sections 14.5.2) to produce and plot the predicted probability for different types of individuals. For example, we could plot the predicted probability of being employed for married and not married men across different ages. Although we cannot compute meaningful marginal effects for the fixed effects logit model, we can still use a Hausman test to decide whether to use the random or the fixed effects logit estimates. We can also use the Hausman test to compare the random effects models with and without the Mundlak correction, and to compare the fixed effects model with the random effects model with Mundlak correction.

Write the commands and compare with the do and log files in the online appendix

As we have already mentioned, pooled logit, probit or LPM will not yield consistent estimates if the individual-specific effects (α_i) are non-zero or are different for all or some individuals. Using the Hausman test we conclude that the fixed effects logit estimates are consistent, while random effects logit estimates are not. So, we should use either the conditional fixed effects logit estimates or the random effects probit with Mundlak correction estimates. As it is not possible to produce marginal effects for conditional fixed effects logit other than at zero fixed effects, we may prefer to show odds ratios for the logit model, or marginal effects estimated using the random effects probit with Mundlak correction. Note also that the number of observations used by the conditional fixed effects logit estimator is very low compared with the number of observations used by the fixed effects linear estimator and by the probit estimator with Mundlak correction.

10.3 Panel Data Methods for Ordered Outcomes

Similar to Equation (8.6) in Chapter 8, we now want to analyse the impact of unemployment on life satisfaction. The model we want to estimate is as follows:

$$y_{it}^* = \eta_0 \text{Unemployed dummy}_{it} + \eta_1 \text{Age}_{it} + \eta_2 \text{Age}_{it}^2 + $$
$$\eta_3 \text{Married dummy}_{it} + \eta_4 \text{Qualification dummies}_{it} + $$
$$\eta_5 \text{Region dummies}_{it} + \text{error term}_{it} \qquad (10.5)$$

where i identifies individuals and t identifies time. Hence, for example, 'Unemployed dummy$_{it}$' is a dummy that is one for those who are unemployed at time t and zero for those who are either employed or self-employed at time t. Since we restrict this model to men only, we have no female dummy.

As we have already mentioned several times, panel data allow us to take into account individual unobserved heterogeneity. This is particularly important in the analysis of satisfaction. The literature has suggested that answers to the questions on satisfaction might reflect cognitive aspects such as personality (such as extraversion or optimism), and emotional aspects such as mood (Argyle 2001). Hence, if we estimate a pooled model, thus neglecting individual unobserved heterogeneity, the residual errors may include measurement error related to mood and personality. If these errors are correlated with the explanatory variables (for example, unemployment or marital status) we might have an endogeneity problem. However, if we are prepared to assume that this endogeneity is due to time-invariant unobserved individual characteristics, then a fixed effects model would eliminate the problem.

Some authors do estimate fixed effects ordered logit models. However, you may notice that Stata does not have an in-built command to estimate this type of model. Various authors have proposed different types of econometric techniques to estimate fixed effects ordered logit models; however, there is still no consensus in the literature on which of these estimators is to be preferred, and on their consistency (for more information see Baetschmann et al. 2011).

An alternative solution is to estimate a random effects ordered probit model. This can be implemented in Stata using the command `reoprob` (more details on this command are given in Frechette 2001); note that we have to install this command before we can use it. If we are using Stata 13 or newer, we can use the commands `xtoprobit` and `xtologit` to estimate random effects ordered probit or logistic models. Remember that these models assume that the random effects are uncorrelated with the explanatory variables. We can partly overcome this problem by estimating a correlated random effects model by including among the explanatory variables the mean of the time-varying characteristics (using the Mundlak correction discussed in Sections 9.4 and 10.2.5).

Identification of the variables that are time invariant – and for which we should include the mean in the model – is sometimes ambiguous. For example, for most people the level of education remains stable during adult life. It is mostly young people – some of which may study and work at the same time – who show changes in levels of education. For this reason many researchers restrict their sample to slightly older people, say aged 23 or older, treat education as a time-invariant characteristic and exclude it from fixed effects models. We follow the same approach here. In our specific case, furthermore, the impact of unemployment on happiness may have a different meaning for young student–workers and for older workers – another reason to exclude younger workers from this analysis.

Another option consists of neglecting the non-linearity and assuming that the difference between any two consecutive levels of satisfaction is constant (see Section 8.5.1). This means that moving from 2 to 3 on the satisfaction scale is the same as moving from 6 to 7, while moving from 2 to 4 increases life satisfaction twice as much as when moving from 2 to 3. This assumption allows us to estimate a linear fixed effects model which, according to some authors, has to be preferred to non-linear random effects and pooled models (Ferrer-i-Carbonell and Frijters 2004).

As a final option, we can aggregate the seven-point scale into a dummy variable which is, for example, one for those who are satisfied and zero for those who are dissatisfied or neither satisfied nor dissatisfied. We can then estimate this model using a fixed effects logit. Although this might seem a simplistic solution, it is nevertheless still quite popular, although it has recently been criticised by some authors (for example, Bond and Lang 2014).

It is interesting to compare the results of these three models. Compute the variables necessary for the analysis and estimate the three models.

Write the commands and compare with the do file in the online appendix

Table 10.2 shows the estimated impact of being unemployed as estimated by the three different methods. The first column shows the results of the random effects ordered probit. The coefficient suggests that unemployment has a negative and statistically significant impact on life satisfaction. You will notice (see also the log file in the online appendix) that the marginal effect is exactly the same as the coefficient. The command margins is not able to compute marginal effects correctly after the reoprob command: by default the marginal effects are computed as a linear prediction.

Table 10.2   Results from the estimation of life satisfaction models for panel data

	Coefficients of random effects ordered probit	Linear fixed effect	Fixed effects binary logit odds ratios
Unemployed	−0.641*	−0.444*	0.421
	(0.049)	(0.042)	(0.064)
Observations	23,262	23,262	9,153

Standard errors in parentheses; + significant at 5%; * significant at 1%.
Other explanatory variables: age and its square, dummy for married or cohabiting, dummies for region, and (in the random effects ordered probit model) means of the time-varying covariates.

The fixed effects linear model, shown in the second column, confirms the negative impact of unemployment on life satisfaction. Since it is a linear model, in this case the coefficient coincides with the marginal effect. The last column of Table 10.2 shows the odds ratios for the fixed effects logit model computed on the binary variable. As we discussed in Section 10.2.4, we cannot compute meaningful marginal effects after this command; hence, the best option in this case is to show odds ratios. Remember that odds ratios higher than 1 mean that the explanatory variable has a positive impact on the dependent variable, and vice versa. Hence, the odds ratio of 0.421 means that for those who are unemployed the odds of them? saying that they are satisfied with their life are 1 − 0.421 = 0.579, lower than for someone who is not unemployed. This, however, does not mean that an unemployed person is half as likely to be satisfied than someone who is not unemployed.

Also note the smaller number of observations that is used in the estimation of the fixed effects logit model compared with the random effects ordered probit and the linear models.

Finally, also in these types of models it is possible to compute different types of standard errors and to use most of the usual post-estimation commands such as predict. The commands are similar to those discussed in Chapter 8. Check the Stata manual for the options that are available for ordered models.

10.4 Summary and Suggestions for Further Reading

In Chapter 8 we discussed various estimation methods that are commonly used in the case of cross-section data. In Chapter 9 we extended the discussion to estimation methods for panel data where the dependent variable is continuous; in this chapter we have extended the discussion further to the case of binary and multinomial dependent variables for panel data. We have also discussed how to account for individual unobserved heterogeneity, how to compute different types of standard errors and how to obtain predictions and residuals.

Key points

- In the absence of unobserved heterogeneity and if the error terms are not correlated with the explanatory variables, then pooled models will produce consistent estimates.
- If there is unobserved heterogeneity which is not correlated with the explanatory variables, the random effects estimators are consistent. Fixed effects estimators are also consistent but less efficient.
- If there is unobserved heterogeneity which is correlated with the explanatory variables, the fixed effects estimators are consistent, while random effects estimators – with the exception of random effects estimators with the Mundlak correction – are inconsistent.

Suggestions for further reading

- For further discussions on methods for binary choice models see:

  - Chapter 2 of Greene, W.H. and Hensher, D.A. (2010) *Modeling Ordered Choices: A Primer*. Cambridge, Cambridge University Press.
  - Chapter 11 of Baltagi, B.H. (2009) *Econometric Analysis of Panel Data*. London, Wiley.
  - Chapter 15 of Wooldridge, J. (2009) *Introductory Econometrics: A Modern Approach*. Mason, OH, South Western, Cengage Learning.

PART III

EVENT HISTORY: DATA PREPARATION AND ANALYSIS

INTRODUCTION TO DURATION ANALYSIS

This chapter is a taster on duration models, including explanations of key terms and of estimation issues. Depending on the discipline, duration analysis is also referred to as event history analysis and survival analysis. These models are used to analyse duration in a particular state or time until a particular event, such as duration of unemployment or time until first marriage. Duration analysis requires the data to be set up in a way that is quite different from what we have dealt with until now. The second part of the chapter deals with these data requirements.

11.1 What Is Duration Analysis?

In duration models, the dependent variable is time, and how long a person stays in a particular state. The aim is to analyse the determinants of exit from that state, one of the determinants being the amount of time already spent in the state. The underlying model of duration analysis treats the time that a person spends in a particular state, such as unemployment, poverty, marriage, as a random variable. This time spent in a particular state is also referred to as spell duration, spell length, time to event or survival time. As long as a person is in that particular state, they are considered to be at risk of leaving the state (see Figure 11.1). You may be interested in the pattern of exit from that state or in the characteristics that are associated with such exits. For example, you may want to know whether the likelihood of leaving unemployment by getting a job is highest right after someone becomes unemployed and reduces over time, and to what extent characteristics such as age, educational qualification, past experiences of unemployment, the region of residence, and so on, play a role. Duration analysis methods are designed to answer these questions. A related class of methods, known as sequence analysis methods, look at not only transitions but also the order in which these events occurred (for reviews on these methods see Abott 1983, 1995).

You may ask why regression methods for categorical dependent variables such as logit or probit cannot be used to model transitions out of a particular state. The reason is that these methods are not able to identify the effect of the time spent in a particular state or that of time-varying variables on the likelihood of leaving this state (for a detailed discussion see Jenkins 2005).

The specific method used for the analysis of duration will depend on the questions you wish to answer, the assumptions you make about the time-varying event, and the data available. You will need to answer a few questions to decide which method to use:

- Is the duration measured in continuous or discrete time?
- Do you want to model duration of multiple spells or just single spells? For example, do you want to analyse duration of every unemployment spell that a person has experienced or just the first one?
- Do you want to model transitions into one state, or multiple states (this last case is known as a competing risks model)? For example, does it matter whether a person leaves the state of unemployment by getting a job rather than by leaving the labour force?
- Do you want to model multiple state durations? For example, do you want to model duration of employment as well as non-employment spells?
- Is the likelihood of leaving a particular state affected by observed factors such as age, sex, ethnic group, marital state and unobserved (by the researcher) factors like motivation? Are these factors fixed or time-varying?
- Are you able to observe the start and end of all spells? If not, are those censoring processes independent of spell durations?

In Chapter 13 we discuss the implementation of duration analysis methods for both continuous and discrete time but restricted to single state transitions, single spells, completed or right-censored spells and time-invariant covariates. Look at Steele (2005) and Jenkins (2005) for duration analysis methods that deal with the different issues.

There are separate sets of methods for analysing spells measured in continuous and discrete time. Most spell durations that we are interested in are determined by certain behavioural processes which are inherently continuous. But when it comes to measuring these spells it is a different story: duration data can be grouped into intervals ranging from something as short as days to something

Figure 11.1   Illustration of event history or spell data

as long as a year. The question to ask is whether this artificial grouping is small relative to the spell duration. For example, if unemployment spells are on average a few months long and the data are measured in days then we can treat the spell durations as continuous. On the other hand, if unemployment spells are typically only a few days long, then we would be better off treating them as discrete if the data measure the length of the spell in days. There is no fixed rule. There are, however, some behavioural processes that result in spell durations that are inherently discrete. This happens when transitions out of a particular state can happen only at specific times, for example winning an annual competition or championship. Also, discrete-time methods can accommodate ties in the data; that is, where more than one person experiences the same event, like becoming unemployed at the same time. See Jenkins (2005) and Yamaguchi (1991) for a detailed discussion.

Ideally, we would like to observe completed spells, but often we do not observe the start and/or end dates of all spells in the dataset for a number of reasons (see Figure 11.2). First, individuals may still be in a particular state under investigation when the survey or the observation period ends. It may also be the case that some people leave the survey while they are still in that state (attrition). A spell for which we do not observe the end date is said to be right censored. Second, in some cases we start observing people who are already in the middle of a spell; that is, we do not observe the start of a spell. Such spells are said to be left censored. If researchers exclude spells that end after a particular period of time, then this is a case of right truncation, while left truncation occurs when spells that end before a particular time are excluded. Note that right (left) truncation implies that long (short) spells are selected out. The terms used to describe these different types of spells vary by discipline (see Yamaguchi 1991; Jenkins 2005; Blossfeld et al. 2007).

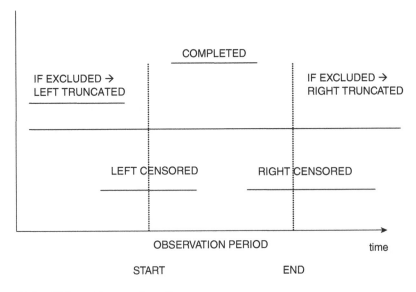

Figure 11.2   Different types of spells

11.2 Key Terms Used in Duration Analysis

In duration models, the survival time or spell duration is treated as a random variable and the actual spell duration is a realisation of that variable. The functional form of this random variable has to be specified at some point during the analysis, based on its distribution. This way of conceptualising the model is very different from any of the econometric methods we discussed in the earlier chapters. We will thus focus on discussing some of the key terms used in duration analysis in this section. Some of these terms have no intuitive explanation and are best explained with the help of mathematical notations. These notations will also be useful when discussing the different types of duration models in Chapter 13.

Let T be the random variable representing spell duration and t the actual realised spell duration. As we have already mentioned, the econometric methods – and concepts – used for the analysis of continuous-time duration differ from those used in the case of discrete-time durations. Below we discuss each in turn.

11.2.1 Continuous Time

If T is a continuous random variable, with a cumulative density function (CDF) $G(t)$ and a probability density function (PDF) $g(t)$, then the failure function, that is the probability that the duration of the spell (T) is shorter than or equal to t, is equal to its CDF:

$$\text{Prob}(T \le t) = G(t) \tag{11.1}$$

and the survivor function, that is the probability that the spell will last at least until time t, is one minus its CDF and can be written as

$$\text{Prob}(T > t) = 1 - G(t) = S(t) \tag{11.2}$$

The hazard function is a useful concept for analysing durations or survival times. It is the ratio of the survival time density function (or the PDF of the spell duration) to the survivor function:

$$\theta(t) = \frac{g(t)}{1 - G(t)} = \frac{g(t)}{S(t)} \tag{11.3}$$

If T is the duration of unemployment then in a very small interval Δt, $\theta(t)$ is the probability of leaving the state of unemployment, conditional on having been unemployed up until t.

From the properties of the CDF (which ranges from 0 to 1) and of the PDF (which is non-negative), it follows that the values of the survivor and the failure functions are always non-negative and less than one, and that the hazard function is always non-negative. The integrated hazard function, or cumulative hazard function, is the 'accumulation' of the hazard function over time and is another way of representing the hazard:

$$H(t) = -\log_e(S(t)) \tag{11.4}$$

Hazard functions are estimated by MLE methods (for details of MLEs of hazard functions see Jenkins 2005). There are different functional forms that can be used for the hazard functions, including parametric, semi-parametric and non-parametric ones. We will discuss some of these in Chapter 13.

11.2.2 Discrete Time

If T is a discrete random variable with a CDF $G(t)$, and a probability mass function (PMF) $g(t)$, then the failure function and the survivor function have the same expressions as in the continuous case, but the hazard function is different. That is,

$$\text{Prob}(T = t \mid T > t) = \theta(t) = \frac{g(t)}{1 - G(t-1)} = \frac{g(t)}{S(t-1)} \tag{11.5}$$

The hazard function in the discrete case can be interpreted as the probability of the spell ending in that time period, conditional on the spell having lasted until the previous period (that is, the probability of failure occurring given that it has not happened until that time). As in the continuous case, the hazard function is non-negative, but in this case it is also less than one. Here, as in the continuous cases, we have assumed that there is no left censoring.

11.2.3 Duration Dependence and Unobserved Heterogeneity or Frailty

We may want to know whether the hazard function changes with spell duration. This is known as duration dependence. There could be many reasons why the likelihood of leaving a particular state changes with the time spent in that state. Let us stick to our example of unemployment. The longer a person is unemployed, the more disheartened they may get and may search less intensively for a job. This may then reduce their chances of leaving unemployment over time.

Quite often there are individual-specific factors such as motivation or personality traits that affect the hazard rate but are not observed in the data. These are referred to as unobserved heterogeneity, or frailty. If we ignore them, we may obtain biased estimates of duration dependence. Why would that happen? Let us assume that there is no duration dependence for unemployment hazard rates, and that motivated individuals search for a job more intensively and leave the state of unemployment faster than others. Over time, the sample will include more and more less-motivated persons with a lower probability of leaving unemployment. So, our estimated hazard rate for the sample will be lower at longer durations. In other words, we may estimate negative duration dependence even though there is no true duration dependence. There are parametric and non-parametric methods for taking account of unobserved heterogeneity, which we discuss in Chapter 13.

11.3 Data Set-Up for Duration Analysis

Data set-up for duration analysis is different from the set-up we have discussed so far in this book. In this section we discuss why and how the data structure for duration analysis is different. We will further discuss the implementation of this data set-up for duration analysis in Chapters 12 and 13.

Event history data, like other longitudinal data, can be collected retrospectively or prospectively (see Chapter 2). A person may be asked at one point in time to provide the history of transitions into and out of different states such as employment, inactivity, unemployment up until the date of the interview. Data collected by this method are known as retrospective data. Alternatively, the same information may be collected by asking individuals at different points in time about their current employment state (that is, the data are collected prospectively) and the employment history may be built up from there. In most cases, event history data are available in the form as shown in Table 11.1. Here you can see that the person with ID = 10001 experiences three activity spells. The first spell is unemployment which started on 17 February 2007 and ended on 17 May 2007. This was followed by a spell of employment that ended on 15 December 2007. The third and last spell was unemployment again; this started right after the employment spell, but was still ongoing at the time of the interview. In other words, this last spell is right censored.

Table 11.1 Event history data on main activity

ID	Spell no.	Start date	End date	Activity status	Spell ended?	Interview date
10001	1	17.02.07	17.05.07	Unemployed	Ended	15.01.11
10001	2	17.05.07	15.12.09	Employed	Ended	15.01.11
10001	3	15.12.09	.	Unemployed	Ongoing	15.01.11
10002	1	01.10.04	15.06.10	Employed	Ended	05.01.11
10003	1	01.10.07	.	Unemployed	Ongoing	05.01.11

Our aim is to transform these data so that they are ready for duration analysis. The key variables we will need for duration analysis are type of spell, spell duration, an indicator of whether the spell is right censored. If we are considering multiple spells we will also need to know the spell number. So, first we need to make sure we have the start and end dates of all spells. By definition, we do not have end dates of right-censored spells, but we could impute them by using the (last) interview date. Note that this would be the day the spell is censored, not the day the spell ended. Some of the start and end dates may also be missing because people forget the exact dates. In such cases we need either to impute these missing dates or drop these observations from the data, the latter being a good idea only if those with missing dates are a random subsample of all spells. We will then end up with a dataset that looks like that in Table 11.2. Sometimes data may be directly available in this form.

Now we are ready to compute the spell duration by subtracting the start date from the end date. Remember that there are two types of spells here: completed spells and right-censored ones. We need to indicate that in the data. We can do this by creating a dummy variable which takes the value 1 when the spell is censored and 0 otherwise.

Table 11.2   Event history data on main activity, end dates for ongoing spells imputed

ID	Spell no.	Start date	End date	Activity status	Spell ended?	Interview date
10001	1	17.02.07	17.05.07	Unemployed	Ended	15.01.11
10001	2	17.05.07	15.12.09	Employed	Ended	15.01.11
10001	3	15.12.09	15.01.11	Unemployed	Ongoing	15.01.11
10002	1	01.10.04	15.06.10	Employed	Ended	05.01.11
10003	1	01.10.07	05.01.11	Unemployed	Ongoing	05.01.11

If we are treating spell duration as a continuous random variable, the data are ready for analysis. Now suppose that a person can continue to be unemployed or leave this state, and that this can happen only once a month. In other words, the duration of unemployment (measured in months) is discrete. The data should show for each month, starting from the month that a person first became unemployed, whether they leave that state in that month or not. We can transform the data shown in Table 11.3 such that each row of observation specifies each month of being in unemployment, and create a new variable which identifies whether the person left the state of unemployment in that month. If there is a completed spell, then this variable ('spell ended') is zero for all months, except for the last month, when it is one. If, on the other hand, it is a right-censored spell, this variable will be zero for all spell months. We will then get a dataset that looks like the one in Table 11.4.

Table 11.3   Event history data on main activity, discrete time

ID	Spellno.	Start date	End date	Activity status	Spell ended?	Interview date	Spell duration	Censored spell?
1	1	17.02.07	17.05.07	Unemployed	Ended	15.01.11	3	0
1	2	17.05.07	15.12.09	Employed	Ended	15.01.11	28	0
1	3	15.12.09	15.01.11	Unemployed	Ongoing	15.01.11	13	1
2	1	01.10.04	15.06.10	Employed	Ended	05.01.11	68	0
3	1	01.10.07	05.01.11	Unemployed	Ongoing	05.01.11	39	1

In the next chapter we discuss what data files collecting retrospective information look like, and what major practical problems need to be solved before the data can be reshaped to look like Tables 11.3 and 11.4. We then discuss how to estimate duration models in Chapter 13.

Table 11.4 Event history data on main activity, continuous time

ID	Spell no.	Activity status	Spell month	Spell ended
10001	1	Unemployed	1	0
10001	1	Unemployed	2	0
10001	1	Unemployed	3	1
10001	2	Employed	1	0
10001	...	...	...	...
10001	2	Employed	28	1
10001	3	Unemployed	1	0
10001	...	...	...	...
10001	3	Unemployed	13	0
10002	1	Employed	1	0
10002	1	Employed	...	...
10002	1	Employed	68	1
10003	1	Unemployed	1	0
10003	...	...	...	0
10003	1	Unemployed	39	0

... = row omitted for illustrative purposes.

11.4 Summary and Suggestions for Further Reading

In this chapter we have discussed duration models and how the individual-level data structure we discussed in Parts I and II of this book differs from the data structure needed for duration types of analyses. Chapter 12 gives more details on what data files containing information on duration spells look like, while Chapter 13 discusses the implementation of the data transformation discussed in the last part of the present chapter.

Key points

- Decide which technique is most appropriate for your analysis; first think of whether the duration in your analysis is continuous or discrete.
- Also verify whether the duration spells are censored and/or truncated.
- Remember that the data need to be set up for duration analyses in different ways for the continuous and discrete cases.

Suggestions for further reading

- For a quick guide to the different methods that deal with different types of duration analysis, see Steele, F. (2005) Event History Analysis: A National Centre for Research Methods Briefing Paper. NCRM Methods Review Papers NCRM/004.
- You can find a good – technical – discussion of duration models in these lecture notes: Jenkins, S. (2005) Survival Analysis. Available at: www.iser.essex.ac.uk/files/teaching/stephenj/ec968/pdfs/ec968lnotesv6.pdf.
- For more gentle introductions see Allison, P.D. (1984) *Event History Analysis: Regression for Longitudinal Event Data.* London, Sage; and Yamaguchi, K. (1991) *Event History Analysis.* London, Sage.

(12)

HOW TO USE RETROSPECTIVE HISTORY DATA FILES: AN EXAMPLE

Aim

Many surveys (both panel and cross-section surveys) collect retrospective information on events referring to the period before the start of the survey or to the period between two consecutive interviews. Examples are employment, fertility and marital histories. These data are meant to give a complete picture of a person's history and are particularly useful for event history analysis. This chapter discusses the general structure of such kinds of data files and problems that are often encountered when combining the history files with data referring to the current status.

12.1 Organisation of Retrospective History Data Files

Because of their nature, the history files are organised in a slightly different way than the individual and household files that we have seen up to now. Instead of containing one observation/row per individual, like, for example, the individual respondent files, the retrospective files contain one observation/row per event/spell.

Hence, individuals who had multiple spells in the reference period will appear multiple times – once per spell – while those individuals who did not have any spell in the reference period may not appear in the file at all.

Besides the person identification number, needed to merge across different types of files, the history files also contain an identifier for the spell so that observations are unique only by combining person and spell identifiers. It is important to consult the documentation and understand how the spell identifier is organised, because different types of files may organise the spell identifiers differently. For example, in the BHPS job history files the most recent spell has a value of 1, and higher values refer to older spells. In the BHPS marital history file the current marriage takes the value 4 and, if the current marriage is not the first marriage, 1, 2 or 3 are the first, second or third previous marriage as appropriate.

The history files normally contain information on the activity during the spell (for example, unemployment, paid job, self-employment), the date of beginning and end of the spell, sometimes the length of the spell, and possibly some information on censoring (whether the spell has ended or whether it is currently ongoing).

If the whole history is contained in a single file, most likely the data are consistent across spells, as for example in the case of the BHPS employment history file (clifejob) which contains information on every employment status spell since the respondent left full-time education. In other cases, as for example in the case of the BHPS wave-on-wave job history files, retrospective data are collected at different points in time and information contained in one file may sometimes be inconsistent with that contained in the other files (the ones collected for the previous and subsequent waves). It is the researcher's job to resolve inconsistencies. Using the wave-on-wave BHPS job history files, we discuss below some of the most common problems encountered when merging data from different files and give hints on how to resolve the most common inconsistencies.

In the examples below we use the first six waves of BHPS data and focus on the wave-on-wave job history files (jobhist). These files contain retrospective information about employment and jobs held between 1 September of the previous year and the date of the current interview. Since interviews occur between August and May, the questions cover between 11 months (for those interviewed in August) and 20 months (for those interviewed in May).

The files are structured as one record for each spell, with the order of the spells going backwards from the most recent to the oldest one; the variable jspno identifies the sequence of the job spells, with 1 being the most recent one. Because of this structure, there might be multiple observations per respondent, but if there was no change between two interviews, in the job history file there is no observation for that respondent. The files also include information on the date the job spell started and ended; however, the day, month and year are in separate variables. Due to recollection problems, there are large numbers of missing values for the day the spell began. Some researchers impute the first day of the month when missing; others impute dates based on previous interviews. For simplicity, here we focus only on the month and year. Note that this choice may have an impact on whether we should consider our duration as continuous or as discrete, and therefore on the type of econometric models we should use for our analysis (see Chapters 11 and 13).

12.2 Merging Data on Previous Spell to Data on Current Spell

In this example we want to merge data from consecutive wave-on-wave job history files, so that the current spell is merged to each of the previous spells. In other words, we want the final file to look like the one in Table 12.1. With data organised in this way we can analyse, for example, the wage impact of a promotion that happened between the two interview dates. This would not lead to a duration type of analysis, but simply to the addition of new information to the individual respondent file. This is one of the many ways in which job history files can be used.

Table 12.1   Output file for Example 1

pid	jspno	current status	previous status	start current spell	start previous spell	spell end (previous)
1001	1	paid empl	looking	1991m4	1991m3	1991m4
1001	2	paid empl	self-empl	1991m4	1991m1	1991m3
1001	3	paid empl	looking	1991m4	1988m11	1991m1
1003	1	paid empl	different job	1991m3	1989m2	1991m3

To obtain a file similar to the one in Table 12.1 we need to merge data from the job history files (which contain information on the previous employment status) with data from the individual respondent files (which contain data on the current employment status) for all waves. Hence, separately for each wave we merge the individual respondent file (indresp.dta) with the corresponding job history file (jobhist.dta). We can start our exercise by opening the file for the first wave (ajobhist), dropping the wave prefix a, generating the wave identifier and recoding missing values.

Write the commands and compare with the do file in the online appendix

What is the maximum number of spells? How many respondents have only one recorded spell? (Hint: use _N; the answers are in the log file in the online appendix.)

Write the commands and compare with the do and log files in the online appendix

We can now construct one variable containing the month and year in which the spell started, and one containing the month and year in which the spell ended. We can construct dates by using the date function ym():

```
generate previous_spellbegin = ym(jhbgy4, jhbgm)

tabulate previous_spellbegin
```

Note that Stata codes date variables using 1.1.1960 as point 0. This means that when we use a day/month/year format, a value of 10 in the date variable corresponds to 1.1.1960 plus 10 days. When we use the month/year format (as in this example) a value of 10 corresponds to January 1960 plus 10 months. When we use year format a value of 10 corresponds to 1960 plus 10 years (1970) etc. This system makes it easy to compute the length of time between two dates (in days, months, years, quarters, etc.); the length of time is computed by subtracting the relevant variables from each other.

To make the variable more readable we can format it using the relevant option, %tm in this case, since we have monthly data (check the Stata manual for the other options):

```
format previous_spellbegin %tm

tabulate previous_spellbegin
```

We can now create a similar variable identifying the end of the spell and save the file with a new name (for example, ajobhistory.dta).

Write the commands and compare with the do file in the online appendix

We then have to prepare the aindresp file for merging with the job history file. We open the file, drop the a prefix, recode missing values and construct the start and end dates of the current job spell. Once the individual respondent file is ready, we merge it with the job history one using the command joinby:

```
joinby pid using ///
    "$dir\ajobhistory.dta", unmatched(both)
```

The command `joinby` matches observations within the groups specified, by forming all pairwise combinations. In this case we match observations in the two files which have the same `pid`. Due to the structure of the two files, it is important that we specify what to do with the unmatched observations; that is, those that appear only in one of the two files. For example, all individuals whose current spell started before 1 September of the previous year are excluded from the job history file. The default for Stata is to ignore all unmatched observations. In our case this would mean for example ignoring all those people who did not have a change in (job) status in the previous year. We use the option `unmatched(both)` to specify that we want to keep all unmatched observations.

Note that for those who appear in the job history files (that is, those who have a valid answer to the question 'which of the descriptions comes closest to what you were doing immediately before then?'), there should be no overlap between the current spell, recorded in the individual respondent file, and the previous one, recorded in the job history file. If there is an overlap, the general suggestion is to give priority to the variable in the individual respondent file (see below). The result of the `joinby` command is a file that looks like the one in Table 12.2.

Table 12.2   File resulting from the `joinby` command

pid	jspno	current status	previous status	start current spell	start previous spell	spell end (previous)
1001	1	paid empl	looking	1991m4	1991m3	1991m4
1001	2	paid empl	self-empl	1991m4	1991m1	1991m3
1001	3	paid empl	looking	1991m4	1988m11	1991m1
1002	.	unempl	.	1988m3	.	.
1003	1	paid empl	different job	1991m3	1989m2	1991m3

Details of the current spell are now merged with details of each of the previous spells. So, for example, individual 1001, who is now in paid employment, had three different employment spells in the previous year. Individual 1002 had no change in employment status in the previous year; hence, since there was no record for this person in the job history file, a missing has been generated for the variables 'previous status', 'start previous spell' and 'spell end'. It is useful at this point to recode jspno to zero when missing. This identifies individuals who did not change their status between the two interviews.

After saving the merged file we need to repeat the same steps for waves b to f before merging the six files (`ajobhistory.dta ... fjobhistory.dta`). We can do this either by repeating all the previous steps for each wave, or by generating a loop.

Write the commands and compare with the do file in the online appendix

Note that from 1992 (wave 2 of the BHPS) the variables jbbgm, jhbgm and jhendm, which refer to the month of beginning and end of the spell, report the season (codes 13 to 16) when the respondent does not remember the exact month. Since this happens in only a few cases, the easiest option is to recode codes 13 to 16 to Stata missing (although in certain circumstances we may prefer to try to impute the month from other information).

We can now append the six files (ajobhistory.dta ... fjobhistory. dta) across waves. The result of the final set of commands is the file jobhistory_final.dta, which should look like the one in Table 12.1.

Write the commands and compare with the do file in the online appendix

We can now use the variable referring to previous status to identify job promotions and job changes. Code 2 in the variable jhstat is 'Empl self/diff emply' and therefore includes those working for a different employer (tabulate jhstat jbsemp). We can create a dummy for those who moved from job to job, that is, those who were in paid employment in wave t and wave $t + 1$, but changed employer between the two waves and had no spells of non-employment. The dummy is zero when the respondent is employed in both waves but does not change employer, and one when the respondent is employed in both waves and changes employer between the two waves. There is no need to exclude those moving to or from self-employment since the wage data we are using (paygu) include only those in paid employment and exclude the self-employed. Finally, for simplicity, in this exercise we keep only those who have at most one recoded spell in the job history file:

```
bysort pid wave: generate TotSpells = _N

drop if TotSpells > 1

* Check that we only keep those with at most

* one spell: (jspno = 0 or jspno = 1)

tabulate jspno

tsset pid wave

generate NewJob = 0 if jbstat == 2 & L.jbstat == 2

replace NewJob = 1 if jhstat == 2
```

We can now run wage regressions similar to the ones in Chapter 9.

Write the commands and compare with the do and log files in the online appendix

12.3 Appending Data on Previous Spell to Data on Current Spell

12.3.1 Merging Files

In the previous example the data on the previous spell were in the same row as the data on the current spell. In some cases we may want the data on the current spell to be in a different row than the data on the previous spells, as in Table 12.3. This is also closer to the format that we discussed in Chapter 11, and which we would need for duration types of analyses.

Table 12.3   Output file for Example 2

pid	jspno	current status	previous status	start current spell	start previous spell	spell end (previous)
1001	0	paid empl	.	1991m4	.	.
1001	1	.	looking		1991m3	1991m4
1001	2	.	self-empl	.	1991m1	1991m3
1001	3	.	looking	.	1988m11	1991m1
1002	0	unempl	.	1988m3	.	.
1003	0	paid empl	.	1991m3	.	.
1003	1	.	different job	.	1989m2	1991m3

We start by opening the individual respondent file and dropping the wave prefix. However, if we want the current and previous spells to be in different records, we need to create a variable in the individual respondent file called jspno (the same name as the variable we find in the job history file), with a value that does not appear in the job history file (for example, zero). We then use the merge command on the pid and jspno variables to combine the individual respondent and the job history files.

We can modify the previous data generating loop to obtain the data in this new format.

Write the commands and compare with the do file in the online appendix

12.3.2 Imputing Missing Values

Since individual respondent and job history files include different variables, the new file will include a large number of missing values (as in Table 12.3). For example, 'current status' and 'start current spell' are included only in the individual respondent file, while 'previous status', 'start previous spell' and 'spell end (previous)' are included only in the job history file. The variables sex and age will only be attached to the records from the individual respondent file (the ones where jspno is zero). We can impute the variables that appear in the individual respondent file but not in the job history file, and that are not job related, by copying their values over:

```
foreach var of varlist sex age qfachi {
bysort pid wave (jspno): replace `var' = ///
   cond(jspno > 0 & ///
            `var' == ., `var'[_n-1], `var')
}
```

As already mentioned in the previous chapters, _n and _N are Stata counters: _n is a running counter so that the first observation has a value 1, the second has a value 2, and so on. The counter in this case is computed separately by pid and wave (sorting within groups by jspno); 1 refers to the smallest jspno in the pid-wave group.

We can then create a variable indicating the job status for each record. Note that this choice is highly subjective and strictly depends on the aim of the analysis. Different choices will lead to different ways of combining the final spells: for example, if we are interested in employment spells, we might want to group spells of employment that are continuous, but refer to different employers. If we are interested in changes in employers we might want instead to keep them separate:

```
* Employment status:
* employment=1, unemployment=2, inactive=3
generate Status = 1 if jbstat == 1 | ///
   jbstat == 2 | ///
   jhstat == 1 | jhstat == 2
replace Status = 2 if jbstat == 3 | jhstat == 3
replace Status = 3 if ///
   (jbstat >= 4 & jbstat <= 10) | ///
   (jhstat >= 4 & jhstat <= 10)
label var Status "Employment Status"
label define ES 1 "Employed" 2 "Unemployed" ///
   3 "Inactive"
label value Status ES
```

We mentioned in Section 4.3.1 that the coding of the variable jbstat in the first wave differs from the coding in all other waves; however, the code above is not affected since all inactive people are in the same group.

12.3.3 Addressing Inconsistencies

Event history datasets that are collected at different points in time, such as the wave-on-wave BHPS job history files, often generate inconsistencies due to the complexity of the data collection and to difficulties that respondents have in remembering exact (start and end) dates. It is therefore good practice to check – and address – inconsistencies.

We now create the start and end dates of each spell. We start by creating the start and end dates of the current spell (data from the individual respondent file), and the start and end dates of the previous spells (data from the job history file) separately. We then create two consistent variables including the start and end dates of each spell. Note that the end date will be missing for the current spells, which are still ongoing.

Write the commands and compare with the do file in the online appendix

The current spell in the last interview (wave w-1) should appear as the oldest spell in the job history file, or as the current spell in the individual respondent file (wave w) if it started before September in the previous wave. However, in some cases there are inconsistencies across spells. Inconsistencies may occur because of a misreported start date, or because more than one job or activity was

Table 12.4   Inconsistencies in spell length

pid	wave	jbstat	jhstat	jspno	previous spell begin	previous spell end	current spell begin
1001	1	employed	.	0	.	.	1991m3[a]
1001	1	.	empl sel	1	1990m2	1991m3	.
1001	2	employed	.	0	.	.	1991m7[b]
1001	3	employed	.	0	.	.	1991m6[c]
1001	4	employed	.	0	.	.	1994m7
1001	4	.	diff job	1	1991m7[d]	1994m7	.
1001	5	employed	.	0	.	.	1994m9
1001	5	.	diff job	1	1991m3[e]	1994m9	.
1001	6	employed	.	0	.	.	1996m4
1001	6	.	diff job	1	1991m3[f]	1996m4	.

[a, b, c, d, e, f] See text.

current at the time of the (previous) interview, and different activities are given priority by the respondent at different times. Furthermore, the questionnaire structure might cause some spells to be suppressed or censored when there is multiple job holding (see the BHPS documentation for further details).

For example, in the dataset in Table 12.4 it is unclear whether the spell started on 1991m7, 1991m6 or 1991m3. Note also that 'diff job' stands for 'different job with the same employer'. In some cases we might want to identify spells by type of job, so that a promotion would count as a different spell; in other cases we might be interested in spells by employer, so that a promotion would not count as a different spell.

In Table 12.4, the spells marked by superscripts b, c and d are inconsistent with that of a, while e and f are consistent with a. There are two main approaches that researchers have taken to derive consistent chronological spells (see Maré 2006: 36–8). One approach consists of giving more weight to the answers that are closest in time to the event, so as to minimise recall error. Another approach consists of giving more weight to the answers that are collected at the same time as a sequence of events. This is because answers are likely to be more accurate when the respondent is asked to talk about the whole sequence of events. This improves internal consistency but gives more weight to retrospective than to interview-date reports.

For simplicity, here we consider only a few cases (this example will still leave some inconsistent spells). We start by putting the spells in chronological order across waves (recall that they are in reverse chronological order within waves). In this case the smallest Cronjspno (chronological ordering of jspno, a variable we need to create) will correspond to the oldest spell within the wave, just as the waves with the smallest values are the oldest:

```
bysort pid wave (jspno): ///
   generate Cronjspno = _N - jspno
```

We then generate the consistent beginning and end dates of the spell starting from the information in the individual respondent file:

```
generate SpellBegin = JBSpellStart if jspno == 0
replace SpellBegin = JHSpellStart if ///
   jspno>0 & jspno~=.
```

We then deal with those cases when there was no change across waves (that is, when jspno == 0):

```
bysort pid (wave Cronjspno): replace ///
   SpellBegin = SpellBegin[_n-1] if ///
   SpellBegin ~= SpellBegin[_n-1] & ///
```

```
SpellBegin[_n-1] ~= . & jspno == 0 & ///

Cronjspno == 1 & wave > 1
```

If there have been intervening spells but the dates do not match, the individual respondent file of wave w should override the job history file at wave w+1. Also note that spells should be consistent not only in terms of dates, but also in terms of employment status and possibly occupation and/or industry. For simplicity, here we consider only (broad) employment status:

```
* JHSpellStart of the oldest spell

* in the job history

* file must be >= JBSpellStart in the indresp file

bysort pid (wave Cronjspno): replace ///

     SpellBegin = JBSpellStart[_n-1] if ///

     SpellBegin<JBSpellStart[_n-1] & ///

     SpellBegin~=. & JBSpellStart[_n-1] ~= . & ///

     Status == Status[_n-1] & wave > 1

bysort pid (wave Cronjspno): replace ///

     SpellBegin = JHSpellStart if ///

     SpellBegin == . & JHSpellStart ~= . & ///

     jspno ~= 0 & Cronjspno == 1 & wave > 1

bysort pid (wave Cronjspno): replace ///

     SpellBegin = SpellBegin[_n-1] if ///

     SpellBegin == . & SpellBegin[_n-1] ~= . & ///

     JHSpellStart == . & Status == Status[_n-1] & ///

     jspno ~= 0 & Cronjspno == 1 & ///

     wave > 1
```

For reasons of space, in this example we stop here. We can use a similar procedure to compute the end of the spell (remember that current spells will have missing end dates). You may also notice that the file still includes a number of missing spell dates. In this exercise we have only included the variables identifying the beginning of job spells, thus excluding, for example, the beginning of a self-employment spell (variables: jsbgd, jsbgm, jsbgy4) and those cases where the beginning of the spell was collected by proxy questionnaire (see the online appendix and the BHPS documentation for more information). We may include or exclude them depending on the aim of our analysis.

Once the individual respondent and job history files are correctly matched, to get complete histories we can merge them with the `clifejob` file, which contains information about jobs held in employment spells in the period since the respondent first left full-time education up to the beginning of data collection in the main panel. We can also merge them with the `blifemst`, `klifemst` and `llifemst` files, which contain information about employment status spells in the period since the respondent first left full-time education.

One thing to note is that respondents may have held more than one job in a single employment status spell, and hence there may be more than one `clife-job` record corresponding to the period covered by a single `blifemst` record (see Volume A of the BHPS documentation). Also note that spells in `clifejob` do not always totally account for the underlying spell in `blifemst`; they may extend into non-employment in `blifemst` spells; some spells in `clifejob` are missing for some `blifemst` spells; and some spells in the two files do not match even when they overlap. Spells in `clifejob` may overlap with each other (see Maré 2006). For more in-depth discussion see Halpin (1997) and Maré (2006). It is also worth remembering that the only people interviewed in wave c have data on past job history (`clifejob`); and that the only people interviewed in wave b (for the original sample), k and l for the Wales, Scotland and Northern Ireland booster samples have data on employment history (`blifemst`, `klifemst`, `llifemst`). All those who have not been interviewed in these waves will not appear in these files and may therefore be dropped from the analysis.

Once we are satisfied with the consistencies of the spells, and our file has one record per spell, we can compute the duration of each spell and drop redundant information. The file at this point should look like the one in Table 12.5.

Table 12.5   Computing overall spell length

pid	wave	empl status	chron jspno	spell begin	spell end[a]	age
1001	1	unemployed	1	1990m2	1990m4	23
1001	1	employed	2	1990m4	.	23
1001	2	employed	1	1990m4	.	24
1001	3	employed	1	1990m4	.	25
1001	4	employed	1	1990m4	1993m6	26
1001	4	employed[b]	2	1993m6	.	26
1001	5	employed	1	1993m6	1994m2	27
1001	5	unemployed	2	1994m2	1994m9	27
1001	5	employed	3	1994m9	.	27
1001	6	employed[b]	1	1994m9	.	28

[a]The spells with missing values are still ongoing at the date of the interview.

[b]This is employment with a different employer: the respondent moved from job to job. If we are only interested in employment spells (as in this case) we will have to sum the duration of these two spells.

Since the spells overlap across waves, we can drop all records with missing end date, with the exception of the most recent observation, which refers to the current spell at the date of the latest interview. We can compute the duration of the most recent spell by substituting the date of the interview as the end date of the spell. In this case, we may want to add a further variable to identify that the spell is still ongoing:

```
generate duration = spellend - spellbegin
bysort pid (wave cronjspno): drop if ///
   duration==. & _n~=_N
```

The dataset now includes only one observation per spell. It includes the duration of the spell, and variables such as Age refer to age at the beginning of the spell. The data are now ready for duration analysis (see Chapter 13).

12.4 Other History Files

12.4.1 Other History Files in the BHPS

Besides the job history files discussed in the previous sections, the BHPS also provides three additional job history files that are derived from dependent interviewing: pjobhistd, qjobhistd and rjobhistd. These files are collected in a different way than the ones collected from wave 1 to wave 15. Specifically, they are based on data fed forward from the job history file in the previous wave, but have essentially the same structure as the job history files derived from independent interviews.

Besides the job history files, the BHPS also provides history files for marriage and cohabitation spells. Marriage spells are in the files bmarriag for the original sample and lmarriag and kmarriag for the booster samples. These files contain information on each reported legal marriage. Individuals are identified by their individual identifier (pid) and marriages are identified by the variable wmarno. As already mentioned, the current or most recent marriage has a value of 4, with values 1, 2 and 3 identifying previous marriages, if any. The data include information on the date the marriage started, whether it was preceded by cohabitation spells with the same partner (and date the cohabitation started), together with date and reason the marriage ended. Similar to the case of the employment history files, there has been no attempt to enforce consistency between the dates within these history files and the information about household composition and relationships in the other files.

The cohabitation history files (bcohab, lcohab and kcohab) contain information about each cohabitation spell outside legal marriage not recorded in the marriage history files. The spell identifier in this case is the variable `wlcsno` and, besides the individual identifier (`pid`), the files contain data on beginning and year of the cohabitation spells.

12.4.2 History Files in the UKHLS

The UKHLS currently provides history data for cohabitation spells and previous marriages (`a_cohab.dta` and `a_marriage.dta`). For a subsample of the respondents it also provides employment histories (`a_empstat.dta`).

Such data are collected for respondents in the first wave only. Individuals are identified by their household identification number and person number within the household; for the spell identifier a value of 1 corresponds to the oldest spell and higher numbers refer to the most recent spells. Due to the data collection, there are no inconsistencies across start and end dates.

The cohabitation file also includes information on the start and end dates of each spell, where the end date of the current spell is coded as inapplicable. The marriage file includes information on the month and year of the marriage, together with data on whether the couple cohabited before the marriage, year in which the cohabitation started and, where applicable, the reason, month and year the marriage ended. The employment history file includes details of the employment status, month and year of beginning and end of the spell. The file also includes information on the very first job, such as occupation and whether employed or self-employed (the variables are coded as inapplicable for subsequent jobs).

12.4.3 History Files in the SOEP

At each interview the SOEP collects information about the main activity status, income received (from different sources) and any changes in marital status and fertility information for the past 12 months. These are referred to in the SOEP documentation as calendar data (same as annual histories in the BHPS). In addition to these annual history files, the SOEP also collects information on past employment, marital and fertility histories when a person is interviewed for the first time (for samples A and B). For the remaining samples, adults were not asked these histories in the year when these samples were added, but asked the following year. These histories are not asked of children turning 16s and 17s (and who were part of the SOEP sample before becoming adults) because they can be retrieved from the information at each (adult) interview.

The employment status and income data collected for the past year are stored in wave-specific flat files named $pkal where $ stands for the wave-specific letter prefix (in the SOEP documentation $ is used to stand for the wave prefix, unlike the BHPS documentation which uses w). This same information is also available in two spell-level files: artkalen and einkalen. Each row of these files represents one specific type of spell (employment status in artkalen and income source in einkalen) for each individual over the entire duration of the survey. The variable spelltyp records the spell type. So, while each row of wpkal is uniquely determined by cross-wave unique individual identifier persnr, each row in these files is uniquely determined by the variable persnr and the spell identifier spellnr.

Also, as the artkalen and einkalen files include all spells, there is no need to combine separate files for each wave as in the case of the wpkal files. In other words, the files artkalen and einkalen contain information already set in the format necessary for duration analysis. As shown in Figure 12.1, these files also contain the household identifier, start and end dates of the spell (measured in months, where 1 means January 1983) and whether the spell was right censored. The spells are ordered such that the current one has the lowest value, namely 1.

```
Contains data from \...\artkalen.dta
  obs:        203,250                        ARTKALEN: 09/10/10 10:14:13-634 DB09
  vars:             7                        10 Sep 2010 11:00
  size:     3,048,750
-------------------------------------------------------------------------------
          storage   display    value
variable name   type    format     label      variable label
-------------------------------------------------------------------------------
hhnr            long    %12.0g                Original Household Number
persnr          long    %12.0g                Never Changing Person Number
spellnr         byte    %8.0g                 Serial Number Of The Event Per Person
spelltyp        byte    %39.0g    spelltyp    Type Of Event
begin           int     %22.0g    begin       Month Event Begins
end             int     %22.0g    end         Month Event Ends
zensor          byte    %37.0g    zensor      Censor Variable
-------------------------------------------------------------------------------


Contains data from \...\einkalen.dta
  obs:         63,079                        EINKALEN: 09/10/10 10:14:13-634 DB09
  vars:             7                        10 Sep 2010 11:02
  size:       946,185
-------------------------------------------------------------------------------
                storage   display    value
variable name   type      format     label    variable label
-------------------------------------------------------------------------------
hhnr            long    %12.0g                Original Household Number
persnr          long    %12.0g                Never Changing Person Number
spellnr         byte    %8.0g                 Serial Number Of The Event Per Person
spelltyp        byte    %26.0g    spelltyp    Type Of Event
begin           int     %22.0g    begin       Month Event Begins
end             int     %22.0g    end         Month Event Ends
zensor          byte    %26.0g    zensor      Censor Variable
-------------------------------------------------------------------------------
```

Figure 12.1   Details about the employment status and income event history files in the SOEP

The initial job history file (jobs since age 15) is merged with information from the annual job history file (artkalen) and is provided in the file pbiospe which has a similar structure to artkalen (each row uniquely determined by persnr and spellnr). As in the file artkalen, this file contains persnr and `spellnr`, information on spell type, beginning and end of a spell (both in months since January 1983 and in years) and whether the spell was censored. In addition to these variables the file contains other variables that are useful for understanding the edits conducted for consistency but can be ignored otherwise. These are variables that show in which year the initial history was collected, whether the information was collected from the initial history questions or from the annual history questions, or both, and so on.

Information on past marriages was combined with information on marriage collected between waves and stored in a spell-level file, `biomarsy`, where each row is uniquely determined by `persnr` and `spellnr`. The start and end dates for these spells are measured in years. Another similarly structured marital status spell-level file only includes marital status spell information collected at each interview (calendar data or annual histories); information starts from the year before the first year the person was interviewed. The spells are measured in months where 1 means January 1983. Both these files contain the variable `spelltyp` which takes on the value of 1 if the person is single, 2 if married, 3 if divorced, and so on, and a variable `remark` which provides information on data quality and source. The spells are ordered such that the oldest spell has value 1.

Information on all births for mothers is reported in an individual-level file `biobirth` consisting of information on number of births, year of birth and sex of up to 15 children (each row uniquely determined by `persnr`). The same information is available for fathers in `biobrthm` (but this has been collected for men since 2000). There is additional information on source and quality of the data.

All these files include household and individual identifiers that can be used to merge these datasets with other individual- or household-level data files. For further details about these data files see Chapter 3 of Haisken-DeNew and Frick (2005).

12.4.4 History Files in the PSID

The PSID provides retrospective data files for marriage and childbirth and adoptions. These files contain details of marriages, childbirth and adoptions for PSID respondents collected in the waves from 1985 onwards, together with retrospective histories prior to 1985. Hence, while data for events before 1985 are collected retrospectively, the data for events from 1985 onwards are effectively collected prospectively.

The marriage file has one record per marriage. Each record includes the person identifier together with the identifier of the spouse, an identifier for the marriage, and data about timing (start and end) and circumstances of the marriage. Additional records identify those who have never been married. Linking to the respondent file can be done using the person identifier or the identifier of the spouse. The childbirth and adoption history file has a structure similar to the marriage file and includes details of the parents; their marital status when the child was born; birthday, birth order and sex of the child; their race; and so on.

12.5 Summary and Suggestions for Further Reading

In this chapter we have discussed the general structure of data files collecting data on past histories, and problems that are often encountered when combining the history files with data referring to current status. This step is a prerequisite for organising the data for duration analysis, which we discuss in Chapter 13.

Key points

- History files usually record multiple spells per individual. Observations are unique by person and spell identifier.
- We need to understand how the spell identifier is organised, because this may be different across files.
- There are different ways to merge the data, which depend on the type of analysis we want to do.
- Care is needed to resolve inconsistencies to prepare the data for duration analysis.

Suggestions for further reading

- In this chapter we have discussed how to use the wave-on-wave job history files. After appending data for all the waves, we could then construct complete job histories starting on the day the respondent left full-time education. For reasons of space we could not do so here, but we refer to Halpin (1997) and Maré (2006) for further suggestions on solving inconsistencies with these additional files:

  o From the UK Data Archive (http://data-archive.ac.uk/) it is possible to download the consistent work–life history data produced by B. Halpin for the period 1990–2005. The dataset goes under the name 'British Household Panel Survey Combined Work-Life History Data, 1990–2005'; the study number is 3954. Details of the methods used by Halpin to derive the data are in: Halpin, B. (1997) Unified BHPS Work-Life Histories: Combining Multiple Sources into a User-Friendly Format. Technical Papers of the ESRC Research Centre on Micro-Social Change, 13, University of Essex.

o Complete documentation on the job and life history files, together with suggestions on how to merge them and resolve inconsistencies, can be found in: Maré, D. (2006) Constructing Consistent Work-life Histories: A Guide for Users of the British House-hold Panel Survey. ISER Working Paper 2006-39.

(13)

ANALYSIS OF EVENT HISTORY DATA

Aim

This chapter discusses how to use the BHPS lifetime employment history file to create an event history file of unemployment spells and how to carry out some basic duration analysis, both in the continuous and in the discrete case. The discussion is restricted to duration analysis of single spells and single state transitions with completed or right-censored spells only.

13.1 Setting Up Data for Duration Analysis

In the second wave of the BHPS, every person in the original (or 'Essex') sample was asked to report their entire lifetime employment status history since they first left full-time education. These data are provided in the file `blifemst`. Similar data were collected for the Scottish, Welsh and Northern Ireland regional boost samples, which were added in later waves. For simplicity, in this chapter we restrict our attention to the `blifemst` file, which only collects data for the original sample. Note that, unlike the wave-on-wave job history files we discussed in Chapter 12, as the information in the `blifemst` file was collected at one point in time, instances of date inconsistencies within this file are less likely. In analysing unemployment duration models, we would like to include additional information in the data, such as interview date, to be able to impute the spell end date for ongoing spells, and some individual characteristics such as sex and region of residence. We can get these variables from the individual respondent data collected in wave 2, bindresp. We also want to include in the analysis data on ethnicity. However, note that some variables, such as ethnicity and date of birth, are collected only once, when a person is first interviewed, so that they would be available for some people in wave 1 and for others in wave 2 (see the online appendix for more details on the BHPS data structure). The easiest way to get these variables is from the fixed information data file called xwavedat. Note that this file and the variables within it do not have a wave prefix.

First, inspect these three datasets: blifemst, bindresp and xwavedat. Check how the data files are arranged using the command duplicates. Next, merge these datasets and drop cases not available in all three. Note that the blifemst data file may have multiple rows of observation for each person, each row corresponding to one employment status spell.

At this point it is a good idea to create some useful variables and do some housekeeping. Create the dummy variables that you will use in the analysis and rename variables such that the new names are easier to understand and remember. Remember to check that the Stata commands you have written are doing what you expect them to do. Another useful tip is to rename the value labels so that they have the same name as the variable name – this makes them easier to remember. At this point it may be a good idea to drop variables that you will not need for the analysis. The data include a variable, bleslen, which records the spell duration but is missing for cases with missing start or end date and ongoing spells. As we will be creating a variable that records spell durations after imputing the start and end dates, it is better to drop bleslen at this point.

Write the commands and compare with the do file in the online appendix

Some end dates are missing because the spell is ongoing. Note that we cannot compute the duration for spells where the end date is missing, such as in the case of spells that are still ongoing. Hence, we substitute the (missing) end date of these spells with the interview date. Note that the variable for the interview year is in a two-digit format, while the years of the start and end of the spell are in a four-digit format. We will need to change the interview year into four-digit format before computing the duration of the spell:

```
replace intv_year = intv_year+1900
replace end_month = intv_month if ///
   spell_ongoing == 1
replace end_year = intv_year if ///
   spell_ongoing == 1
```

Additionally, some start and end dates are partially or wholly missing because people often have problems remembering exact dates of non-significant events.

Some people who did not remember the exact start or end month of a spell could remember the season. This is also a form of missing data. We need either to impute these missing values or to drop such cases from the analysis. A simple form of imputation is to decide on a practical rule. For example, when 'winter' is reported you can impute the value to be 1 (for January), and so on. Finally, to measure the duration of each spell of unemployment we will need to identify unemployment spells and then compute the duration of these spells using their start and end dates. To compute the duration of unemployment spells (after identifying unemployment spells and imputing start and end dates when missing) we can use the following command:

```
generate unempdur=((end_year-start_year)*12) + ///
   (end_month-start_month) if activity_status==4 ///
   & start_year>0 & end_year>0 & start_month>0 ///
   & end_month>0 ///
   & start_year<. & end_year<. & start_month<. ///
   & end_month<.
```

The next step is to create a dummy variable that takes on value 1 when the spell is right censored and 0 otherwise:

```
generate censored = 1 if spell_ongoing == 1
replace censored = 0 if spell_ongoing == -8
```

As always, it is worth listing out a few cases and looking at the frequency distribution of the new variable unempdur to see whether the Stata commands you have written are doing what you want them to do. Alternatively, open the Data Editor (Browse). You will notice that not all unemployment durations are positive. It is worth double-checking that these negative durations are not the result of wrong commands. If negative durations are a small proportion of all durations, and are the result of mis-coded dates in the data, we can drop them from the dataset. Also check that unemployment duration is missing for all types of spells other than unemployment spells.

Write the commands and compare with the do file in the online appendix

The data are now in the form shown in Table 13.1 (this corresponds to Table 11.3 of Chapter 11).

The final step for the analysis we want to do is to keep only the first unemployment spell for each person. As we have mentioned, in this chapter we focus only on single spells and on the first spell. Hence, drop all spells other than unemployment spells (keep if activity_status==4) and keep only the

Table 13.1 Event history data on main activity

ID	Spell No.	Start date	End date	Activity status	Spell ended?	Interview date	Spell duration	Censored spell?
1	1	17.02.07	17.05.07	Unemployed	Ended	15.01.11	3	0
1	2	17.05.07	15.12.09	Employed	Ended	15.01.11	28	0
1	3	15.12.09	15.01.11	Unemployed	Ongoing	15.01.11	13	1
2	1	01.10.04	15.06.10	Employed	Ended	05.01.11	68	0
3	1	01.10.07	05.01.11	Unemployed	Ongoing	05.01.11	39	1

first of the unemployment spells (bysort pid (spellno): keep if _
n==1). The data are now in the form shown in Table 13.2.

Table 13.2 Event history data on main activity, keeping the first spell

ID	Spell No.	Start date	End date	Activity status	Spell ended?	Interview date	Spell duration	Censored spell?
1	1	17.02.07	17.05.07	Unemployed	Ended	15.01.11	3	0
3	1	01.10.07	05.01.11	Unemployed	Ongoing	05.01.11	39	1

Finally, create a variable that measures the age at the start of a spell and save the data set as duration_continuous.dta.

Write the commands and compare with the do file in the online appendix

We discussed in Chapter 11 that the set-up of the data should be different depending on whether we consider our duration as continuous or discrete. If we treat the duration variable as continuous, the dataset is ready for analysis. If we treat these unemployment spells as discrete, we need to transform the dataset further, such that the new dataset looks like Table 13.3 (which is similar to Table

Table 13.3 Event history data on main activity, in person–spell–time format

ID	Spell no.	Activity status	Spell month	Spell ended
10001	1	Unemployed	1	0
10001	1	Unemployed	2	0
10001	1	Unemployed	3	1
10003	1	Unemployed	1	0
10003	...	...	...	0
10003	1	Unemployed	39	0

11.4 in Chapter 11). In other words, we would have to create as many copies of the data as the spell duration using the command expand.

The command expand creates as many copies of the data as the value of the variable (or the number) specified after it. The copies of the dataset are added to the same file as the original dataset. In our case we need as many copies of the datasets as the length of the unemployment spell. The command

```
expand unempdur
```

creates different number of copies for each person, depending on the length of their unemployment spell (unempdur). Now that we have transformed the data into person-month observations we create a new variable to identify the person-month, using the command bysort ... gen. Finally, we create a variable that tells us if each particular person-month observation was the one where the spell ended. Remember that for censored spells this variable will be zero for all person-month observations. We then save the dataset as duration_discrete.dta.

Write the commands and compare with the do file in the online appendix

13.2 Estimating Continuous-Time Duration Models

13.2.1 Stata sts Suite of Commands

The sts suite of commands is especially designed for survival analysis when survival time is considered to be continuous. Similar to the case of the xtset and svy commands, in the case of survival analysis we have first to specify that the data are intended for duration analysis. In this case we stset the data, that is, we tell Stata that the data are survival time (st) data and specify their structure:

```
stset timevar, failure(failvar) id(idvar)
```

where timevar is the survival time or spell duration variable. The option failure() is used to specify the variable identifying whether the spell is censored instead of being completed. If the option failure() is not specified, every record is assumed to end in a failure (that is, all spells are considered completed). In the case of multiple record data, this condition must be specified. If you just type failure(failvar) then Stata interprets the spell to be censored whenever failvar is zero or missing, and completed otherwise. Alternatively you can explicitly specify the censoring condition by using failure(failvar==numlist), where a spell is considered to be censored if it does not take on any of the values of numlist. The option id() is used to specify the variable that identifies individuals. If you do not specify the option id(), then Stata assumes that each record (identified by the variable `timevar`) refers to a different individual. So, in the case of single-spell data we do not need to specify this option. In our case, to set up the data in `st` format, the command is

```
stset unempdur, failure(censored==0)
```

Once specified, Stata remembers the `stset` specifications until they are respecified.

The `stset` command creates some internal Stata variables. One such variable is `_t`, which signifies the survival time. If you want to create a generic program that will work no matter what the actual survival time variable is called, then you should use `_t` instead of the name of the survival time variable, which is `unempdur` in our case.

If you want to know the details of the data set up in survival time form, use the command `st`.

13.2.2 Estimating Non-parametric Survivor, Failure and Hazard Functions

The equivalent of frequency tables, histograms and kernel density functions for duration data are non-parametric estimations of survivor functions. These methods do not account for differences in these functions due to individual differences, although you can estimate separate functions for sub-groups. Some commonly used estimators are the Kaplan–Meier (also known as the product-limit) estimator of the survival and integrated hazard functions; the Nelson–Aalen estimator of the cumulative hazard function; and lifetable estimators (see Jenkins 2005). If the duration time is considered to be continuous then Kaplan–Meier and Nelson–Aalen estimators are used. If the spell duration is considered to be discrete or represents intervals during which the event occurred, then the lifetable estimator is used. These estimators can handle right censoring. We will focus our discussion on the Kaplan–Meier survivor function estimator.

At each point when a transition out of a state, say unemployment, is observed, the survivor function is estimated as the proportion of people who continue to be unemployed among those who were unemployed prior to this point in time (also referred to as 'at risk of failure'). Those who leave the state of unemployment are referred to as 'failed' and those who were still unemployed at a time point, but were no longer observed by the next time point, are referred to as 'net lost' (right censored). Table 13.4 shows an example of these types of data and how to compute the Kaplan–Meier estimator of the survivor function.

In Table 13.4 we see that, in January, among the 100 people in the sample, 20 became employed and 5 were still unemployed but left the survey or were not observed by the next time point in March. So, the survivor function in

Table 13.4   Estimating survivor function using Kaplan–Meier estimator

Time	At risk	Failed[a]	Net lost[a]	Survivor Function
January	100	20	5	$1 - (20/100) = 0.80$
March	75	10	0	$0.75 \times (1 - (10/75)) = 0.69$
September	65	5	0	$0.69 \times (1 - (5/65)) = 0.64$
December	60	1	0	$0.64 \times (1 - (1/60)) = 0.63$

[a] Net lost means right censored and Failed means completed spells. These terms are used primarily in survival analysis discussions.

January is 0.80. But by March only 75 are at risk of failure or could transition out of unemployment. Of these 10 do, and the survivor function in March is 0.69. The resulting survivor function is shown in Figure 13.1. The only information we have about transitioning out of a state are the observed failure times, but we do not know how this varies in the intervening period. This is why the survivor function in this case is a step function. The height of the step reflects differences in estimates of the survivor functions at each time point, and the width of the step varies because of differences in failure time intervals.

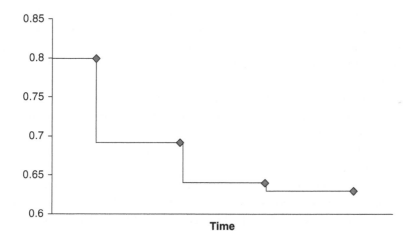

Figure 13.1   Kaplan–Meier survivor function

Note that we have not made any assumptions about the functional form for the hazard or survivor functions, but we let the data determine the shapes. For this reason, we say that the Kaplan–Meir estimator is a non-parametric estimator (it makes no assumptions on the parameters of the distribution).

To produce the Kaplan–Meier estimator of the survivor function in table form we use the command sts list, and to draw its graph we use the command sts graph. Now we can draw a graph of the Kaplan–Meier failure function; the Nelson–Aalen cumulative hazard functions, and the smoothed hazard function can be produced by specifying the options `survival (default)`, `cumhaz` and `hazard`.

Write the commands and compare with the do file in the online appendix

As expected, the Kaplan–Meier failure function and the Nelson–Aalen cumulative hazard functions are very similar. They both measure the proportion of those at risk who leave the state. Also, as the survivor function measures the proportion of those at risk who remain in the state, the Kaplan–Meier survivor function is the mirror image of the Kaplan–Meier failure function.

If we consider the unemployment durations as intervals during which individuals transition out of unemployment, then we should use the lifetable estimators. The command is called `ltable` and does not require the `stset` command:

```
ltable unempdur
```

13.2.3 Proportional Hazard Models

The estimators that we have discussed up to now do not take into account any individual characteristics. In the case of linear regression, this would be the same as computing a simple correlation coefficient between two variables. We use regression analysis to take into account that the correlation may also vary across groups and depend on individual characteristics. If we want to include individual characteristics in our duration analysis we can use, for example, proportional hazard models.

Proportional hazard (PH) models represent a class of hazard models which comprise two multiplicative parts: a duration dependence function common to all individuals; and a part which is a function of individual characteristics. In other words, the PH models assume that the duration dependence is common to all individuals, and each person's hazard function is a parallel shift of this common duration dependence, where this shift factor depends on each person's characteristics. The PH models are also known as multiplicative hazard models or as log relative hazard models (Jenkins 2005). All PH models are of the form

$$\theta(t, X) = \psi(X)\phi(t) \tag{13.1}$$

where X is a vector of explanatory variables, $\psi(X)$ is the shift factor function and $\varphi(t)$ specifies the duration dependence function, which is often referred to as the baseline hazard. Different PH models assume different forms for these two functions. A commonly used form for $\psi(X)$ is the exponential function. Most PH models use the exponential function for $\psi(X)$ and only differ in terms of the functional forms for the baseline hazard, $\varphi(t)$. The general case, where $\psi(X)$ is exponential and $\varphi(t)$ is left unspecified, is

$$\theta(t,X) = [\exp(\beta'X)]\phi(t)$$

(13.2)

This is the multivariate regression counterpart for duration models. In these models, everyone shares a basic hazard rate, $\varphi(t)$, but this function shifts based on the person's individual characteristics. If $\varphi(t)$ decreases as time increases, it means that the longer someone is unemployed, the lower is their unemployment hazard. If one of the factors X_k represents spousal income and we find that its coefficient β_k is negative, it means that, if all else remains the same, the person whose spouse earns more has a higher hazard rate of unemployment.

Two of the most common functional forms for the baseline hazard are the exponential and Weibull functions. The exponential model assumes no duration dependence ($\varphi(t)$ is a constant) which depends on the explanatory variables X but not on the length of the spell t, so that Equation (13.2) becomes

$$\theta(t) = \exp(\beta'X)$$

(13.3)

The Weibull model assumes that $\varphi(t) = \alpha t^{\alpha-1}$. The Weibull model therefore allows for zero, positive and negative duration dependence, and Equation (13.2) becomes

$$\theta(t) = \alpha t^{\alpha-1} \exp(\beta'X)$$

(13.4)

In the Weibull model the type of duration dependence is not assumed a priori but is inferred based on the estimated value of the parameter α. If α is greater than one, then the hazard is increasing with time spent in that state (there is positive duration dependence); if it is less than one then the hazard is decreasing with time spent in that state (there is negative duration dependence). If α is equal to one then there is no duration dependence and the Weibull is identical to the exponential function.

A useful property of the PH model is that, at any point in time t, the ratio of the hazard rates for two people is independent of the survival time:

$$\frac{\theta(t,X_i)}{\theta(t,X_j)} = \exp[\beta'(X_i - X_j)]$$

(13.5)

where i and j are two individuals and X_i and X_j the vectors of their characteristics. So, at any point in time the absolute difference in the individuals' characteristics X_i and X_j is reflected as a proportional difference in their hazard rates. A one-unit difference between the two individuals in one of the characteristics, say X^k, while keeping the other characteristics the same across the two individuals, equals the exponential function of the coefficient of that characteristic, say β^k:

$$\frac{\theta(t, X_i)}{\theta(t, X_j)} = \exp[\beta^k] \qquad (13.6)$$

For this reason, $\exp[\beta k]$ is known as the hazard ratio. From Equation (13.2), it also follows that

$$\beta^k = \frac{\delta \log \theta(t, X)}{\delta X^k} \qquad (13.7)$$

so that each coefficient measures the proportional effect on the hazard of an infinitesimal small change in the value of the factor. For example, if the estimated coefficient of a variable A is a, it implies that, as A changes by one unit, the hazard rate increases by a%.

As we have already stset the data, we are ready to estimate a PH function using the command streg. This command estimates parametric regression survival time models using maximum likelihood estimation. A number of different models can be fitted in Stata including the Weibull and exponential functions. The model to be fitted can be specified using the option distribution (distname). By default, Stata reports hazard ratios ($\exp[\beta]$) rather than the coefficients (β). You can ask Stata to produce coefficients instead of hazard ratios using the option nohr. This option is valid only for models with a PH ratio parameterisation: exponential, Weibull and Gompertz.

When Stata reports the results it reports α as 'p' and you can deduce the nature of the duration dependence from the estimated value of p. Stata also provides the standard errors and p-values for the natural logarithm of p (namely, $\ln(p)$) and tests if $\ln(p) = 0$ (which is the same as testing if $p = 1$). To estimate a Weibull model with individual characteristics such as age, gender, ethnic group, the command is

```
streg age female white north midlands stheast ///
    wales scotland, distribution(weibull)
```

The results of this command are reported in Figure 13.2. At the bottom of the results table we can see the test on p. We can see that the data reject the hypothesis that $p = 1$ (or $\ln p = 0$). As the estimated value of p is less than 1 (0.821), there is negative duration dependence. Reading off the estimated hazard ratios and their p-values, we can also say that, at any point in time, women are as likely as men to leave the state of unemployment (the hazard ratio is very close to 1 and not statistically different from it), but whites are more likely to leave unemployment than non-whites (the coefficient is larger than 1 and statistically significant). As this is a duration model, 'more likely to leave unemployment' translates into leaving unemployment faster.

To plot the cumulative hazard, survival and hazard functions at the mean value of the covariates, we use the command stcurve after the streg command.

```
. streg age female white north midlands stheast wales scotland, distribution(w)

        failure _d:  censored == 0
  analysis time _t:  unempdur

Fitting constant-only model:

Iteration 0:   log likelihood =  -2578.099
Iteration 1:   log likelihood = -2499.6539
Iteration 2:   log likelihood = -2499.6204
Iteration 3:   log likelihood = -2499.6204

Fitting full model:

Iteration 0:   log likelihood = -2499.6204
Iteration 1:   log likelihood = -2481.1111
Iteration 2:   log likelihood = -2480.9469
Iteration 3:   log likelihood = -2480.9468

Weibull regression -- log relative-hazard form

No. of subjects =         1518              Number of obs    =       1518
No. of failures =         1391
Time at risk    =        18355
                                            LR chi2(8)       =      37.35
Log likelihood  =    -2480.9468             Prob > chi2      =     0.0000
```

_t	Haz. Ratio	Std. Err.	z	P>|z|	[95% Conf. Interval]	
age	.9992463	.0004714	-1.60	0.110	.9983227	1.000171
female	.9967321	.0545715	-0.06	0.952	.8953128	1.10964
white	1.413103	.2031441	2.41	0.016	1.066123	1.873011
north	.7468838	.0775322	-2.81	0.005	.6093852	.9154069
midlands	.7286552	.0809123	-2.85	0.004	.5861407	.9058207
stheast	1.03511	.1062957	0.34	0.737	.8464013	1.265892
wales	.8521687	.119173	-1.14	0.253	.6478699	1.120891
scotland	.9809616	.1208389	-0.16	0.876	.7705441	1.248839
_cons	.1137205	.018722	-13.21	0.000	.0823576	.1570268
/ln_p	-.1969252	.0187625	-10.50	0.000	-.233699	-.1601514
p	.8212521	.0154087			.7916001	.8520148
1/p	1.217653	.0228462			1.173689	1.263264

Figure 13.2   Estimation results for a PH Weibull model of unemployment duration

Specifically, to plot the hazard function, use stcurve, hazard. We can also plot the cumulative hazard, survival and hazard functions separately for men and women and for white and non-white groups and save these graphs.

Write the commands and compare with the do file in the online appendix

The hazard functions estimated separately for men and women are shown in Figure 13.3, while the hazard functions estimated separately for whites and non-whites are shown in Figure 13.4.

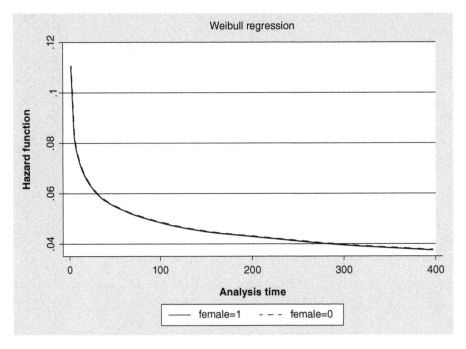

Figure 13.3   Predicted hazard function for men and women based on a PH Weibull model of unemployment duration

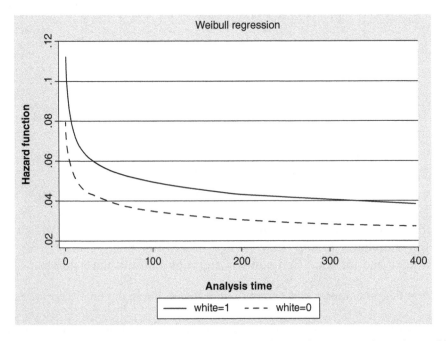

Figure 13.4   Predicted hazard function for white and non-white groups based on a PH Weibull model of unemployment duration

As you can see, these graphs reflect what we had deduced from the estimated coefficients of the PH model. The hazard functions for white and non-white groups are different, while those for men and women are almost identical (see Figures 13.3 and 13.4). In other words, the pattern of leaving unemployment is similar for women and men, but non-white groups are less likely to leave unemployment at any point in time than white groups.

If you want to predict the hazard rate for each person at their completed or censored spell durations, you can use the command `predict predHaz, hazard`. All those individuals with the same completed or censored spell durations, same gender, ethnic group and age at the start of the unemployment spell will have the same predicted hazard.

The median survival time for an individual with a particular set of characteristics is the spell length at which the survival probability for such a person is expected to become half (note that the survival probability at the start of a spell is one). Starting from time 0, and assuming that individual characteristics do not change over time, the median survival time can be estimated in Stata in the following way:

```
predict survMd, median time
```

From the results of this command (see the online appendix), we find that for all 30-year old white women living in the North, the median survival time is 8.7 months while for those living in the South East it is 5.9 months and averages at 7 months. In other words, on average, for white women the chances of being unemployed for at least as long as 7 months are 50%.

13.2.4 Unobserved Heterogeneity

There are different ways to model unobserved heterogeneity (also called frailty). In parametric methods unobserved heterogeneity is modelled as a random variable with a specific probability distribution. If the frailty is denoted by v, then the new hazard function is specified as

$$\theta(t, X_i \mid v) = v\theta(t, X_i)$$

(13.8)

As the parameters of the PDF of v are known, the likelihood function is written such that it includes only the parameters of v rather than specific values of v, also known as 'integrating out' (Jenkins 2005). We will not discuss non-parametric methods here but refer to Ham and Rae (1987) and Heckman and Singer (1984) for more information.

For parametric models, in the continuous case the distribution of the unobserved heterogeneity is generally assumed to be a gamma or an inverse Gaussian distribution with mean equal to 1. To estimate a Weibull PH model, where the distribution of the unobserved heterogeneity is assumed to be a gamma distribution, we can use the command

```
streg age female white, ///

   distribution(weibull) frailty(gamma)
```

The estimation results, in addition to the standard parameter estimates, will contain an estimate of the variance of the frailties and a likelihood ratio test of the null hypothesis that this variance is 0. When this null hypothesis is not rejected, there is no unobserved heterogeneity. A specified frailty() is remembered and used from one estimation to the next when the option

```
. streg age female white north midlands stheast wales scotland, distribution(w) frailty(gamma)

         failure _d:  censored == 0
   analysis time _t:  unempdur

Fitting Weibull model:

Fitting constant-only model:

Iteration 0:   log likelihood = -2350.9182
Iteration 1:   log likelihood = -2266.9769
Iteration 2:   log likelihood = -2257.5748
Iteration 3:   log likelihood = -2257.5218
Iteration 4:   log likelihood = -2257.5218

Fitting full model:

Iteration 0:   log likelihood = -2338.1931
Iteration 1:   log likelihood = -2252.4494
Iteration 2:   log likelihood = -2249.6643
Iteration 3:   log likelihood =  -2249.625
Iteration 4:   log likelihood =  -2249.625

Weibull regression -- log relative-hazard form
               Gamma frailty

No. of subjects =        1518              Number of obs   =       1518
No. of failures =        1391
Time at risk    =       18355
                                          LR chi2(8)      =      15.79
Log likelihood  =    -2249.625            Prob > chi2     =     0.0454
```

_t	Haz. Ratio	Std. Err.	z	P>|z|	[95% Conf. Interval]	
age	.9997252	.0012321	-0.22	0.824	.9973132	1.002143
female	1.105371	.145839	0.76	0.448	.8535	1.431571
white	1.425484	.4656287	1.09	0.278	.7514857	2.703983
north	.778096	.1831065	-1.07	0.286	.4905948	1.23408
midlands	.6871682	.1760256	-1.46	0.143	.4159284	1.135292
stheast	1.267106	.2987059	1.00	0.315	.7982733	2.011287
wales	.7596392	.258767	-0.81	0.420	.389628	1.481032
scotland	1.175706	.3433751	0.55	0.579	.6632819	2.084009
_cons	.0277925	.0107252	-9.28	0.000	.0130451	.0592118
/ln_p	.8590572	.0661397	12.99	0.000	.7294257	.9886887
/ln_the	.9524716	.1101693	8.65	0.000	.7365437	1.1684
p	2.360934	.1561515			2.073889	2.687708
1/p	.4235612	.0280142			.3720643	.4821858
theta	2.592108	.2855709			2.088704	3.21684

```
Likelihood-ratio test of theta=0: chibar2(01) =   462.64 Prob>=chibar2 = 0.000
```

Figure 13.5 Estimation results for a PH Weibull model with gamma frailty specified

distribution() is not respecified. When you respecify the option distribution(), the previously used specification of frailty() is forgotten.

Figure 13.5 shows the results of a Weibull model with frailty following a gamma distribution.

The theta at the bottom of the results table is the estimated variance of the frailty distribution. The likelihood ratio test of theta = 0 below the table is the test for the null hypothesis that the unobserved heterogeneity is zero. In this case we find that the test rejects the null hypothesis, thus suggesting that there is unobserved heterogeneity. Once we have corrected for unobserved heterogeneity, as expected, the negative duration dependence (the value of ln_p in the middle of the table) reduces and in this case becomes positive and statistically significant. We now find a statistically significant positive duration dependence ($p = 2.4$). This suggests that people with certain unobserved characteristics (for example, motivation) are more likely to leave unemployment faster and that those remaining in the pool of unemployed for longer have comparatively 'worse' unobserved characteristics.

Note that the hazard ratios displayed represent the proportional changes in the hazard only if all other covariates, including frailty, remain the same over time. But in the case of population hazards, that is, the average hazard rate in the sample at any point in time, the average value of the frailty decreases over time. This is because cases with higher frailty drop out of the sample, the remaining sample is more homogeneous and the remaining cases have lower values of frailty (see StataCorp 2013c: 378). So, the hazard ratios have the proportional change interpretation only at $t = 0$.

13.2.5 Semi-Parametric PH Models (Cox Model)

In this section we discuss semi-parametric models. The specific one that we discuss is the Cox proportional hazard model (Cox 1972; Yamaguchi 1991). This model allows us to relax any restriction on the functional form of the baseline hazard. The Cox PH model, like all PH models, consists of two multiplicative parts (see Section 13.1.3). The difference with the parametric hazard models is that the functional form of the part specifying the duration dependence (or the baseline hazard) is non-parametric. This means that the baseline hazard is estimated from the data and does not rely on parametric assumptions (such as an exponential or a Weibull distribution). Another useful feature of the Cox model is that the baseline hazard is allowed to vary by categorical variables such as gender, ethnicity or level of education (stratified Cox models). On the other hand, the Cox model has a number of disadvantages as well. One of them is that it does not handle tied events very well and different approximations have to be used to deal with tied events. If the data include many tied events, Yamaguchi (1991) suggests using discrete-time models instead.

Once the data have been `stset`, you can estimate a Cox model using the `stcox` command. This command will produce estimates of the coefficients of the individual specific shifts, but not of the baseline hazard. By default Stata uses the Breslow method (Breslow 1974) to treat cases of tied failure times; other methods can be specified in the options.

If you want to estimate the so-called null model, that is, without any covariates, you can use the command in the following form:

```
stcox, estimate
```

If you just type `stcox`, Stata will not estimate the null model but replay the results of the last Cox model estimated. The baseline survivor function estimated using the Null model is the same as that estimated using the Kaplan-Meier method. To estimate a Cox model with covariates, it is enough to add the list of explanatory variables. By specifying the option `basesurv(newvar)`, Stata produces a new variable `newvar` which records the value of the estimated baseline survivor function at each point in time. Similarly, the baseline hazard is recorded by specifying the option `basehc(newvar)`. The command and its results are shown in Figure 13.6.

```
. stcox age female white north midlands stheast wales scotland, basesurv(baseline1)

        failure _d:  censored == 0
  analysis time _t:  unempdur

Iteration 0:   log likelihood = -8958.1018
Iteration 1:   log likelihood = -8948.9096
Iteration 2:   log likelihood = -8948.8935
Iteration 3:   log likelihood = -8948.8935
Refining estimates:
Iteration 0:   log likelihood = -8948.8935


Cox regression -- Breslow method for ties

No. of subjects =        1518                    Number of obs   =       1518
No. of failures =        1391
Time at risk    =       18355
                                                 LR chi2(8)      =      18.42
Log likelihood  =   -8948.8935                   Prob > chi2     =     0.0183
```

_t	Haz. Ratio	Std. Err.	z	P>|z|	[95% Conf. Interval]	
age	.999646	.0004755	-0.74	0.457	.9987146	1.000578
female	1.055755	.0577613	0.99	0.321	.9484036	1.175258
white	1.28588	.1839285	1.76	0.079	.9715095	1.701978
north	.8401644	.086903	-1.68	0.092	.6859929	1.028985
midlands	.8131374	.0898658	-1.87	0.061	.6547739	1.009803
stheast	1.042128	.10702	0.40	0.688	.852134	1.274483
wales	.9025372	.1260886	-0.73	0.463	.6863542	1.186812
scotland	.9852311	.1213103	-0.12	0.904	.7739818	1.254139

Figure 13.6   Estimation results for a Cox model

The estimates of the coefficients of this Cox model are very similar to those estimated for a PH Weibull model (see Figure 13.2); the hazard ratio for the group of white people is slightly lower, and that of the regions north and midlands slightly higher in the Cox than in the Weibull model. Note that the main difference between the two models is in the specification of the baseline hazard, which was restricted to be exponential in the PH Weibull model but not restricted to any parametric form in the Cox model.

Stratified Cox models can be estimated by specifying the option strata(varlist); Stata allows estimation for up to five strata. To estimate the Cox model stratified by gender, use

```
stcox age white north midlands stheast ///

    wales Scotland, strata(female) nolog
```

If we are not interested in the log of the iterations we can specify the option nolog. The results of the estimation of this command are shown in Figure 13.7.

```
. stcox age white north midlands stheast wales scotland, basesurv(baseline2) ///
> strata(female) nolog

        failure _d:  censored == 0
  analysis time _t:  unempdur

Stratified Cox regr. -- Breslow method for ties

No. of subjects =        1518              Number of obs   =        1518
No. of failures =        1391
Time at risk    =       18355
                                           LR chi2(7)      =       17.21
Log likelihood  =    -8005.3278            Prob > chi2     =      0.0161
```

_t	Haz. Ratio	Std. Err.	z	P>|z|	[95% Conf. Interval]	
age	.9996126	.0004765	-0.81	0.416	.9986793	1.000547
white	1.29252	.1854231	1.79	0.074	.9757194	1.71218
north	.836367	.0865662	-1.73	0.084	.6828028	1.024468
midlands	.8118454	.0897863	-1.88	0.059	.6536336	1.008352
stheast	1.038813	.106732	0.37	0.711	.84934	1.270555
wales	.8994849	.1257549	-0.76	0.449	.683895	1.183037
scotland	.9792639	.1206687	-0.17	0.865	.7691505	1.246775

```
                                                    Stratified by female
```

Figure 13.7   Estimation results for a Cox model stratified by gender

We find that the hazard ratio for age is 0.99. The estimated coefficient of age is the natural log of 0.99 and from Equation (13.7) we know that $\ln(0.99) = -0.01$ measures the proportional change in the hazard rate from a one-unit increase in age. So, the hazard rate of leaving unemployment is lower for older people, although the effect is not statistically significant. Instead of having to do these conversions we can ask for the estimated coefficients to be displayed in place of hazard ratios by specifying the nohr option. Also, if all we are interested in is the sign of the effect, then we can use this mathematical relationship: if a number is less than one then its natural log is negative, otherwise positive. We also find that white men and women are likely to leave unemployment earlier than non-white men and women.

We can compare the estimated unstratified baseline hazard, baseline1, with the baseline hazards estimated separately for men and women with the help of a graph. We restrict the graph to the first 30 time points (months):

```
twoway line baseline2 _t ///

  if female==1 & e(sample)& _t<30, sort || ///

  line baseline2 _t ///

  if female==0 & e(sample) & _t<30, sort || ///

  line baseline1 _t ///

  if female!=. & e(sample)& _t<30, sort ///

  legend(label(1 women) label(2 men) ///

  label(3 all)) scheme(s2mono)
```

Figure 13.8 shows that the baseline survivor function for women is slightly lower than that of men up to the first 20 months in unemployment, but is hardly any different after that. This implies that at the start of the unemployment period, women are more likely to leave unemployment than men, but the difference between men and women decreases over time.

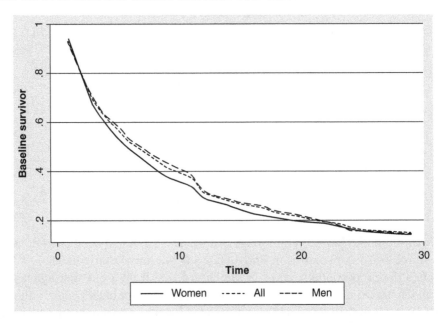

Figure 13.8   Baseline survivor function (for unemployment) by gender

Note that Stata by default draws graphs from one observation to the next and, unless the data are sorted on the X variable, it produces weird-looking graphs. The sort option sorts the data by the variable on the X-axis.

13.3 Estimating Discrete-Time Duration Models

If we want to estimate duration models where time is discrete, we need the data structured as in Table 13.3. If we specify the hazard function as a logit model, then we are in effect estimating a logit model where each time period is treated as a separate observation, and the binary dependent variable is the variable which specifies whether the individual left the state of unemployment in that time period (measured by the variable spellended). So, we can estimate such a model using the command logit.

We can specify a functional form for the duration dependence, which could be as simple as the duration itself (measured by monthid), or a polynomial of the duration, or the natural log of the duration. We then include this variable among the explanatory variables. Jenkins (2005: 85) shows that if we specify the functional form of the duration dependence as $\alpha \log(t)$ then this is very similar to the specification of the baseline hazard in the Weibull distribution where the duration dependence is positive if $\alpha > 1$, and so on.

The estimation command and its results are shown in Figure 13.9:

```
generate logdur=log(monthid)

logit spellended logdur age female white ///

    north midlands stheast wales Scotland
```

```
Logistic regression                          Number of obs    =      18396
                                             LR chi2(9)       =     480.59
                                             Prob > chi2      =     0.0000
Log likelihood =    -4768.17                 Pseudo R2        =     0.0480
```

spellended	Coef.	Std. Err.	z	P>|z|	[95% Conf. Interval]	
logdur	-.4249297	.0219809	-19.33	0.000	-.4680115	-.3818479
age	-.0006812	.0004948	-1.38	0.169	-.001651	.0002885
female	.0192601	.0570202	0.34	0.736	-.0924975	.1310177
white	.3245344	.1490394	2.18	0.029	.0324225	.6166463
north	-.2124501	.1086396	-1.96	0.051	-.4253797	.0004795
midlands	-.2639251	.1161745	-2.27	0.023	-.491623	-.0362273
stheast	.055605	.1081671	0.51	0.607	-.1563987	.2676087
wales	-.1276934	.1467027	-0.87	0.384	-.4152254	.1598385
scotland	-.0027928	.1296715	-0.02	0.983	-.2569442	.2513586
_cons	-1.78081	.169664	-10.50	0.000	-2.113345	-1.448274

Figure 13.9 Estimation results for a discrete duration model with logistic hazard function

The results of this model can be interpreted as you would interpret the results in a logit model, which here represents the probability of leaving unemployment, conditional on being unemployed up until that time. Hence, for ease of interpretation, we compute the marginal effects of this model. The results are given in Figure 13.10.

```
. margins, dydx(*)

Average marginal effects                      Number of obs    =      18396
Model VCE      : OIM

Expression    : Pr(spellended), predict()
dy/dx w.r.t.  : logdur age female white north midlands stheast wales scotland
```

	dy/dx	Delta-method Std. Err.	z	P>|z|	[95% Conf.	Interval]
logdur	-.0295023	.0015999	-18.44	0.000	-.032638	-.0263667
age	-.0000473	.0000344	-1.38	0.169	-.0001146	.00002
female	.0013372	.0039588	0.34	0.736	-.006422	.0090964
white	.022532	.0103541	2.18	0.030	.0022384	.0428256
north	-.0147501	.0075463	-1.95	0.051	-.0295406	.0000404
midlands	-.018324	.0080711	-2.27	0.023	-.0341431	-.0025049
stheast	.0038606	.0075101	0.51	0.607	-.0108589	.0185801
wales	-.0088656	.0101862	-0.87	0.384	-.0288302	.011099
scotland	-.0001939	.0090029	-0.02	0.983	-.0178393	.0174515

Figure 13.10   Marginal effects of model specified in Figure 13.9

As in the PH Weibull model, here we estimated the model without accounting for frailty, and we find that there is negative duration dependence since the marginal effect for the variable logdur is negative and statistically significant. While there is no difference in the conditional probability of leaving unemployment between men and women, we find that white people are more likely to leave unemployment than non-white people. But note that this is the average effect on the conditional probability of leaving unemployment over the entire duration of unemployment. Also note that the duration dependence specification is the discrete-time counterpart of the baseline hazard. To see if there is a difference in the duration dependence by gender or ethnic group we could either interact gender and ethnic group by monthid or estimate separate models. Estimate separate models for men and women and compare the estimated duration dependence for men and women.

Write the commands and compare with the do file in the online appendix

There are different methods of accounting for unobserved heterogeneity in discrete-time models. If we assume that the unobserved heterogeneity is normally distributed with zero mean and finite variance then we can estimate this model using random effects methods. Use the xtlogit command to estimate the model (see Chapter 10), but remember first to declare the data as a panel dataset where the time dimension is identified by the variable monthid. The results of the xtlogit command are given in Figure 13.11, while the estimated marginal effects are shown in Figure 13.12:

```
xtset pid monthid

xtlogit spellended logdur age female white ///

    north midlands stheast wales scotland, re
```

```
Random-effects logistic regression          Number of obs      =      18396
Group variable: pid                          Number of groups   =       1559

Random effects u_i ~ Gaussian                Obs per group: min =          1
                                                            avg =       11.8
                                                            max =        397

Integration method: mvaghermite              Integration points =         12

                                             Wald chi2(9)       =      34.17
Log likelihood  = -4725.9576                 Prob > chi2        =     0.0001
```

spellended	Coef.	Std. Err.	z	P>|z|	[95% Conf. Interval]	
logdur	1.858135	.3299491	5.63	0.000	1.211447	2.504824
age	-.0014969	.0017551	-0.85	0.394	-.0049369	.0019431
female	.1235313	.1944873	0.64	0.525	-.2576568	.5047194
white	.9025535	.5003579	1.80	0.071	-.07813	1.883237
north	-.4843737	.3663224	-1.32	0.186	-1.202352	.2336049
midlands	-.7634782	.3961922	-1.93	0.054	-1.540001	.0130443
stheast	.3085841	.3642315	0.85	0.397	-.4052966	1.022465
wales	-.4189843	.5029236	-0.83	0.405	-1.404696	.566728
scotland	.0875062	.4382564	0.20	0.842	-.7714605	.946473
_cons	-5.121941	.7868293	-6.51	0.000	-6.664098	-3.579784
/lnsig2u	2.477658	.2565855			1.974759	2.980556
sigma_u	3.451569	.4428114			2.684192	4.43833
rho	.7836068	.0435085			.6865226	.8568916

```
Likelihood-ratio test of rho=0: chibar2(01) =    84.42 Prob >= chibar2 = 0.000
```

Figure 13.11 Estimation results for a discrete duration model with logistic hazard function and controlling for unobserved heterogeneity

```
. margins, dydx(*) predict(pu0)

Average marginal effects                        Number of obs    =      18396
Model VCE      : OIM

Expression    : Pr(spellended=1 assuming u_i=0), predict(pu0)
dy/dx w.r.t. : logdur age female white north midlands stheast wales scotland
```

	dy/dx	Delta-method Std. Err.	z	P>|z|	[95% Conf. Interval]
logdur	.2264818	.0108952	20.79	0.000	.2051277	.247836
age	-.0001825	.0002126	-0.86	0.391	-.0005992	.0002343
female	.0150568	.0236406	0.64	0.524	-.0312779	.0613915
white	.1100092	.0593027	1.86	0.064	-.0062219	.2262402
north	-.0590387	.0443257	-1.33	0.183	-.1459154	.0278381
midlands	-.0930578	.0472956	-1.97	0.049	-.1857554	-.0003602
stheast	.0376123	.0440445	0.85	0.393	-.0487134	.1239379
wales	-.0510686	.0611621	-0.83	0.404	-.1709441	.0688069
scotland	.0106658	.05337	0.20	0.842	-.0939374	.1152691

Figure 13.12   Marginal effects of model specified in Figure 13.11 (estimated assuming unobserved heterogeneity is zero)

From Figure 13.11 we can see that the likelihood ratio test rejects the null hypothesis that the random effect is zero. In other words, we cannot reject the presence of unobserved heterogeneity. As in the case of the PH Weibull model, once we control for unobserved heterogeneity, the duration dependence becomes positive (see Figure 13.12) and the marginal effects of other covariates become stronger. For example, the conditional probability of leaving unemployment is 11 percentage points higher for white people than non-white people, but this was estimated to be only 2 percentage points higher in the earlier model (see Figure 13.10).

13.4 Summary and Suggestions for Further Reading

In this chapter we have discussed how to use the BHPS lifetime employment history file to create an event history file of unemployment spells and how to carry out some basic duration analysis in cases of continuous and of discrete durations.

Key points

- Remember that the data may not be available in the particular structure necessary for duration analysis.
- For a description of the nature of duration data, use non-parametric estimators of survival and hazard functions such as the Kaplan–Meier, Nelson–Aalen and lifetable estimators.
- For duration analysis where spell duration is treated as a continuous variable, use the `sts` set of commands. Use `stset` to define the duration data, `sts graph` and `sts list` to produce Kaplan–Meier survivor functions, `streg` for estimating PH models, and `stcox` for Cox models.
- For duration analysis where the spell duration is treated as a discrete variable, set up the data such that the duration of each spell is a separate variable and then use standard estimation techniques for binary dependent variables such as logit models.
- Remember to take into account unobserved heterogeneity since it may bias the duration dependence estimates downwards.

Suggestions for further reading

- Stata has a manual focusing on the `st` set of commands, which are typically used for duration analysis: StataCorp. (2013c) *Survival Analysis and Epidemiological Tables Reference Manual.* College Station, TX, Stata Press.
- You can find a good – technical – discussion of duration models in: Jenkins, S. (2005) Survival Analysis. Available at: www.iser.essex.ac.uk/files/teaching/stephenj/ec968/pdfs/ec968lnotesv6.pdf.
- For a gentler introduction see:

  o Yamaguchi, K. (1991) *Event History Analysis.* London, Sage;
  o Blossfeld, H., Golsch, K. and Rohwer, G. (2007) *Event History Analysis with Stata.* Mahwah, NJ, Lawrence Erlbaum Associates; and
  o Cleves, M. et al. (2010) *An Introduction to Survival Analysis Using Stata,* 3rd Edition. College Station, TX, Stata Press.

PART IV

PRESENTING YOUR RESULTS

14

PRODUCING OUTPUT TABLES AND GRAPHS

Aim

The previous chapters discussed various estimation techniques and highlighted the correct way of interpreting the results of the analysis. This chapter concludes this book by discussing how to use Stata to produce output tables for descriptive statistics and regression results and how to visualise the results using graphs.

14.1 Introduction

In the previous chapters we have shown how to compute tables of descriptive statistics, how to estimate regression models and how to interpret their results. Often we may want to export the tables of descriptive statistics or the regression results into a spreadsheet or text document to be included in a paper. There are various options to achieve this result. The easiest one is to highlight the set of results in the Stata 'Results' window and then copy and paste them into another application. To make the copy we first highlight the results that we want to export, then either use Ctrl + C, or use the Stata menu Edit → Copy, Copy Table, or Copy Table as HTML. However, this means we have to copy/paste all our tables every time we make small changes to our analysis. Furthermore, the tables of results that Stata displays by default contain much more information than we may need to show in a paper (for example, both t-statistics and p-values, together with confidence intervals).

Besides being quite time-consuming, this copy/paste approach may also generate errors, for example if we forget to select one or more rows of results. It is good practice to automate the process by using the Stata saved results. This will also save time, especially if we have a large number of tables to produce. In some cases user-written commands such as `outreg`, `estout` or `esttab` may speed up the process even more. Although at first it may seem quite challenging to implement some of the methods we discuss below, they give the best chance of generating consistent and reproducible results.

In the following sections we discuss various ways in which we can save our results into tables. To keep things simple we use only the data from wave `r` of the BHPS that we used for the examples in Chapter 8.

Sometimes, when working on a number of different projects, it is a good idea to store the outputs in project-specific folders. Stata allows the creation of folders from within the do file using the command `mkdir`. To illustrate its usefulness we use this command in some of our do files:

```
capture mkdir "C:\My Documents\chapter14"
```

We can then use a global macro to point to this folder and store all outputs such as log files, graphs, new datasets in this folder:

```
global analysisdir "C:\My Documents\chapter14"

log using ///

   "$analysisdir\Example_Chapter14.log", replace
```

14.2 Saving Tables of Descriptive Statistics

In this section we want to tabulate how the proportions of married or cohabiting people in our dataset are distributed across the UK countries (England, Wales, Scotland and Northern Ireland) and save the results in a spreadsheet that we can use for ad hoc formatting of our table. For simplicity, here we use unweighted proportions. Below we suggest two methods. The first one uses the `bysort` and `egen` commands. This method is a bit simpler but less flexible than the second method, which uses the Stata saved results (see also Chapter 5). The second method may look complicated at first, but it is more flexible and allows various extensions, some of which can be used to save tables of marginal effects (see Section 14.4.2).

For the purpose of this first exercise we want to produce and export a table that looks like Table 14.1. We discuss how to produce such a table in Sections 14.2.1 and 14.2.2.

Table 14.1   Distribution of married and not married residents across UK countries

	T_NotMarried	T_Married
England	0.454	0.519
Wales	0.184	0.175
Scotland	0.180	0.167
Northern Ireland	0.181	0.139
Total	1	1
Observations	5,128	9,167

In Section 14.2.3 we discuss how to produce and export a table that looks like Table 14.2. This table tabulates the proportion of married people in England, Wales, Scotland and Northern Ireland. For this kind of exercise we use the command `collapse`.

Table 14.2   Proportion of married people in UK countries

	Proportion_Married	Number_Observations
England	0.671	7,087
Wales	0.629	2,547
Scotland	0.624	2,548
Northern Ireland	0.578	2,203
UK	0.641	14,295

14.2.1 Using the `bysort` and `egen` Commands

To create a table similar to Table 14.1, as a first step we open the dataset saved in Chapter 8 (`DatasetR.dta`) and recode the variable `region2` into the UK countries. We then label the new variable and its values.

The table we want to create is similar to the one which results from the command `tab Country Married`. We use the `bysort` and `egen` commands to create one variable which sums the total number of people who are not married or cohabiting (`X_NotMarried`), and one which sums the total number of people who are married or cohabiting (`X_Married`) by `Country`. We then create two additional variables which include the number of observations for married and non-married people (`N_Married` and `N_NotMarried`). Since we are interested in the overall number of observations, in this last case we do not need the `bysort` part of the command.

Write the commands and compare with the do file in the online appendix

If we look at the Data Editor, we can see that the content of the first two new variables (X_NotMarried and X_Married) varies only by country, while the other two variables (N_Married and N_NotMarried) are constant across countries. Hence, without loss of information we can keep just one observation per country. One way to keep one observation per country and only the variables of interest is to use the bysort and keep commands:

```
keep Country X_* N_*
bysort Country: keep if _n == 1
```

The first command selects the variables (columns) we want to keep, while the second one selects the observations (rows) we want to keep. As an alternative, the same result can be obtained using the command collapse X_* N_*, by(Country); for more details on this command see Section 14.2.3. Note that in the command bysort ... keep we can use a combination of variables, for example country and year if we have panel data and want to obtain a time series (see also Section 14.2.3).

The new dataset contains five variables (Country, X_NotMarried, X_Married, N_NotMarried and N_Married) and four values (one for each country). At this point we can compute the proportion of married and non-married people by country, label the variables and drop unwanted observations (for example, when Country == .).

Write the commands and compare with the do file in the online appendix

We still need to add the last two rows of Table 14.1. To do this, we first add two new empty rows of observations, using the command set obs:

```
set obs 6
```

This command increases the number of observations in the dataset, to the specified number. As we have four rows of observations in our dataset, the command adds two additional rows. Next, we replace the missing values in the last row with the total number of observations for married and non-married people: N_Married and N_NotMarried. We also assign a value to the variable Country, which we can label 'Observations' (see Table 14.1):

```
replace T_Married = N_Married[1] if _n==6
replace T_NotMarried = N_NotMarried[1] if _n==6
replace Country = 6 if _n==6
```

In the fifth row we replace the missing values in the variables N_Married and N_NotMarried with the value 1 (the sum of all proportions in that column, see

Table 14.1), and the missing values in the variable Country with a value which we will later label 'Total %':

```
replace T_Married = 1 if _n==5

replace T_NotMarried = 1 if _n==5

replace Country = 5 if _n==5
```

Finally, we save the new dataset with a new name to avoid overwriting the individual-level dataset. We can then open the Data Editor, copy its content and paste it in any other program.

Note that in this case Country is a numeric variable. If we copy the data from the Stata browser into Excel, the value labels are not carried over. However, we can generate a new string variable where we store the name of the country that corresponds to the numeric value in Country as shown below:

```
generate CountryString = "England" if Country == 1

replace CountryString = "Wales" if Country == 2

replace CountryString = "Scotland" if Country == 3

replace CountryString = "Northern Ireland" ///
    if Country == 4

replace CountryString = "Total" if Country == 6
```

Manually copying these tables from Stata into Excel is a tedious and error-prone process. A better alternative is to automate the process by directly exporting the new dataset into an Excel spreadsheet (or to any other format) using the command

```
order Country T_NotMarried T_Married

export excel using ///
    "$analysisdir\TableMethod1.xls", ///
    replace firstrow(variable)
```

The command order orders the variables in Stata in the preferred order, while the command export creates the Excel file. The option firstrow(variable) is used to export the variable names as the first row.

We can now format the table following the publisher's standards.

14.2.2 Using Stata Saved Results

In this section we suggest a different method to automate the process of producing tables of descriptive statistics by using the results that Stata automatically saves after running the command `tab`. The objective is again to produce a table similar to Table 14.1. Also in this case we will have to modify the dataset: we will produce a table of results within the open dataset, then keep only the rows and columns where the table is stored and save it with a new name to avoid overwriting the original dataset. Although this is sub-optimal – ideally we would like to save the table in a new dataset – it is the only option in this case, since Stata does not allow us to have two datasets open at the same time. (As an alternative, we could save the result in a matrix and then convert the matrix into a dataset to be exported into other formats.)

As before, we open the dataset, recode the variable `region2`, and label the variable and its values. We then start by creating a string variable which contains the labels that we want to have in our output table; this will become the first column of our table of descriptive statistics. We can call this variable `Names`. In the first row of this new variable (in 1) we add the value 'England'; in the second row (in 2) we add the value 'Wales'; and so on. We also want to record the column percentage in the fifth row and the number of observations in the sixth row. We can leave any row free if we want:

```
generate Names = ""

replace Names = "England" in 1

replace Names = "Wales" in 2

replace Names = "Scotland" in 3

replace Names = "Northern Ireland" in 4

replace Names = "Total %" in 5

replace Names = "Observations" in 6
```

Hence, this new variable will have non-missing values only in the first six rows. Note that with these commands we assign the values to a specific cell; if we later sort the dataset, the position of these cells may change thus compromising our table of results. Hence, if any sorting is needed, it has to be done before we start producing our table of results.

It is useful to create the first column of our table of results before computing the actual values we want to put in the table. When we want to produce large tables of results or descriptive statistics it is easy to forget in which row each value needs to be placed. After creating the variable `Names` we can create two new variables containing only missing values, in which we will save the results of our tabulation; we can call them `T_NotMarried` and `T_Married`. The dataset at this point looks like the one in Table 14.3.

Now we use the command `tabulate`:

```
tabulate Country Married, col matcell(Total)
```

Table 14.3   Original dataset including the table of descriptive statistics

pid	mastat	region2	Married	Names	T_NotMarried	T_Married
1001	1	1	1	England	.	.
1002	1	5	1	Wales	.	.
1005	1	8	1	Scotland	.	.
2015	3	12	0	Northern Ireland	.	.
2045	2	5	1	Total %	.	.
2245	3	4	0	Observations	.	.
3511	.	1	.		.	.
3604	2	1	1		.	.
5741	2	3	1		.	.
6858	3	5	0		.	.

The option `matcell` saves the frequencies in the matrix `Total` (Total is a name of our choice). Note that it is only possible to save frequencies, not proportions, and that no results are saved after the command `tab` unless we use the option `matcell`. We can tabulate the stored matrix to verify its structure: `mat list Total`. At this point we need to study this matrix carefully and check in which column and row each frequency is stored (see Figure 14.1).

```
. mat list Total

Total[4,2]
        c1      c2
r1    2330    4757
r2     944    1603
r3     925    1533
r4     929    1274
```

Figure 14.1   Matrix 'Total'

In this case the matrix has four rows and three columns. Each row refers to the country (the four different values in the variable `Country`), one column includes the labels, and each of the two remaining columns refer to the marital status (the two different values in the variable `Married`). We now sequentially pick each frequency and store it in the right row of the right variable (either T_NotMarried or T_Married). In this particular case the values that we want to record in the T_NotMarried variable are in the first column of the matrix, while the values that we want to record in the T_Married variable are in the second column of the matrix. We can use a loop over the four rows (countries):

```
local i = 1
while `i' <= 4    {
   replace T_NotMarried = Total[`i',1] in `i'
   replace T_Married = Total[`i',2] in `i'
   local i = `i' + 1
}
```

We should also double-check that the table of results we are creating includes the right frequencies (browse Names T_*). At this point we have a table of the overall frequencies, which we now have to convert into proportions. If we want the proportions by row we can create a new variable called, for example, Total which contains the sum of the two variables (T_NotMarried and T_Married). Note that, similar to the case of local and global macros, variables and matrices may have the same name; Stata will not confuse them because the syntax for using variables and matrices is different. We now divide the values of each variable by the total. These are the same proportions as in the command tab Country Married, row.

Write the commands and compare with the do file in the online appendix

If we want proportions by column (as in the command tab Country Married, col), we need to compute them separately for each of the two values that the variable Married can have. Hence, we need an extra step: we first tabulate the variable Country if Married is zero. At this point Stata saves the total number of observations in the variable r(N). This contains the total number of observations that we need for the variable T_NotMarried. We then store the total number of observations in the right cell (in 5/6) and generate a temporary variable in which we store this total (generate Tempo = r(N) in 1/5). After this step we can divide the variable T_NotMarried by this temporary variable and repeat for the variable T_Married.

Write the commands and compare with the do file in the online appendix

We can easily compute proportions by cells by combining the two procedures: computing proportions by columns and by row. Finally, we can save our table of descriptive statistics in a spreadsheet. We keep only the variables (columns) and cells (rows) that form part of our table and use the command export to save our new dataset in spreadsheet form.

Write the commands and compare with the do file in the online appendix

We can now use the spreadsheet or text software to format our table following the publisher's standards.

14.2.3 Using the `collapse` Command

In this section we describe how to obtain a table of descriptive statistics similar to Table 14.2. The best way to obtain such a table is to use the command `collapse` which converts the dataset open in memory into a new dataset of means, medians, sums, etc. Execution of the `collapse` command means that the dataset open in memory is lost, if it was not saved prior to using the command.

Again, we start by opening the dataset saved in Chapter 8 (`DatasetR.dta`), recoding the variable `region2` into the UK countries and labelling the new variable. This time we hold off on labelling the values of the variable `country` since value labels are lost when we use the `collapse` command. We then save this new dataset.

Write the commands and compare with the do file in the online appendix

Next, we use the `collapse` command to produce a table of the proportion of married people and the total number of people (married and not married) in each of the four countries:

```
collapse (mean) ProportionMarried = Married ///
    (count) Number_Observations = ///
    Married, by(Country)
```

This command generates a new variable called `ProportionMarried` which contains the mean of the variable `married`, and a new variable called `Number_Observations` which contains the total number of non-missing observations in the variable `married`. Since the variable `married` is a dummy which has value 1 for married people and 0 for non-married people, its mean corresponds to the proportion of people who are married. The `by(Country)` option requests that these descriptive statistics are computed separately for each `Country`. After a `collapse` command, only the descriptive statistics are retained; all other variables are dropped. The new dataset only contains the variables `ProportionMarried`, `Number_Observations` and `Country`.

If we wanted to produce statistics by country and wave, we would have included both variables `Country` and `wave` in the `by()` part of the command: `by(Country wave)`. This is possible since `by()` allows a list of variables.

At this point we have the first four rows of Table 14.2: the proportion of people who are married and the total number of people in each of the four countries. What is missing is the last row which contains the UK-level statistics. To produce the same statistics for the UK as a whole, we use a similar set of commands but this time we do not include the option `by(Country)`. Remember that this dataset only contains the variables `ProportionMarried` and `Number_Observations`. We therefore have to create the variable `Country` and give it a value of 5. The reason for giving `Country` a higher value than any of the existing values is that, when we later sort the merged data by `Country`, the UK-level statistics will appear in the last row. Next, we append to this dataset the saved dataset with country-level statistics. This is the time to define and attach value labels to the variable `Country`. When we sort the data by `Country`, the UK-level statistics are in the last row and the dataset looks like Table 14.2. We can now export and save this dataset in Excel format by using the command `export excel`. The complete sequence of commands is in the do file in the online appendix.

14.3 Graphs of Descriptive Statistics

14.3.1 Bar Graphs

We discussed histograms and kernel density graphs in Chapter 3 and event history graphs in Chapter 13. Here we discuss a few more types of graphs which are particularly useful for descriptive statistics and refer to Mitchell (2012) for more types of graphs and options.

Let us start with the dataset in Section 14.2.3. To produce a bar chart to show the proportion of married people across the UK countries, we can use the command

```
graph bar ProportionMarried, ///
   over(Country, label(angle(45))) ///
   ytitle("Proportion") ///
   scheme(s1manual) ///
   title("Proportion married - UK countries") ///
   note("Source: BHPS wave 18") ///
   saving("$analysisdir\PropMarried1.gph", replace)
```

The option `over` creates separate bars for each value of the categorical variable `Country`. If we do not specify the option `over(Country)` Stata produces a graph with one single bar, which is the overall mean of the variable `ProportionMarried` across all five values of the variable `Country`. The

Stata graph options discussed in Chapter 3 can be applied here, for example ytitle. By specifying the label option within over(Country, label(angle(45))), the country labels appear at a 45 degree angle. If we prefer horizontal bars we can use the graph hbar instead of bar. It is also useful to add notes to the graph, for example to specify the data source by making use of the note option.

The resulting graph looks like the one in Figure 14.2.

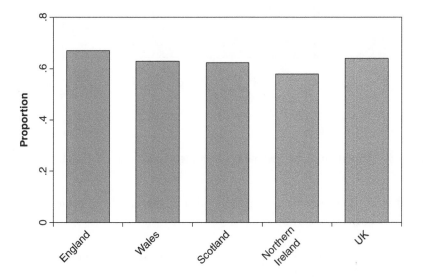

Figure 14.2   Bar graph of proportion married across UK countries

It is also possible to save Stata graphs in a different format, such as pdf, using the command graph export, so that they can be opened using software such as Adobe Reader: graph export "$analysisdir\ PropMarried1.pdf", replace. See the Stata help for a complete list of file formats supported.

We can also produce a graph for the proportion of married women across the UK countries. First, we produce a table with the proportion of married people separately for men and women across the UK countries, remembering to attach value labels after the collapse command. Now we can produce a bar graph separately by gender and country.

Write the commands and compare with the do file in the online appendix

The resulting graph looks like the one in Figure 14.3.

If we want to produce a graph showing the proportion of people with different levels of education across the UK countries, we first need to produce

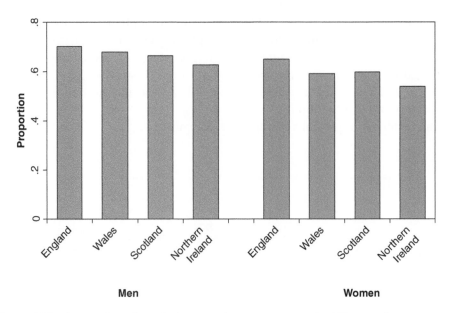

Figure 14.3   Proportion of married men and women across the UK countries

a dataset with the proportions of people with different education levels (Q1–Q6 variables in `DatasetR.dta`).

Write the commands and compare with the do file in the online appendix

Now we can produce a horizontal bar graph of the proportions of people with each of the six levels of education across the UK countries. We specify the option `stack` to get a stacked bar graph.

There is one important difference between this graph and earlier ones: in those earlier graphs there was one variable for which we were drawing the graph, `ProportionMarried`, while in this graph there are six variables, Q1–Q6. Hence in this graph we can specify a different colour for each of the six bars, although we are not using this option here because our graphs are only in black and white. The resulting graph should look like the one in Figure 14.4.

This graph highlights that a higher (lower) proportion of adults in England and Scotland have a first degree or higher (no educational qualifications) than adults living in Wales and Northern Ireland. However, it is worth remembering that these are unweighted proportions: the graph shows descriptive statistics for our dataset, which may or may not coincide with those in the population. To produce a graph that can be interpreted in terms of the population we should use weighted statistics (see Chapter 7).

It is not necessary to produce a dataset of descriptive statistics to obtain a graph: we could produce a bar graph directly from the individual-level dataset.

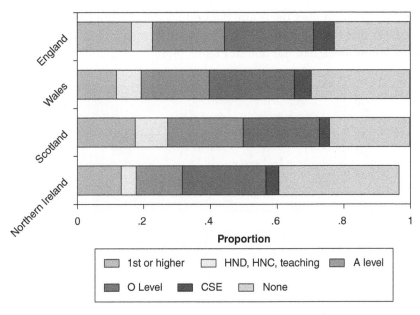

Figure 14.4   Educational composition across UK countries (method 1)

Source: BHPS wave 18

The following code produces the same bar graph as in Figure 14.5 but without using the collapse command:

```
graph hbar Q1 Q2 Q3 Q4 Q5 Q6, stack ///
   over(Country, relabel(1 "England" 2 "Wales" ///
   3 "Scotland" 4 "Northern Ireland") ///
   label(angle(45))) ///
   ytitle("Proportion") ///
   title("composition across UK countries") ///
   scheme(s1manual) ///
   note("Source: BHPS wave 18") ///
   legend(label(1 "1st or higher") ///
      label(2 "HND,HNC,teaching") ///
      label(3 "A level") ///
      label(4 "O level") ///
      label(5 "CSE") ///
      label(6 "None")) ///
saving("$analysisdir\PropEdu2.gph", replace)
```

As this type of graph uses the entire data rather than just the reduced dataset of means as in the earlier example, this graph may take longer to compute. The resulting graph looks like the one in Figure 14.5.

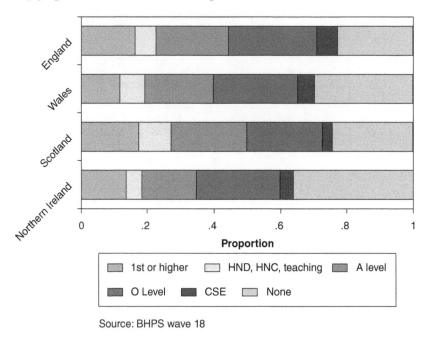

Source: BHPS wave 18

Figure 14.5   Educational composition across UK countries (method 2)

To produce this type of graph separately for men and women we can use the by option.

Write the commands and compare with the do file in the online appendix

14.3.2 Time-Series Graphs

When we have panel data we may want to analyse how some aggregate variables of interest may covary over time. For example, we may be interested in the proportion of married and non-married people and how these proportions vary over time in the BHPS (remember that we need to use weights if we want to generalise our results to the population; this is, however, beyond the scope of this section). We can go back to the file DataFile.dta which we saved at the end of Chapter 4 and which includes all waves of the BHPS. We open the file and create the variables of interest if they are not already in the dataset. Similar to Section 14.2.1 we compute the number and proportions of married and non-married people. The only difference here is that in this case the groups will vary by both Country and wave rather than by Country only.

Write the commands and compare with the do **file in the online appendix**

If we open the dataset (edit or browse) we can clearly see that we have a panel of countries across waves. We can plot the time series of the proportion of married and non-married people using the command twoway:

```
twoway (tsline PropMarried, lcolor(black))   ///

   (tsline PropNotMarried, lpattern(dash)) ///

   if Country == 1, ///

   ytitle(Proportion) ytitle(, size(medsmall)) ///

   ttitle(year) ttitle(, size(medsmall)) ///

   scheme(s1manual) ///

   legend(cols(1) nobox region(lpattern(blank)))
```

The command twoway allows us to combine different types of graphs. In this case we want two time-series graphs, one for PropMarried and one for PropNotMarried (tsline PropMarried and tsline PropNotMarried). The command tsline generates a time-series graph/line.

Note that the commands for the two sub-graphs, including all their specific options, are within parentheses. We want the line of the first command to be black (lcolor(black)) and the line of the second graph to be dashed (lpattern(dash)). After specifying the options of each sub-graph we specify

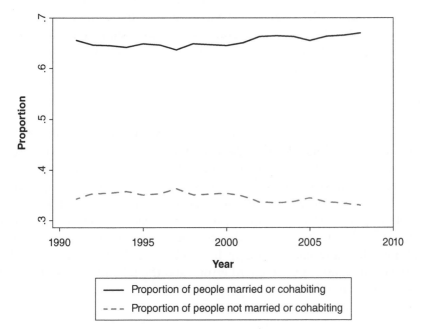

Figure 14.6   Time-series graph

the options of the overall graph; for example, we want the graph to include only England (if Country == 1) and we can specify a legend for the y-axis (ytitle) and for the x-axis (ttitle; it is called 't' because it is a time-series graph). The sub-option size(medsmall) refers to the size of the legend (medium–small in this case). We can also specify that we want the overall legend of the graph to be in one column (legend); look at the Stata manual for more options. The resulting graph looks like the one in Figure 14.6.

Remember that we need to use the command tsset or xtset before we can use the tsline command. To have a more meaningful legend on the time-series axis we should generate a variable which corresponds to the year of the BHPS interview, from the variable which includes the waves of the interview. The complete sequence of commands is in the do file in the online appendix.

14.4 Saving Regression Results

14.4.1 Saving Results of a Linear Regression

It is relatively easy to save tables of regression coefficients thanks to a number of user-written commands which we can install in our version of Stata (see also Section 3.3 on how to install additional commands). One of these commands is estout (see Jann 2005, 2007b). The command estout works in two steps. After estimating each regression model we use the command estimates store, followed by the name we want to give to the estimation results, for example R_OLS1. This saves the results of the last estimation with the given name. Once the results of all our models have been saved, we can produce output tables using the command estout:

```
estout R_OLS1 R_OLS2 using FileName.out, replace
```

where R_OLS1 and R_OLS2 are the names that we gave to the results of the two models we have estimated. With the command estout we can save the estimated regression coefficients, their standard errors and other statistics in an 'output' file. When we open the file FileName.out in Word, the output appears as text, which we can convert into a properly formatted table in a few steps. After selecting the text we want to convert into a table, we use the menu Table → Convert → Text to Table. Note that for the conversion to work properly we should not select any note we might have added to the table: we should only select the coefficients, their standard errors, and the R2 and number of observations at the bottom of the table.

Useful options of the command estout are:

1. `keep(keeplist)`, which keeps only the parameters of interest, in case we want to show in the table only some of the estimated coefficients. If we do not specify this option, all the regression coefficients are saved.
2. `cells(array|none)`, which refers to the contents of the table cells. For example, `cells(b(star fmt(%9.3f)))` specifies that we want to show only three decimals of the estimated coefficients (`...b...`), and we want Stata to include stars/asterisks to identify the level of statistical significance (`...b(star...)`). We can use the option `starlevels()` to specify how many stars (or other symbols) would identify the level of statistical significance. The option `cells(se(par fmt(%9.3f)))` specifies that we want to show only three decimals of the estimated standard errors (`...se...`), and we want Stata to put them within parentheses (`...se(par...)`).
3. `stats(scalarlist[, subopts])`, which displays summary statistics at the bottom of the table. For example, `N` shows the number of observations; `r2` shows R^2; `r2_a` shows the adjusted R^2; `aic` shows the Akaike Information Criterion.
4. `postfoot(stringlist)`, which adds a specified text after the table footer, for example table notes.

You can find more details and the complete sequence of commands in the do file in the online appendix, where we estimate a model to analyse individual wages, similar to the one in Chapter 8, Equation (8.1), save the results of our estimates and then use the `estout` command to produce the output table. In the online appendix, see also the do file for Chapter 8.

As an alternative to the command `estout` we can use the command `esttab` which works in a similar way (see the Stata manual for more details). The commands `outreg` and `outreg2` are similar to `estout`. The main difference is that the commands `outreg` and `outreg2` have to be placed after each estimation command because they do not rely on the command `estimates store`.

These commands can be used after any type of estimation command, even after non-linear models such as `logit` or `probit`. However, these commands store coefficients and only in some specific cases are able to store marginal effects (for example, after the command `dprobit` and in some cases after the command `mfx`, but not after the command `margins`).

14.4.2 Saving Marginal Effects

We can produce a table of results showing the marginal effects and their standard errors (*t*-stats and so on) using the results that Stata automatically saves after each estimation command. Similar to Section 14.2.2 we start by creating a string variable which contains the labels that we want to appear in our table. If we want to show the standard errors (or *t*-stats or *p*-values) below the coefficients, then we need to leave one empty row between two consecutive labels:

```
generate Variable = ""

replace Variable = "age" in 1

replace Variable = "age2" in 3

replace Variable = "Married" in 5

replace Variable = "Q1" in 7

replace Variable = "Q2" in 9

replace Variable = "Q3" in 11

replace Variable = "Q4" in 13

replace Variable = "Q5" in 15

replace Variable = "Log likelihood" in 18

replace Variable = "Observations" in 19
```

We then run our models, for example a probit model to describe the probability of being in employment, similar to the one in Chapter 8, Equation (8.2), and compute the marginal effects (note that we can only use the command margins after the estimation of a model: the command margins does not stand alone). We then create a variable that will contain the marginal effects, the standard errors and everything else we want to appear in that column of our table. For example, one of the Stata saved estimation results is called e(ll) and contains the value of the (maximum) log likelihood, which we want to save in row 18; r(table) is a matrix which contains the marginal effects, their standard errors, *t*-statistics, *p*-values, and so on. We use the command mat list r(table) to view the full content of the matrix. For simplicity we save r(table) in a matrix which we call R. We then identify the position of the marginal effects and of the other statistics in the R matrix and save them in the appropriate row and column of the output table we want to create. You can find more details and the complete sequence of commands in the do file in the online appendix.

We can automate the process of saving the marginal effects and their standard errors using a loop:

```
local i = 1

local j = 1

while `i' <= 8    {

   * Save the coefficient/marginal effect:

   replace Men = R[1,`i'] in `j'

   local j = `j' + 1

   * Save standard error in row below

   * marginal effect:

   replace Men = R[2,`i'] in `j'

   local j = `j' + 1
```

```
local i = `i' + 1

}
```

where the local variable `i' goes up to the number of variables we have in the R matrix, while `j' is an additional counter which identifies the row in our output table where we want to save the values. Hence, the counter `i' has to go up only after we have saved both marginal effects and standard errors, while the counter `j' has to go up each time we save one value in a cell (it goes up twice for each time `i' goes up). Note that the marginal effects are in the first row of the R matrix (hence replace Men = R[1,`i'] in `j'), and the standard errors are in the second row (replace Men = R[2,`i'] in `j'). Since *t*-stats are in the third row, if we wanted to save them rather than standard errors we would have used R[3,`i'] rather than R[2,`i'].

Once again, after completing all rows and columns of our output table we keep only the variables and observations relevant to our output table and export it for example to a spreadsheet. The table does not yet look as nice as the ones produced by the estout commands (Section 14.3.1); parentheses around the standard errors and asterisks for statistical significance have to be added by hand in the spreadsheet. However, this requires much less effort than copy/paste from the Stata 'Results' window.

A new user-written routine has recently become available, which can be used along with the commands estout and esttab to save results from margins. This user-written routine is called estpost. If estpost is not installed, we install it after locating it using the command findit (see Section 3.2.1). As this is part of the estout program, when we search for estpost the link provided refers to the command estout. If an older version of estout is already installed on the computer, we forcefully replace the old version with the new one.

After running the estimation command (for example, probit) we use est-post margins, dydx(*) to 'post' the marginal effects estimated by the command margins, dydx(*). If we are using the command estout, we can use the command estimates store right after the command estpost. No additional changes are needed for the estout part of the command. If we are using the command esttab and specify the option cell("b se"), the table will show the marginal effects instead of the coefficients.

14.5 Graphs of Regression Results

14.5.1 The Command parmest

Sometimes, especially for oral presentations, it may be easier to show graphs of the regression coefficients and their standard errors rather than to discuss tables. A useful command, called parmest, has been proposed by Newson (2003). This command converts the estimation results into a dataset which contains the parameter estimate, the confidence intervals, *p*-values, and so on. This dataset contains one observation per parameter and can be used to plot the regression parameters together with, for example, their confidence intervals. When the dataset is in this form we can use for example the command `eclplot` to produce a graph of estimates and confidence intervals.

Similar to the commands we discussed in Section 14.4 to produce output tables, the command `parmest` works in two steps. After each regression we save its results with the command

```
parmest, format(estimate min95 max95) ///

saving("$analysisdir\RegGraph", replace)
```

The option `format` specifies that the new data files should contain the estimate of the parameter (`estimate`) and the 5% confidence intervals (`min95 max95`). The new dataset is saved in the file `RegGraph.dta`; as usual, the option `replace` overwrites the previously created dataset.

Once the new dataset is saved, we open it and drop the observations referring to the coefficients we do not want to show in our graph (for example, the intercept).

Write the commands and compare with the do file in the online appendix

The variable `parm` in this dataset contains the name of the explanatory variables in our regression and, since it is a string, in order to create our graph we need to encode it into a numeric value using, for instance, the command `sencode`. For example, the command `sencode parm, gen(parmid)` generates a new variable, called `parmid` (parameter identifier), which contains the numerical values associated with the string `parm`. Now we can create our graph using the command `eclplot`, which plots estimates with confidence intervals:

```
eclplot estimate min95 max95 parmid, ///

    horizontal xline(0) scheme(s1manual) ///

    ylabel(1 "age" 2 "age square" 3 "female" ///

    4 "married" 5 "Q1" 6 "Q2" 7 "Q3" 8 "Q4"   ///

    9 "Q5", labsize(small)) ///

    title(Wage Regression)
```

where `estimate` is the name of the variable containing the estimated parameters, `min95` and `max95` are the two variables containing the confidence interval, and `parmid` is the numeric variable we have just created. Most of the options in this graph are discussed in the previous sections and chapters. The option `horizontal` specifies that we want the variables to be shown on the vertical – rather than on the horizontal – axis, while the option `xline(0)` draws a vertical line where the horizontal axis is zero. This facilitates the reading of the graph since confidence intervals that cross this line show that the parameter is not statistically significant. The resulting graph looks like the one in Figure 14.7.

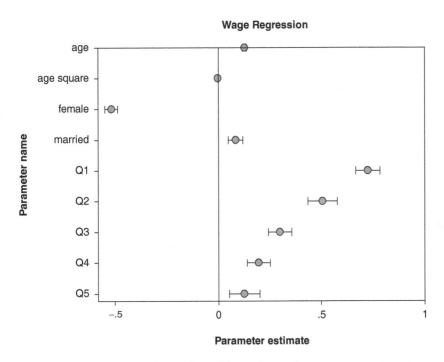

Figure 14.7 Parameter estimates and confidence intervals

The figure clearly shows the estimates and their precision. In our case, only the variable age square is not statistically significant. The only negative coefficient is that of the female dummy and there seems to be a clear gradient for education: although any level of education pays more than having no education, the two highest levels of qualification pay wages that are on average much higher than the other levels of education.

Other options for the command parmest are available; check the Stata manual for details. For example, the command parmby works in a similar way to the command parmest but produces a dataset that contains an estimation parameter and other statistics for each group specified by the by variables.

14.5.2 The Command marginsplot

In previous chapters we learned how to use the command margins. This command is particularly useful for estimating marginal effects which vary with values of the explanatory variables, such as when the model includes polynomials of explanatory variables, interactions, and when we use non-linear models such as probit or logit. Stata has recently introduced a new command called marginsplot, which allows us to plot the output of the command margins (the command marginsplot has to be preceded by the command margins). The options available with graph commands are also available with marginsplot.

Let us estimate a probit of the probability of being married for individuals between the ages of 18 and 59 and include age, age-squared, education dummies, region dummies, employment status and number of own children in the household as explanatory variables. Particularly if there are polynomials or interactions, it is useful to include the explanatory variables in factor variable format. The command to estimate this model is

```
probit Married c.age##c.age i.Female ///
    ib7.edu ib7.region2 nchild i.Employed ///
    if age>=18 & age<60, vce(robust)
```

We now estimate the average marginal effects of age on the probability of marriage at different ages so that we can plot them on a graph. As we are interested in the graph based on the margins output rather than the values of the margins, we use the option quietly:

```
quietly margins, at(age = (25(1)45))
```

We can use quietly before any estimation command when we want to prevent Stata from showing the results of the command in the 'Results' window. This is particularly useful when the estimation command is an intermediate step, as in this case. The command above computes (but does not show on screen) the predicted probability of marriage by assuming that everyone in the dataset is aged 25 years, 26 years, 27 years, and so on, while the other variables are kept at their actual values. If we add the option atmeans, then the other variables are assigned their mean values. What we obtain with the command margins, at() is the probability of being married at different ages. We now plot these marginal effects using the command marginsplot:

```
marginsplot, scheme(s1manual) xlabel(25(5)45) ///
    xtitle("Age as of date of interview") ///
    note("Source: BHPS wave 18") ///
    saving("$analysisdir\predprob_age", replace)
```

The resulting graph looks like the one in Figure 14.8.

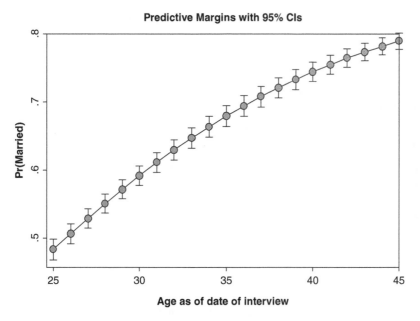

Figure 14.8   Predicted probability of marriage at different ages

Source: BHPS wave 18

We know that the estimated coefficient of age is positive (0.119) and the coefficient of age-squared is negative (−0.001); both are statistically significant. As already mentioned, unlike in a linear model, we cannot read off the marginal effect of age based on these coefficients. Looking at the graph we find that the predicted probability of marriage increases with age, at a slightly decreasing rate. We can also plot the marginal effects of the variable age at different ages.

Write the commands and compare with the do file in the online appendix

The resulting graph looks like the one in Figure 14.9.

The figure shows that the average marginal effects are positive, as expected, but that they decrease with age. This is consistent with what we see in Figure 14.8, which shows that the probability of marriage increases with age, but at a slightly decreasing rate.

The command margins also allows us to compute the predicted probabilities of being married for employed and not employed men and women, separately at different ages. We can then plot them using the command marginsplot.

Write the commands and compare with the do file in the online appendix

The resulting graph looks like the one in Figure 14.10.

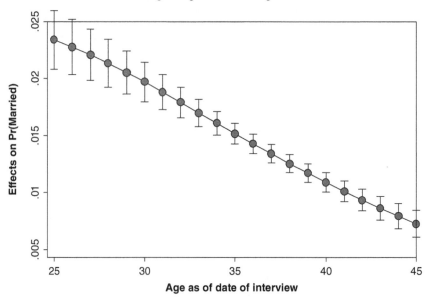

Figure 14.9   Average marginal effect of age on the probability of marriage at different ages

Source: BHPS wave 18

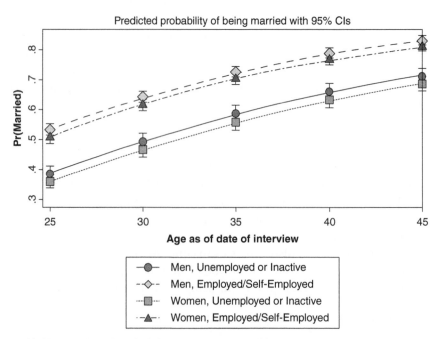

Figure 14.10   Predicted probability of being married by sex, age and employment status

Source: BHPS wave 18

The figure shows a clear difference in the probability of being married between people who work and those who do not: employed men and women are more likely to be married than their unemployed or inactive counterparts at all ages. The figure also shows that at all ages women are slightly less likely to be married than men with the same employment status. In this case, however, the confidence intervals (CIs) overlap, and we can see directly from the figure that the difference between men and women is not statistically significant, while the difference between the two employment statuses is statistically significant.

14.5.3 The Command `marginsplot` and Interaction Effects

In the above model we have reported marginal effects and predicted probabilities at different points of the distribution of the explanatory variables, but we have not assumed any heterogeneity of marginal effects. To allow the gender coefficient to vary with age, we can include an interaction between the `Female` and `age` variables, and estimate and plot the different predicted probabilities of men and women across ages.

Write the commands and compare with the do file in the online appendix

The resulting graph looks like the one in Figure 14.11.

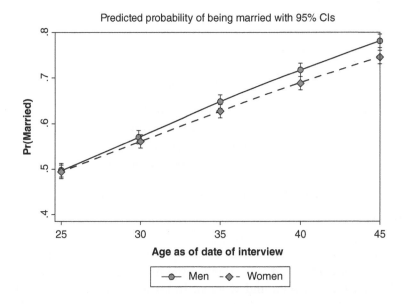

Figure 14.11   Predicted probability of being married by sex and age

Source: BHPS wave 18

The figure shows that the probability of being married increases with age for both men and women and that, although men and women are almost equally likely to be married at younger ages, at older ages men are more likely to be married. The confidence intervals plotted in the figure show that the difference between men and women is not statistically significant at the age of 35. It is statistically significant at the age of 40, although the confidence intervals are rather close, and it is clearly statistically significant at the age of 45.

To allow the gender coefficient to vary with employment status we include interactions between the Female and employment status dummies, and estimate the average marginal effects of being employed for men and women separately before plotting them.

Write the commands and compare with the do file in the online appendix.

The resulting graph looks like the one in Figure 14.12.

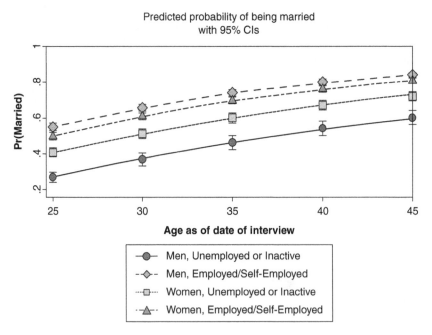

Figure 14.12   Predicted probability of being married by sex, age and employment status

Source: BHPS wave 18

Figure 14.12 looks very similar to Figure 14.10 but there is one important difference: in Figure 14.12 we have allowed the marginal effect of employment status to be different for men and women. In terms of estimations, for Figure 14.10 we have not included the interaction term in the probit model, but we have estimated the marginal effects of the interaction, while for Figure 14.12 we have included the interaction term in the probit model. The second model allows the marginal effect of employment status to be different for men and women.

As before, the figure shows that those who are unemployed or inactive are less likely to be married than those who are employed. In this case, however, we can see that the difference is much higher for men than women. In contrast to Figure 14.10, Figure 14.12 suggests that men and women who are employed are more likely to be married at any age than those who are not employed. The difference between men and women in this case is not statistically significant. Among those who are unemployed or inactive, women are much more likely to be married than men and the difference is statistically significant.

14.5.4 Combining Multiple Graphs

In Chapter 8 we learned one method of combining multiple graphs. In this subsection we discuss another. We continue with the example in Section 14.5.3 but we now want to produce two graphs, the first showing the estimated probability of being married for those who are employed separately by sex and age, and the second showing the same probabilities, but for those who are either unemployed or inactive. We then want to put these two graphs side by side. To do this we need to produce the two graphs separately using the command marginsplot and then save them as memory graphs using the name option. Finally we use the command graph combine to combine the two graphs. A user-written routine (grc1leg) allows us to use one common legend for both graphs:

```
quietly margins Female if Employed==0, ///
    at(age = (25(5)45))
marginsplot, scheme(s1manual) name(gr1) ///
    yscale(r(.3(.2).9)) ylabel(.3(.2).9) ///
    title("Not employed")
```

We use a similar set of commands for the employed.

Write the commands and compare with the do file in the online appendix

Finally we produce the combined graph:

```
graph combine gr1 gr2, ///
    title("Predicted Prob. of Being Married", ///
    size(medium)) ///
    scheme(s1manual) note("Source: BHPS wave 18") ///
```

```
saving("$analysisdir\ predprob_sexempage3", ///

replace)
```

The resulting graph looks like the one in Figure 14.13 and provides the same information as in Figure 14.12. Some people may find Figure 14.12 easier to read, while others may prefer Figure 14.13.

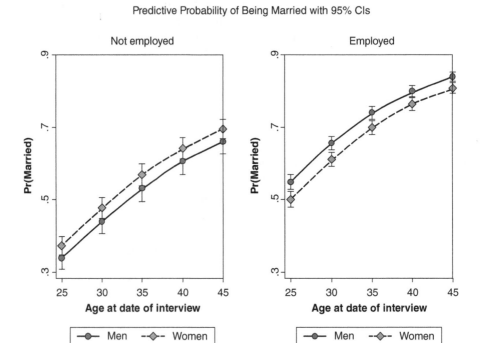

Figure 14.13   Predicted probability of being married by sex, age and employment status

Source: BHPS wave 18

14.6 Summary and Suggestions for Further Reading

In the previous chapters in this book we discussed the correct way of interpreting the results of the analysis. In this final chapter we have discussed how to produce output tables and graphs for descriptive statistics and regression results.

Key points

- To save tables of descriptive statistics use the Stata saved results, the `egen` and `bysort` commands or the command `collapse`.
- You can produce graphs of descriptive statistics using the `graph` command and save them in Stata, pdf or other formats.
- To save tables of regression coefficients use the `estout`, `esttab` or `outreg` commands.
- To save tables of marginal effects use the Stata saved results or use the command `estpost`.
- Consider producing graphs of the estimated parameters and standard errors to complement tables of results.
- Use the command `marginsplot` to visualise marginal effects and predicted probabilities at different values of the explanatory variables.

Suggestions for further reading

- In this chapter we have discussed a few ways to use matrices. For a discussion of advanced programming, see StataCorp (2013g) *Stata Programming Reference Manual*. College Station, TX, Stata Press. For a discussion of how to use matrices see StataCorp (2013h) *Mata Reference Manual*. College Station, TX, Stata Press.
- For a discussion of other types of graphs and their additional options see Mitchell, M.N. (2012) *A Visual Guide to Stata Graphics*, 3rd Edition. College Station, TX, Stata Press.

GLOSSARY

Balanced panel A panel dataset where every unit of observation appears in all waves.

Bias The difference between the mean or expected value of the sampling distribution of an estimator and the true value of the population parameter.

Biased estimator An estimator with a non-zero bias.

Binary variable A variable that takes on only two (non-missing) values.

Censoring Cases where entry or exit into a specific state, such as unemployment or marriage, is not observed in data. When entry is not observed the case is said to be left censored. When exit is not observed then it is referred to as being right censored.

Clustered random sample A sample where the first groups of population units (clusters) are chosen by random sampling. Then either all units within that cluster (one-stage cluster sampling) or only some units within that cluster (multi-stage cluster sampling) are chosen by random sampling. The sample selection process need not be restricted to just two clustering stages.

Consistency The quality of an estimator, such that, as the sample size increases, the value of the estimator (or the parameter estimate) approaches (converges in probability to) the true parameter value (the value in the population).

Consistent estimator An estimator for which, as the sample size increases, the parameter estimate approaches (converges in probability to) the true parameter value (the value in the population).

Cumulative density function (CDF) A function of a random variable X that reflects the probability that X is less than a specific value. The CDF is based on an underlying probability distribution of X.

do file A text file where a list of Stata commands is saved.

Dummy variable A binary variable that takes on a value of 1 or 0.

Efficient estimator The estimator of a population parameter which has the smallest standard error among all (consistent) estimators of that parameter.

Estimator   A measure computed on a sample, such as sample mean pay, proportion of sample members who are employed, or regression coefficients which are used to estimate population parameters.

Failure function   The probability that a spell is shorter than a specific length.

First difference   The difference between the value of a variable in one time period and the time period prior to it.

Government Office Region (GOR)   The nine administrative areas into which England is divided: North East, North West, Yorkshire and The Humber, East Midlands, West Midlands, East of England, London, South East, and the South West.

Hazard function   For continuous time: the ratio of the probability density function of spell duration to its survival function. For discrete time: the probability of the spell ending in a period conditional on its having lasted until the previous period.

Heteroscedasticity   The case where the variability of a random variable is different for different sub-groups.

Homoscedasticity   The case where the variability of a random variable is the same across different sub-groups.

Instrument   Any variable which does not explain the dependent variable but is correlated with the endogenous variable.

Inverse Mills ratio (IMR)   The correction factor to be included in a model suffering from selection bias to correct for the selection equation.

log file   File which records the Stata output produced.

Macros   Variables stored within the Sata memory that are available only while the program (either the do file, or a loop while working interactively) is running (local macros) or within each Stata session (global macros).

Marginal effect   The increase in the predicted value of the dependent variable for a unit change in the explanatory variable.

Mean square error (MSE)   Sum of the square of the bias and the square of the standard error of an estimator.

Odds   Ratio of the probability of an event occurring to the probability of the event not occurring.

Odds ratio Ratio of the odds of an event occurring if an explanatory variable takes on a particular value, to the odds of the event occurring if the explanatory variable takes on another value.

Ordered choice Choice between alternatives that are in a particular order, for example the choice from a scale from 1 to 7.

p-**value** Generally interpreted as the probability of observing the estimated coefficient, or the test value, if the hypothesis that the true coefficient is zero is true.

Population Any group of objects or units about which we are interested in gathering information.

Primary sampling unit The clusters chosen at the first (or only) stage of a clustered sample.

Probability density function (PDF) For continuous time, a function of a random variable X that equals the relative likelihood that X will take on a specific value.

Probability mass function (PMF) For discrete time, a function of a random variable X that gives the probability that X will take on a specific value.

Probability sample A sample selected by using a method that allows every population member to have a known and positive chance of selection into the sample. Also called random sample.

Random sample A sample selected by using a method that allows every population member to have a known and positive chance of selection into the sample. Also called probability sample.

Robust standard error A consistent estimator of the standard error of the regression coefficient when the error in the data is heteroscedastic.

Sample A group of objects or units which are a subset of the population or drawn from the population.

Sample design The method used for drawing a sample from the population; also called sampling plan.

Sample statistic A measure based on sample data, such as mean pay, proportion of women who are employed, etc.

Sampling fraction The probability of each population unit being selected into the sample; also called selection probability.

Sampling frame   The list of all population units from which to draw a sample.

Sampling plan   The method used for drawing a sample from the population; also called sample design.

Selection probability   The probability of each population unit being selected into the sample; also called sampling fraction.

Simple random sample (SRS)   A sample design where every population unit has the same selection probability and every possible sample of the same size that can be drawn from the population has the same probability of selection.

Spell   Length of time the unit of observation (individual, household, firm) spent in a particular state, such as unemployment or marriage.

Standard error   The standard deviation of the sampling distribution of an estimator.

Stratified random sample   A sample design where the population is divided into mutually exclusive and exhaustive groups based on known characteristics (strata) and then a sample is drawn from each stratum by random sampling.

Survivor function   The probability that a spell is longer than a specific length.

t-**statistic**   The ratio of the difference of the estimated value from the true value of the parameter, to the standard error of the estimator.

Unbalanced panel   Data where not every unit of observation appear in all waves.

Unbiased estimator   An estimator with a zero bias.

Unobserved heterogeneity   All unobserved factors (or characteristics) that are specific to an individual (or unit of analysis).

Unordered choice   Choice between alternatives that are in no particular order; for example, the choice between different types of cars.

Wave   Interview year in a panel survey.

BIBLIOGRAPHY

Abott, A. (1983) Sequences of Social Events: Concepts and Methods for the Analysis of Order in Social Processes. *Historical Methods* 16(4): 129–47.

Abott, A. (1995) Sequence Analysis: New Methods for Old Ideas. *Annual Review of Sociology* 21: 93–113.

Allison, P.D. (1984) *Event History Analysis: Regression for Longitudinal Event Data*. London, Sage.

Anderson, T. and Hsiao, C. (1981) Estimation of Dynamic Models with Error Components. *Journal of the American Statistical Association* 76: 598–606.

Anderson, T. and Hsiao, C. (1982) Formulation and Estimation of Dynamic Models Using Panel Data. *Journal of Econometrics* 18: 47–82.

Angrist, J.D. and Pischke, J.-S. (2009) *Mostly Harmless Econometrics – An Empiricist's Companion*. Princeton, NJ, Princeton University Press.

Arellano, M. and Bond, S. (1991) Some Tests of Specification for Panel Data: Monte Carlo Evidence and an Application to Employment Equations. *Review of Economic Studies* 58(2): 277–97.

Arellano, M. and Bover, O. (1995) Another Look at the Instrumental Variable Estimation of Error-Components Models. *Journal of Econometrics* 68: 29–51.

Argyle, M. (2001) *The Psychology of Happiness*. Hove, Routledge.

Baetschmann, G., Staub, K.E. and Winkelmann, R. (2011) Consistent Estimation of the Fixed Effects Ordered Logit Model. IZA Discussion Paper No. 5443.

Baltagi, B.H. (2009) *Econometric Analysis of Panel Data*. Chichester, Wiley.

Bardasi, E. and Taylor, M. (2008) Marriage and Wages: A Test of the Specialization Hypothesis. *Economica* 75: 569–91.

Blossfeld, H., Golsch, K. and Rohwer, G. (2007) *Event History Analysis with Stata*. Mahwah, NJ, Lawrence Erlbaum Associates.

Blundell, R. and Bond, S. (1998) Initial Conditions and Moment Restrictions in Dynamic Panel Data Models. *Journal of Econometrics* 87: 115–43.

Bond, T.N. and Lang, K. (2014) The Sad Truth About Happiness Scales. NBER Working Paper 19950.

Breslow, N. (1974) Covariance Analysis of Censored Survival Data. *Biometrics* 30: 89–99.

Breusch, T.S. and Pagan, A.R. (1979) A Simple Test for Heteroscedasticity and Random Coefficient Variation. *Econometrica* 47: 1287–94.

Cameron, C.A. and Trivedi P.K. (2005) *Microeconometrics: Methods and Applications*, USA, Cambridge University Press.

Cameron, C.A. and Trivedi, P.K. (2010) *Microeconometrics Using Stata*, College Station, TX, Stata Press.

Carstairs, V. and Morris, R. (1991) *Deprivation and Health in Scotland*. Aberdeen University Press, Aberdeen.

Citro, C.F. and Michael, R.T. (1995) *Measuring Poverty: A New Approach*. Washington, DC, National Academy Press.

Cleves, M., Gould, W., Gutierrez, R.G. and Marchenko, Y.V. (2010) *An Introduction to Survival Analysis Using Stata*, 3rd Edition. College Station, TX, Stata Press.

Cook, R.D. and Weisberg, S. (1983) Diagnostics for Heteroscedasticity in Regression. *Biometrika* 70: 1–10.

Coudouel, A., Hentschel, J.S. and Wodon, Q.T. (2002) Poverty Measurement and Analysis. In the *PRSP Sourcebook*. Washington, DC, The World Bank, Chapter 1. Available at: http://go.worldbank.org/0C60K5UK40.

Cox, D.R. (1972) Regression Models and Life-Tables. *Journal of the Royal Statistical Society, Series B (Methodological)* 34(2): 187–220.

Creedy, J. and Sleeman, C. (2005) Adult Equivalence Scale, Inequality and Poverty. *New Zealand Economic Papers* 39(1): 51–81.

De Leeuw, W. (2005) To Mix or Not to Mix Data Collection Modes in Surveys. *Journal of Official Statistics* 21(2): 235–55.

Dillman, D.A. (2007) *Mail and Internet Surveys: The Tailored Design Method*. Hoboken, NJ, Wiley.

Doornik, J.A. and Hansen, H. (2008) An Omnibus Test for Univariate and Multivariate Normality. *Oxford Bulletin of Economics and Statistics* 70: 927–39.

DuMouchel, W.H. and Duncan, G.J. (1983) Using Sample Survey Weights in Multiple Regression Analyses of Stratified Samples. *Journal of the American Statistical Association* 78(383): 535–43.

Elliot, D. (1991) *Weighting for Non-Response: A Survey Researcher's Guide*. London, Office of Population Censuses and Surveys, Social Survey Division.

Faiella, I. (2010) The Use of Survey Weights in Regression Analysis. Bank of Italy Working Paper 739.

Ferrer-i-Carbonell, A. and Frijters, P. (2004) How Important Is Methodology for the Estimates of the Determinants of Happiness? *The Economic Journal* 114(497): 641–59.

Frazer, H. (2009) Poverty and Inequality in the EU, Social Inclusion Working Group, Brussels.

Frechette, G.R. (2001) Random-Effects Ordered Probit. *Stata Technical Bulletin* 59: 23–7.

Frey, B.S. (2008) *Happiness: A Revolution in Economics*. Cambridge, MA, MIT Press.

Froot, K.A. (1989) Consistent Covariance Matrix Estimation with Cross-Sectional Dependence and Heteroskedasticity in Financial Data. *Journal of Financial and Quantitative Analysis* 24: 333–55.

Gelman, A. (2007) Struggles with Survey Weighting and Regression Modeling. *Statistical Science* 22(2): 153–64.

Gouskova, E., Heeringa, S.G., McGonagle, K. and Schoeni, R.F. (2008) Panel Study of Income Dynamics Revised Longitudinal Weights 1993–2005. Survey Research Center, Institute for Social Research, University of Michigan.

Gouskova, E., Heeringa, S.G., McGonagle, K., Schoeni, R.F. and Stafford, F. (2009) Panel Study of Income Dynamics Construction and Evaluation of the Longitudinal Sample Weight 2007. Survey Research Center, Institute for Social Research, University of Michigan.

Greene, W.H. (2003) *Econometric Analysis*. Harlow, Pearson Education.

Greene, W.H. and Hensher, D.A. (2010) *Modeling Ordered Choices: A Primer*. Cambridge, Cambridge University Press.

Grossbard, S. (ed.) (2006) *Jacob Mincer – A Pioneer of Modern Labor Economics*. Berlin, Springer.

Groves, R.M. (2006) Non-Response Rates and Non-Response Bias in Household Surveys. *Public Opinion Quarterly, Special Issue: Nonresponse Bias in Household Surveys* 70(5): 646–75.

Groves, R.M. and Couper, M.P. (1998) *Nonresponse in Household Interview Surveys*. New York, Wiley.

Groves, R.M., Dillman, D.A., Eltinge, J.L. and Little, R.J.A. (2001) *Survey Nonresponse*. New York, Wiley.

Groves, R.M., Fowler, J.F.J., Couper, M.P., Lepkowski, J.M., Singer, E. and Tourangeau, R. (2004) *Survey Methodology*. Hoboken, NJ, Wiley-Interscience.

Haisken-DeNew, J.P. and Frick, J.R. (2005) *Desktop Companion to the German Socio-Economic Panel (SOEP)*. Berlin. Available at: www.diw.de/documents/dokumente-narchiv/17/diw_01.c.38951.de/dtc.409713.pdf.

Halpin, B. (1997) Unified BHPS Work-Life Histories: Combining Multiple Sources into a User-Friendly Format. Technical Papers of the ESRC Research Centre on Micro-Social Change, 13, University of Essex.

Ham, J.C. and Rae, S.A.J. (1987) Unemployment Insurance and Male Unemployment Duration in Canada, *Journal of Labor Economics* 5(3): 325–53.

Harmon, C., Oosterbeek, H. and Walker, I. (2003) The Returns to Education: Microeconomics. *Journal of Economic Surveys* 17(2): 115–55.

Haughton, J. and Khandker, S.R. (2009) *The Handbook on Poverty and Inequality*. Washington, DC, The World Bank. Available at: http://go.worldbank.org/7JGPK76TM0.

Hausman, J.A. (1978) Specification Tests in Econometrics. *Econometrica* 46(6): 1251–71.

Heckman, J.J. (1979) Sample Selection Bias as Specification Error. *Econometrica* 47(1): 153–62.

Heckman, J.J. and Singer, B. (1984) A Method for Minimising the Impact of Distributional Assumptions in Econometric Models for Duration Data. *Econometrica* 52(2): 271–320.

Heeringa, S.G., Berglund, P.A., Khan, A., Lee, S. and Gouskova, E. (2011) PSID Cross-Sectional Individual Weights, 1997–2009. Survey Research Center, Institute for Social Research, University of Michigan.

Henze, N. and Zirkler, B. (1990) A Class of Invariant Consistent Tests for Multivariate Normality. *Communications in Statistics, Theory and Methods* 19: 3595–617.

Hill, M. (1992) *The Panel Study of Income Dynamics: A User's Guide*. London, Sage.

Hox, J. (2002) *Multilevel Analysis, Techniques and Applications*. Mahwah, NJ, Lawrence Erlbaum Associates.

Hsiao, C. (2003) *Analysis of Panel Data*. Cambridge, Cambridge University Press.

Huber, P.J. (1967) The Behavior of Maximum Likelihood Estimates under Nonstandard Conditions. *Proceedings of the Fifth Berkeley Symposium on Mathematical Statistics and Probability*. Berkeley, CA, University of California Press. pp. 221–33.

Imbens, G.W. (2014) Instrumental Variables: An Econometrician's Perspective. NBER Working Paper 19983.

Jann, B. (2005). Making Regression Tables from Stored Estimates. *The Stata Journal* 5(3): 288–308.

Jann, B. (2007a) FRE: Stata Module to Display One-Way Frequency Table. Available from http://ideas.repec.org/c/boc/bocode/s456835.html.

Jann, B. (2007b). Making Regression Tables Simplified. *The Stata Journal* 7(2): 227–44.

Jenkins, S. (2005) Survival Analysis. Available at: www.iser.essex.ac.uk/files/teaching/stephenj/ec968/pdfs/ec968lnotesv6.pdf.

Jepsen, L.K. and Jepsen, C.A. (2002) An Empirical Analysis of the Matching Patterns of Same-Sex and Opposite-Sex Couples. *Demography* 39(3): 435–53.

Kan, M.Y. and Heath, A. (2006) The Political Values and Choices of Husbands and Wives. *Journal of Marriage and the Family* 68(1): 70–86.

Knies, G. (ed.) (2014) *Understanding Society – UK Household Longitudinal Study: Wave 1-4, 2009–2013, User Manual*. Colchester: University of Essex.

Layard, R. (2005) *Happiness – Lessons from a New Science*. London, Penguin.

Levy, H. and Jenkins, S. (2012) Documentation for Derived Current and Annual Net Household Income Variables, BHPS Waves 1–18.

Levy, P.S. and Lemeshow, S. (1999) *Sampling of Populations: Methods and Applications*. New York, Wiley.

Lewbel, A. and Pendakur, K. (2006) Equivalence Scales. In *The New Palgrave Dictionary of Economics*, 2nd Edition. Basingstoke, Palgrave Macmillan.

Long, J.S. (1997) *Regression Models for Categorical and Limited Dependent Variables.* London, Sage.

Long, J.S. (2009) *The Workflow of Data Analysis Using Stata.* College Station, TX, Stata Press.

Lynn, P. (2006) Quality Profile: British Household Panel Survey Waves 1 to 13: 1991–2003, Version 2.0.

Lynn, P., Burton, J., Kaminska, O., Knies, G. and Nandi, A. (2012) An Initial Look at Non-Response and Attrition in Understanding Society. Understanding Society Working Paper (2012-02).

Lynn, P. and Clarke, P. (2006) Separating Refusal Bias and Non-Contact Bias: Evidence from UK National Surveys. *Journal of the Royal Statistical Society, Series D (The Statistician)* 51(3): 319–33.

Magee, L., Robb, A.L. and Burbidge, J.B. (1998) On the Use of Sampling Weights When Estimating Regression Models with Survey Data. *Journal of Econometrics* 48(2): 251–71.

Mardia, K.V. (1970) Measures of Multivariate Skewness and Kurtosis with Applications. *Biometrika* 57: 519–30.

Maré, D.C. (1991) Five Decades of Educational Assortative Mating. *American Sociological Review* 56(1): 15–32.

Maré, D.C. (2006) Constructing Consistent Work-Life Histories: A Guide for Users of the British Household Panel Survey. ISER Working Paper 2006-39.

McFadden, D.L. (1974) Conditional Logit Analysis of Qualitative Choice Analysis. In P. Zarembka (ed.), *Frontiers in Econometrics*. New York, Academic Press. pp. 105–42.

McGonagle, K., Schoeni, R.F., Sastry, N. and Freedman, V.A. (2012) The Panel Study of Income Dynamics: Overview, Recent Innovations, and Potential for Life Coures Research. *Longitudinal and Life Course Studies* 3(2): 268–84.

Mitchell, M.N. (2012) *A Visual Guide to Stata Graphics*, 3rd Edition. College Station, TX, Stata Press.

Morris, R. and Carstairs, V. (1991) Which Deprivation? A Comparison of Selected Deprivation Indexes. *Journal of Public Health Medicine* 13(4): 318–26.

Mundlak, Y. (1978) On the Pooling of Time Series and Cross Section Data. *Econometrica* 46(1): 69–85.

Newson, R.B. (2003) Confidence Intervals and P-values for Delivery to the End User. *Stata Journal* 3: 245–69.

Nezlek, J.B. (2008) An Introduction to Multilevel Modeling for Social and Personality Psychology. *Social and Personality Psychology Compass* 2(2): 842–60.

Noble, M., Wright, G., Smith, G. and Dibben, C. (2006) Measuring Multiple Deprivation at the Small-Area level. *Environment and Planning A* 38: 169–85.

Payne, R.A. and Abel, G.A. (2012) UK Indices of Multiple Deprivation – A Way to Make Comparisons Across Constituent Countries Easier. *Health Statistics Quarterly* 53: 1–16.

Pfeffermann, D. (1993) The Role of Sampling Weights When Modeling Survey Data. *International Statistical Review* 61(2): 317–37.

Polachek, S.W. (2006) Proving Mincer Right: Mincer's Overtaking Point and the Lifecycle Earnings Distribution. In S. Grossbard (ed.), *Jacob Mincer – A Pioneer of Modern Labor Economics*. New York, Springer. pp. 81–108.

Powdthavee, N. (2011) *The Happiness Equation*. London, Icon Books.

Rabe-Hesketh, S. and Skrondal, A. (2012) *Multilevel and Longitudinal Modeling Using Stata*. College Station, TX, Stata Press.

Roberts, C. (2007) Mixing Modes of Data Collection in Surveys: A Methodological Review. NCRM Review Papers (NCRM/008).

Singer, E. (2006) Introduction: Non-Response Bias in Household Surveys. *Public Opinion Quarterly* 70(5): 637–45.

Solon, G., Haider, S.J. and Wooldridge, J. (2013) What Are We Weighting For? NBER Working Paper 18859.

StataCorp (2013a) *Stata: Release 13. Statistical Software*. College Station, TX: Stata Press.

StataCorp (2013b) *Stata Longitudinal-Data/Panel-Data Reference Manual Release 13*. College Station, TX, Stata Press.

StataCorp (2013c) *Stata Survival Analysis and Epidemiological Tables Reference Manual Release 13*. College Station, TX, Stata Press.

StataCorp (2013d) *Stata Data Management Reference Manual Release 13*. College Station, TX, Stata Press.

StataCorp (2013e) *Stata Graphics Reference Manual Release 13*. College Station, TX, Stata Press.

StataCorp (2013f) *Stata User's Guide Reference Manual Release 13*. College Station, TX, Stata Press.

StataCorp (2013g) *Stata Programming Reference Manual Release 13*. College Station, TX, Stata Press.

StataCorp (2013h) *Mata Reference Manual Release 13*. College Station, TX, Stata Press.

Steele, F. (2005) Event History Analysis: A National Centre for Research Methods Briefing Paper. NCRM Review Papers (NCRM/004).

Taris, T.W. (2000) *A Primer in Longitudinal Data Analysis*. London, Sage.

Taylor, M.F., Brice, J., Buck, N. and Prentice-Lane, E. (2010) *British Household Panel Survey User Manual Volume A: Introduction, Technical Report and Appendices*. Colchester, University of Essex.

Townsend, P. (1987) Deprivation. *Journal of Social Policy* 16: 125–46.

Townsend, P., Phillimore, P. and Beattie, A. (1988) *Health and Deprivation: Inequality and the North*. London, Routledge.

Uhrig, N.S. (2008) The Nature and Causes of Attrition in the British Household Panel Study. ISER Working Paper Series (2008-05).

van der Klaauw, B. (2014) From Micro Data to Causality: Forty Years of Empirical Labor Economics. IZA Discussion Paper No. 8047.

Verbeek, M. (2008) *A Guide to Modern Econometrics*. Chichester, Wiley.

Weichselbaumer, D. and Winter-Ebmer, R. (2005) A Meta-Analysis of the International Gender Wage Gap. *Journal of Economic Surveys* 19(3): 479–511.

White, H. (1980) A Heteroskedasticity-Consistent Covariance Matrix Estimator and a Direct Test for Heteroskedasticity. *Econometrica* 48: 817–30.

Williams, R.L. (2000) A Note on Robust Variance Estimation for Cluster-Correlated Data. *Biometrics* 56: 645–6.

Winkelmann, R. and Boes, S. (2006) *Analysis of Microdata*. Heidelberg, Springer.

Wooldridge, J. (2002) *Econometric Analysis of Cross Section and Panel Data*. Cambridge, MA, MIT Press.

Wooldridge, J. (2009) *Introductory Econometrics: A Modern Approach*. Mason, OH, South Western, Cengage Learning.

Wooldridge, J. (2010) *Correlated Random Effects Models with Unbalanced Panels*. Department of Economics, Michigan State University.

Yamaguchi, K. (1991) *Event History Analysis*. London, Sage.

INDEX

administrative data, 11
attrition, 6, 15

BHPS, xxv, 9, 12–14, 17–18, 21
  data structure, 36
  household data, 80, 86–8, 106–8, 109, 115–6
  missing data labels, 42
  retrospective data, 225–7, 237–8
  weights, 137–8
bias, 130

census, 10
CNEF, 19
cohort survey, 12–13
comments in Stata, 30
coverage error, 134–5
cross-section data, 3–5

data management commands
  _n, 100–1
  _N, 87, 100–1
  append, 59
  bysort, 84
  capture, 30, 32, 61–2
  collapse, 271–2, 277
  compress, 27–8
  drop, 54–5
  duplicates, 87
  egen, 47, 84–5, 102, 113–4, 120
  ereturn, 92
  foreach, 61, 66
  forvalues, 67
  fre, 41
  generate, 44–6
  index, 61–2
  indexnot, 61–2
  joinby, 228–9
  keep, 55
  merge, 88–91
  mvdecode, 42
  quietly, 290
  recode, 42, 45
  rename, 44, 59
  reshape, 64
  return, 92
  save, 55
  set more, 30–1
  stset, 247–8
  svy, 142–5
  tsset, 67
  use, 35
  xtset, 67
dates format in Stata, 228

descriptive statistics commands
  correlate, 123, 148–9
  describe, 35, 40, 67
  summarize, 26
  tabstat, 97
  tabulate, 43–4
do files, 28–30
duration analysis, 215–9
  censoring, 217, 221–2, 245–7
  for continuous time, 219
  Cox model, 257–8
  for discrete time, 219–20
  duration dependence, 220, 250–1, 257, 261–2, 264
  failure function, 219–20
  hazard function, 219–20
  hazard ratio, 252, 257
  Kaplan–Meier estimator, 248–50
  life tables, 250
  Nelson–Aalen estimator, 248–50
  product limit estimator, *see Kaplan–Meier*
  proportion hazard model, 250–5
  survivor function, 219–20
  truncation, 217
  unobserved heterogeneity, 220, 255–7, 263–4, 265

ECHP, 19
endogeneity, 180–1
estimator, 10, 129–31
EU-SILC, 20
event history analysis, *see duration analysis*

first difference estimator, 187–9
fixed effects estimator
  in linear models, 186–93
  in non-linear models, 200, 203–10
fixed life surveys, 13

graphs
  combine graphs, 295–296
  of descriptive statistics, 278–84
  exporting to pdf, 279
  of hazard functions, 250, 253–5
  histogram, 46–53
  of Kaplan–Meier survivor function, 249
  of kernel density, 53–4, 74–7
  of marginal effects, 289–96
  of normal density, 53–4
  of regression results, 287–95
  saving graphs, 52
  scatter plot, 122–3, 148–9
  of survivor function, 260